Lenin on the Train

ALLEN LANE

UK | USA | Canada | Ireland | Australia
India | New Zealand | South Africa

Allen Lane is part of the Penguin Random House group of companies
whose addresses can be found at global.penguinrandomhouse.com

First published 2016
001

Copyright © Catherine Merridale, 2016

The moral right of the author has been asserted

Set in 13.5/16 pt Garamond MT Std
Typeset by Jouve (UK), Milton Keynes
Printed in Great Britain by Clays Ltd, St Ives plc

A CIP catalogue record for this book is available from the British Library

ISBN: 978–0–241–01132–4

Lenin on the Train

CATHERINE MERRIDALE

ALLEN LANE
an imprint of
PENGUIN BOOKS

Contents

List of Illustrations

Every effort has been made to contact all copyright holders. The publishers will be pleased to make good any errors or omissions brought to their attention.

A Note on the Text

Two complications threaten to confound any English-speaker who writes about Russia in 1917. The first is the Russian alphabet, which defies consistent transliteration. In my text, I have opted to use the simplest and most familiar-looking versions of Russian names wherever possible (which is why I have ended up with Trotsky and not Trotskii or even Trockij), but the endnotes follow the precepts of the Library of Congress, which is still the best system for tracking Russian material through online catalogues.

Yet more problems arise with dates. In 1917, Russia still used the Julian calendar, which almost always trailed behind the rest of Europe and the United States (and most of the world) by thirteen days. Since I have had to deal with telegrams (and people) travelling between both worlds, I have often been forced to give both dates at once.

Meanwhile, of course, there are two Easters in this story, for Lenin left Zurich on Catholic Europe's Easter Monday afternoon (the date in Zurich was 9 April) and arrived in Petrograd a week later on Orthodox Russia's Easter Monday night (which was 3 April to the supporters who were waiting for him).

LENIN'S ROUTE: APRIL 1917

100 50 0   100   200   300
miles

Arctic Circle

Romanov
(Murmansk)

N O R W A Y

S W E D E N

Grand Duchy of Finland

Karungi
Boden Tornio
Haparanda

Gulf of Bothnia

Bräcke

Tampere

Bergen

CHRISTIANIA
(Oslo)

STOCKHOLM

Helsingfors
(Helsinki)

Gulf of Finland

Beloostrov
PETROGRAD
(St. Petersburg)

Reval
(Tallinn)

NORTH
SEA

B A L T I C   S E A

DENMARK

COPENHAGEN

Malmö
Trelleborg

Sassnitz

Stralsund

RUSSIAN

EMPIRE

BERLIN

Warsaw

GERMANY

Frankfurt

Kiev

Karlsruhe
Stuttgart

Cracow

A U S T R I A

Singen

VIENNA

BERN Zürich

BUDAPEST

Odessa

SWITZERLAND
Geneva

H U N G A R Y

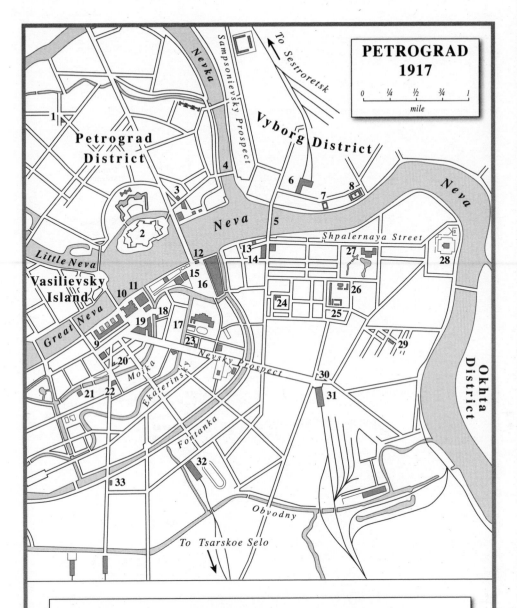

PETROGRAD 1917

0   ¼   ½   ¾   1
mile

Nevka

To Sestroretsk

Sampsonievsky Prospect

Vyborg District

Petrograd District

Neva

Little Neva

Vasilievsky Island

Great Neva

Neva

Okhta District

Shpalernaya Street

Moika

Nevsky Prospect

Ekaterinsky

Fontanka

Obvodny

To Tsarskoe Selo

1 Elizarov Apartment	12 British Embassy	23 Europe Hotel
2 Peter-Paul Fortress	13 French Embassy	24 Litovsky Barracks
3 Kshesinskaya Mansion	14 Artillery Department	25 Volhynsky Barracks
4 Sampson Bridge	15 Pavlovsky Barracks	26 Preobrazhensky Barracks
5 Liteiny Bridge	16 Mars Field	27 Tauride Palace
6 Finland Station	17 Michael Theatre	28 Smolny Institute
7 Kresty Prison	18 Pravda Offices	29 Alliluev Apartment
8 Arsenal	19 General Staff Building	30 Znamenskaya Square
9 Admiralty Building	20 Astoria Hotel	31 Nicholas Station
10 Winter Palace	21 Yusupov Palace	32 Tsarskoe Selo Station
11 Hermitage	22 Mariinsky Palace	33 Izmailovsky Barracks

Introduction

*The masses must always be told the whole truth, the
unvarnished truth, without fearing that the truth will
frighten them away.*

N. K. Krupskaya

It was Thomas Cook who said it. There are three places in
the world that anyone who claims to be a global traveller
really must see. The desert citadel of Timbuktu is one of
them, another is the old city of Samarkand. The third is a
small town in Sweden. A hundred and fifty years ago, it
may have been the Northern Lights that drew Cook up to
Haparanda. The locals boasted of pirates, too, but every har-
bour round that coast claimed to have those. Perhaps what
really did the trick was the report of a man in a swirling coat,
a magic healer, skilled with herbs, who flew above the Arctic
night like a great bird.

It was not simply that the small town was remote. The
place was thrilling, dangerous, right at the end of the known
world. Haparanda is situated at the apex of the Gulf of Bothnia, the sea that separates Sweden's northern territories from
Finland. The area is dominated by a river delta, and at one
time the town encompassed a string of low-lying islands as
well as some more solid ground towards the west. Other
settlements sprang up along the waterside, including a
much larger town called Tornio, but life for everyone meant

sharing: hunting the region's winter game, taking cattle to pasture on the nearby hills and wading out in the brief thaws to catch the eels that flashed between the floating mats of reed.

The population had nothing much in common with Stockholm (most people spoke a local patois), but the whole zone was part of Sweden until the early nineteenth century. In 1809, however, a treaty concluded at the end of one of Russia's many wars with the Swedes decreed that the eastern bank of the river, including the busiest central island, should be transferred to the Grand Duchy of Finland, a territory that the Russians had just snatched for their empire. Marooned on the Swedish bank, Haparanda faced its bigger sister, Tornio, across the river. The two of them were now estranged.

From the moment of its creation, the border never felt entirely safe. The Swedish government could not forget that Russia had ambitions to expand. When vast reserves of iron ore were discovered at Kiruna, less than 300 miles to the north-west, investors in Stockholm were forced to curb their plans for a new railway out of fear that Haparanda might become a gateway for some fresh wave of invading Russian hordes. Sweden's age of steam was at its height, but as the lines reached on, like nerve pathways, towards the north, no track was laid to Haparanda. In summer, when the hunters' sledges could no longer cross the ice, the only solid link to Finland was a wooden bridge.

What changed things was the First World War. The great powers of Europe's Atlantic coast, Britain and France, were allied with the Russian empire now. They needed to send people back and forth, and they had also agreed to provide the Russians with vital war materials, with fuses and precision sights, but direct contact between west and east was blocked. The routes through Germany were shut, of course, and where they were not packed with mines the sea-lanes in the North Sea and the Baltic were patrolled by submarines. Only the land-based route through northern Sweden was viable, albeit gruelling and remote. Thomas Cook died in 1892. If he had thought that Haparanda was exotic once, he should have seen it in 1917.

The rail link was completed in 1915. It was only a branch line, single track, and engines had to steam down from Karungi, some way to the north. Although the route was now an artery for vital wartime trade, the line still stopped short of Finland itself, whose railways (like all those that Russia controlled) used a different gauge in any case. Because the two sides had remained so nervous of each other, everything (including passengers) had to be unloaded at Haparanda station, ferried across the river, hauled up the high bank opposite and reloaded on Russian trains. In winter, sledges dragged by reindeer or stout little horses plied the route; in summer, every boat that could be found was busy on the water.

The bottleneck was clumsy, a time-consuming irritation, but Haparanda was set for a boom. Together with its sister on the Finnish side, it soon became the busiest commercial crossing-point in Europe. Where local herdsmen had once been the only drinkers, the small town's bars now swelled with hustlers, spivs and the secret policemen whose lives slipped by as they observed them. The rooms in the only hotel were booked up for the diplomats and politicians, mainly British, French and Russian, who suddenly began to pass through town. They did not like the climate or the tedious slow trains, but there were no easier options left.

That inconvenient fact also led to the most unlikely of visitations. The Dowager Empress of Russia, Maria Fedorovna, had been in western Europe when the war broke out. She managed to get home herself, but her imperial train was stuck in Denmark and officials in the German government refused to let it steam to Russia along any track of theirs. The situation was awkward, but it was saved by the record freeze of January 1917. When the ice was at its thickest, an army of workmen arrived to lay temporary rails across the Tornionjoki river between Haparanda and the station at Tornio. The imperial train (including boudoir, throne room, kitchens and a mobile electricity generator) was then pulled over, two carriages at a time, and coupled on to a Finnish locomotive on the opposite side. Special castors had been fitted to accommodate the wider gauge. The carriages had barely vanished into Finland when the men were back out on the ice with crowbars to rip up the track.[1]

Wartime photographs from the local museum show creatures who might well be from another world. Stiff, corseted and alien, they look outlandish in their uniforms, their gold braid and a range of feathered hats. Today, the landscape bears no trace whatever of their ghosts. The twin towns on the Tornionjoki have combined – the tourist guidebooks talk about 'HaTo' – and you can stroll from Sweden into Finland and back by crossing the square outside the shopping mall.[2] The Finnish part is permanently one hour ahead of the Swedes, which complicates the bus timetable, but the usual border annoyances – passports, customs, traffic queues – have all been smoothed out like crisp euro notes. The only monument of any size is a massive dark-blue box, the world's largest Ikea store. In April, it is surrounded by a wasteland of oily puddles and filthy heaps of gritty snow, but when that melts the car park will be full. The Russians are still coming, then, as well as Finns and reindeer-herders from Lapland. The man whose story I am here to tell would certainly have understood. He wrote a lot about world trade. He also crossed this river on the ice. It was a journey that changed the world.

In April 1917, at the height of the First World War, the exiled leader of the Bolsheviks, Vladimir Ilyich Lenin, travelled back to Russia by train. Before the year was out he had become the master of a revolutionary new state. Lenin's ultimate achievement was to turn ideas that Karl Marx had outlined on paper forty years before into an ideology of government. He created a Soviet system that ruled in the name of working people, ordering the redistribution of wealth and sponsoring equally radical transformations in culture and social relations. Lenin's programme offered hope and dignity to many of his country's poor, not least by granting an unprecedented measure of equality to women. Among the costs were countless human lives, beginning with tens of thousands of murders in Lenin's lifetime. Some died for no crime more heinous than their possession of a pair of spectacles. Over the seven decades of the Soviet Union's existence the number of its guiltless victims would rise to the low millions. At the same time, its practical, unsentimental advocacy of the dispossessed established Leninism as a blueprint for revolutionary parties from China and Vietnam to the Indian sub-continent and the Caribbean. The starting-point for all these things, from infant Soviet state to world Cold War, was that momentous wartime ride.

Lenin was in Switzerland when the story began. Condemned to exile by the tsarist courts, the Bolshevik leader was safe enough in his new home, but he was endlessly impatient to see the revolution that he had been forecasting for more than twenty years. Like many socialists, he expected it to begin somewhere in western Europe, but the early months of 1917 brought news of large-scale protests in the Russian capital, Petrograd. That shock had barely been absorbed when the world learned that the tsar had abdicated. On the eve of the campaigning season, with plans afoot for a major offensive in the west, the future of the Russian empire was suddenly uncertain. In Petrograd, the people cheered. Their country had become a republic, at least until a constitution was approved.

Like almost every Russian exile, Lenin was delighted when he heard this news. As the leader of Russia's most militant revolutionary party, his first priority was to get home. The trouble was that he was trapped. Neither Britain nor France was inclined to assist with his travel plans. They knew him as a fierce opponent of the war, and their entire diplomatic effort was focused on persuading Russia, free or not, to keep on fighting so that they could win. This unhelpful position left only one route for Lenin to take. It involved catching a train through Germany, crossing to Sweden by ferry, and continuing north to the border at Haparanda. The problem there was Germany itself, for its army had been butchering Russian soldiers in their hundreds of thousands on the eastern front since 1914. Lenin's dilemma looked unresolvable. To go through Germany was treachery, to stay in Switzerland was to ignore the call for which he had been waiting all his life.

Lenin, naturally, chose the first. What made it possible was the unexpected co-operation of the German High Command. The stalemate in the trenches had forced all Europe's major powers to search for ways of gaining an advantage somewhere other than the battlefield. By 1917, a small group of officials inside the German foreign ministry had come to favour the idea of using insurgents to destabilize their enemies. They sponsored military mutineers in France, they armed the Irish nationalists and dreamed of sparking a rebellion on the borders of India. When Lenin's name was recommended, they were quick to grasp his potential for disrupting Russia's war effort. If all went well, and the German army took the opportunity to land a truly crushing blow against Britain and France, they would not need his help for long.

With that delightful thought in mind, German officials saw no difficulty in arranging for the Bolshevik leader's safe transport across their country, even acceding to his request that the carriage transporting his group be treated as an extra-territorial entity, sealed off from the surrounding world and therefore innocent of any contact with the enemy popu-lation. More controversially, they also organized financial backing – the infamous 'German gold' – for some of his revolutionary operations. The French and British knew about the journey, and though they found it hard to separate the rumours from the facts, Lenin's reputation gave them ample cause for alarm. Some even urged that he be stopped, perhaps in Sweden's Arctic woods. When the time came, however, no one was willing to accept responsibility and shoot.

It was a story that might easily have come from the pen of John Buchan. Only a few months previously, indeed, Buchan had published a spy-thriller, *Greenmantle*, whose eponymous villain also preached against the wartime British and their friends. Greenmantle's home was not Russia (Buchan opted to use the Middle East), but the plot depended on a special agent's willingness to cross the whole of Germany to get to him. 'I had expected a big barricade and barbed wire with entrenchments,' the hero, Richard Hannay, explains in the book. 'But there was nothing to see on the German side but half a dozen sentries in . . . field grey. We were all shepherded into a big bare waiting-room where a large stove burned. They took us two at a time into an inner room for examination . . . They made us strip to the skin . . . The men who did the job were fairly civil, but they were mighty thorough.'[3] Lenin was to suffer this ordeal in real life, and the location was the customs house in Tornio. While a group of sceptical Russian border guards looked on, moreover, the person who was being mighty thorough was a British officer.

The journey ended at the Finland Station in Petrograd. A triumphant Lenin, barely showing strain after his eight-day ride, stepped through the ranks of his adoring followers and on to change the course of Russia's history for ever. The Bolsheviks created an admiring myth based on the tale, but the most memorable verdict was passed by Winston Churchill. 'Full allowance must be made for the desperate stakes to which the German war leaders were already committed,' he commented in retrospect. 'Nevertheless it was with a sense of awe that they turned upon Russia the most grisly of all weapons. They transported Lenin in a sealed truck like a plague bacillus from Switzerland to Russia.'[4]

The 'truck', in fact, was not exactly sealed; the trackside doors were seldom locked and people did get on and off. The journey was also much tougher than Churchill's words suggest. It took the Russians three whole days to cross Germany, and for that time they could not buy a meal, let alone step out to stretch their legs. If they slept at all, it was in their packed hard-class compartments, heads lolling on their neighbours' chests, dreams perfumed with stale bread and socks. The idea of a bacillus, however, is something that I recognize at once. Just as the First World War gave rise to great intrigues, there have been many global games – diplomatic, economic and military – in my lifetime.

There is almost as much instability across the planet now as there once was in Lenin's day, and a slightly different collection of great powers is still working hard to make sure that they stay on top. One technique that they use in regional conflicts, since direct military engagement tends to cost too much, is to help and finance local rebels, some of whom are on the ground, but some of whom must be dropped in exactly as Lenin was. I think of South America in the 1980s, of all the dirty wars in Central Asia since that time. I shudder at the current conflicts in the Arab world. The history of Lenin's train is not exclusively the property of the Soviets. In part, it is a parable about great-power intrigue, and one rule there is that great powers almost always get things wrong.

I knew that I would have to do the train-ride for myself. A journey is not only places, distances and times, but there are things that must be seen. The first task was to make sure the itinerary was right. Historians have offered plenty of accounts, but I have yet to see a map that shows the route that Lenin really took. Most experts send him north along a line that was not even built in 1917, and at least one book – a classic that has been reprinted many times – gets the journey wrong by well over 1,000 miles.[5] The route is not a mere detail. There is a difference between a boat across the Baltic and a long haul through the Lapland snow. A track through lonely forest with no light or road in sight is still a proposition far more menacing than steaming past a jaunty string of seaside towns.

Thick though it is, and splendid in its colourful jacket, Bradshaw's 1913 *Continental Railway Guide* is not a great deal of help. The wartime train schedules varied from week to week, and new tracks were still being laid as late as 1916. Leaving Bradshaw on the bookshelf, I armed myself with archive timetables from 1917, my notes from the fifty-five volumes of Lenin's *Collected Works* and a very large map. Apart from a notebook and pen, my bag was also packed with a small digital sound recorder. As I play it back at my desk now, what I hear is the song of Europe on the move: a chorus of languages, the roar of traffic from the streets near by, then engines, tannoys, brakes and hissing doors. If the device had gone on running after that, it would have picked up hours of conversation: muted, bored, confiding, brash, but seldom rising much above the soothing background clatter of the rails.

I planned to keep to Lenin's schedule as well as his exact route. I would leave Zurich on 9 April and arrive in St Petersburg eight days and well over 2,000 miles later. It promised to be a headlong rush, even on Europe's fastest-moving trains, but Lenin was impatient and I took my cue from him. Though every connection had to be met at breakneck speed, I was also to enjoy what seemed like endless hours of leisure, as Lenin did, watching the changing scene. A hundred years have passed since the great Russian came this way. The little German towns he saw, huddled neatly like wooden toys, are now ringed by commercial blocks and high-speed roads. The urban landscape sprawls for miles beyond the old suburbs. Most striking of all, however, is the absence of any sense of danger. As my train crossed from Switzerland into

Germany it did not even stop, but the border bristled with guns in Lenin's time and the land beyond had a murderous reputation. My journey was smooth, fast and safe; as Europe's war raged all around him, Lenin's was arduous and frightening.

Lenin might also have struggled to recognize the towns and cities where I stopped. In Zurich, waiting to set off, I wandered up the narrow street where he once lived. Strolling towards the lake, I visited the cafés where the Russian exiles used to meet. The district was a poor one then, but now even the short walk to the library where Lenin liked to work is lined with shops, and the only frightening things in sight are the prices on the hand-made shoes and imported designer paint. The working class has disappeared, the factories are gone. The sumptuous Baur au Lac, the city's most luxurious hotel, is one of the few landmarks that remains more or less as it was when Parvus, the enigmatic go-between who handled some of Lenin's German funds, set up in one of its suites in 1915. A century on, the rich at least have things exactly as they wish.

It was refreshing, having mused on that, to find one cottage industry that had somehow survived the years. Lulled by the ultra-modern German trains I had forgotten it, but the seaway between Sassnitz and the Swedish port of Trelleborg has been a smugglers' route for centuries. By the time I wheeled my suitcase through the metal door, the ferry's airline seats, upright as Presbyterian church pews, had all been occupied by families and men with flickering laptops, but the saloon, a carnival of plastic palms and blue banquettes, felt more like Tirana or Bucharest, especially when everyone began to shout. We were still in port at Sassnitz when the cursing began. It centred round a monstrous stretch-wrapped pallet-load of beer, as awkward as a restaurant-size fridge, which several men were attempting to heave over a step. I was thirsty from the latest train, to say nothing of weary and crumpled, so my instinct was to track this to the nearest pas-senger bar, but as the tenth crate-trolley wobbled in, and the twentieth, all of them laden with German canned beer, I understood that I was travelling along an artery for tax-free booze. The contraband – heaped under groundsheets, bound with cords – created looming walls around the groups of traders as they dealt their playing cards and checked their phones.

Those smugglers – businessmen, of course – were heirs to an impressive line. Their predecessors worked this route throughout the First World War, sometimes conveying phar-maceutical supplies and sometimes coded letters in primitive secret ink. What made the current lot so special, however, was an irony of history, for all these small-time beer tycoons came from societies where private trade had once been out-lawed by a communist regime. That rapid turnabout helps to explain why Lenin's countrymen have cooled to him in recent times. They have embalmed him like a rubber doll, and they have made exhaustive studies of his brain, but no one really loves him now; the corpse has been preserved without a heart. His reputation is worst of all in the places where Soviet power was forcibly imposed. In one, western Ukraine, his ideas are so execrated that a new word, *Lenina-pad*, had to be coined when Maidan protesters brought down dozens of Lenin statues at once in 2014.

One of my fellow passengers turned out to have come from Sofia. As we chatted in a canyon between many crates of beer, she remembered Bulgarian communism and clicked her tongue against bare gums. She was surprised enough that I was not transporting freight. If I had told her of my quest for Lenin she would probably have given me up for a halfwit. What that dead man has come to symbolize in countries such as hers – corruption, hardship, lies and the abuse of power – is a system so rotten that it does not even qualify to be described as a fossil. But I knew that it had once been alive. Like fossil-hunters everywhere, I dreamed of stepping back into the world where it had breathed.

It was springtime six days ago when I left Zurich. In the snowdrifts of Tornio, it is as cold as death. The station here, another relic of the First World War, is a brick building that now stands abandoned on a stretch of bank. Back across the river, albeit not precisely opposite (as usual, no one was willing to risk that), Haparanda's station was a more elaborate affair, but both places are empty now and the lines have been closed to passengers for years. To get to Haparanda station from the town, indeed, I had to pass the regional prison. The Finnish side is prettier, at least today, and certainly less forbidding. The station also has a plaque commemorating Lenin's famous journey; it is the only one that I have found in Haparanda–Tornio. It must have been the Soviets who got the Finns to put it there. In the 1960s, when they were celebrating fifty years of proletarian dictatorship, Russia's diplomats in Europe attempted to persuade their hosts to screw a bit of metal like this to any site Lenin passed through.

The trouble with memorials is that people stop seeing them. Two days ago, I had gone looking for a brass plaque in Malmö's Savoy Hotel. Lenin and his hungry comrades had dined there after their ferry-ride from Germany, and I had read about a gorgeous room and famously efficient staff. The concierge was mystified. 'Lenin?' she asked eventually. 'You mean John Lennon?' It turned out that there was indeed a plaque across the hall, and when I saw it I could tell why Lenin's name had not occurred to the young woman (despite the astonishing revelation that she was herself from Russia). The brass is mainly polished to a lovely shine, but the bit that carries Lenin's name is dim enough to be eclipsed by stars of a quite different magnitude: Judy Garland and Brigitte Bardot, Abba and Henning Mankell.

At least the man in Stockholm knew who Lenin was. I had only one day in town (as Lenin did), and several people asked me why I had to leave so soon. 'You are following Lenin?' this shopkeeper exclaimed. 'Don't you know? You are about a hundred years too late!' We both laughed, but in fact that was the point of the whole thing. I was not there merely to tell an old story again. Whatever new details may have emerged from Russia's archives recently, I wanted to do something more than fill history's gaps. I took the train to recreate a journey from a century ago, but I am writing this book because we all live in a different world.

The Cold War used to exercise a stranglehold on everyone's imagination. It arranged everything along a line between two poles – for or against, right or left – and ultimately drained the colour out of history. Most of us turned instead to books about the Romanovs and pretty princesses in white. As I thought about Europe in 1917, however, and tried to picture Lenin there, I kept seeing reflections of the times we live in now. Lenin's legacy is often treated as an abstract thing, a list of texts and speeches, formal stuff. The weight of all that writing makes it difficult to see the living strands, the ones that matter in the light of recent world events. The list of those is long, but it includes global power realignment, espionage and dirty tricks, fanaticism and complex multiple insurgencies.

The old books told the story in the best way for their times. In 1940, Edmund Wilson used Lenin's journey to the Finland Station as a way of writing about socialism, labouring for decades to construct a classic tale of disappointed hope.[6] In the 1950s, Alan Moorehead produced a more sober account, financed in part by *Life* magazine, whose aim was to investigate the truth behind the German gold that Lenin was supposed to have received.[7] Michael Pearson went over that ground again in the 1970s, this time with drama on his mind.[8] His work was good on German trains and English gossip but weak, indeed evasive, on the politics. For that, you had to read the socialist Marcel Liebman, for whom the Lenin story (like Lenin's writings as a whole) was 'one of the brightest torches available to aid our observation of present-day political phenomena'.[9] Views like Liebman's seem antiquated now, and almost no one goes to Lenin for enlightenment. But revolutions are still happening, and leaders are still preaching anger and armed struggle to receptive crowds.

The universe of Marx and Lenin used to be my own. I made my first visit to Russia when its government was Soviet and its cities grey, devoid of coffee, barely lit at night. I made my pilgrimage to Lenin's tomb, I marvelled at the reverence some people genuinely felt. Later, as Moscow turned into the Dubai of the north, I spent my time amid the dust and relics of the past. Thanks to the Russian people's kindness, I explored the costs and hardship of the Soviet years as if I were researching my own family. Listening to people's memories of arrest and exile to the labour camps, or visiting the mass graves that survive from Stalin's time, I was a witness to some of the tragedies that communism inflicted on its citizens. I was not one of those who thought all aspects of the Soviet Union evil, false or misguided, but its effects were catastrophic just the same. I understood why its end was celebrated across Europe, North America and wealthy countries everywhere. There was a celebration of a kind in Russia, too. But though we all wept tears of happiness when the Berlin Wall came down, outsiders' crowing self-congratulation was bound to leave a sour taste.

The truth, which took a while to dawn, is that not everyone turned out to be as enchanted by the values of the so-called 'West' as some leaders of the free world thought they should be. It is too soon to talk of any victory; the term is as misleading as it is unwise. The British diplomats in Russia made the same mistake in Lenin's time when they assumed that every individual across the globe would want to be a decent chap just like they were. They never really understood that Lenin was not some imported species of demon, deflecting Russians from their destiny to be like meek versions of Englishmen. As I would find, the British sponsored Russian exiles of their own, escorting them to Petrograd to preach to waiting crowds. They failed, while Lenin's mission ended in success because he promised things that mattered more than British decency and yet more guns.

The dogma of Marxism-Leninism-Stalinism was an empty shell by the time I studied at Moscow State University in the 1980s (and a tactful leadership had dropped the Stalinism part), but I knew that there had once been a time when it felt alive. The brightest moments were in 1917. The spring and summer of that year saw Lenin at his most creative. Whatever happened when he was in power, the man who came back on the sealed train was popular because he offered clarity and hope. His message spoke to a large section of the Russian people, the ones who wanted more than their old leaders thought they had a right to ask from life. Although the route I have been following is a fact of geography, I have also been travelling in time, rattling north in search of a landscape of forgotten possibilities.

The journey ends in the magical city of St Petersburg, Lenin's wartime Petrograd, the second Russian capital. Thirty years after the end of communism, the traces of the leader's fateful journey are disappearing even here. Wrapped in gold leaf and painted in fresh pastel shades, the city has decided to revive its glamorous, imperial phase. There remain a few places, however, where the flame of revolution is still allowed a controlled burn. One of them stands in a quiet street on the Petrograd Side, not too far from Chkalovskaya metro. As is the case with many old apartment blocks, its crumbling entrance lobby hits you with a smell of dogs, stale smoke and beer. The pushchairs parked along the wall are all new and expensive brands, but no one cares to pool their money and provide a lift of sufficient size to carry the things upstairs. Like the graffiti on the wall outside, the present one proclaims the nation's verdict on collectivism. Above, the doors to the private apartments are of a calibre more usually associated with bank vaults. The building's walls are fragile, with enormous cracks, but if the whole thing ever does come down those doors will still be there.

When I get to the top floor, the portrait of Vladimir Putin on the office wall tells me which version of Lenin I can expect to encounter today. The staff in here are keener on the one they think of as a great leader and teacher than on the revolutionary whose aim was global civil war. The woman who extends her hand for me to shake is neat, precise and spotless. She is also generous, however, and once it is clear that I really want to listen, and that I also need to see and understand, she blossoms into the ideal guide. It helps that I once lived, as she did, in the Soviet world. We have a language in common, a language that young Russians do not even know.

The place that she curates is the Elizarov museum, the apartment where Lenin's sisters lived with his brother-in-law and, for a short time in the last years of her life, his mother. In April 1917, in the small hours of the morning, Lenin came here after the reception that greeted his arrival at the Finland Station. As I peer into the bedroom, I can imagine him throwing his jacket on the bed while Nadezhda Krupskaya, his wife of nearly twenty years, unpins her hat and glides about, in borrowed slippers, to arrange the room. The couple lived here for the next six weeks, displacing the two sisters and sharing their tea.

To say that it has been preserved is an understatement. The flat iron is still leaning on the kitchen range, the copper bath awaits. The twin beds where the couple slept are draped with the linen that Lenin's sister Mariya loved to decorate with fussy hand-embroidery. His mother's things are in the main bedroom, but with them is a travelling-case, left open to show brushes, shaving kit and bottles for cologne. Its battered leather is a reminder that Lenin spent the best years of his life packing a bag like this and travelling, his homes no more than rented rooms in foreign towns. Though the vanity case is splendid in its way, its purpose here in the museum is to represent the life of a renunciate, a wanderer, the Lenin who was part of Soviet myth.

What I had not expected was the primness, an atmosphere as suffocating as that of any Dickensian parlour. Frilled pillows and embroidered cushions have been scattered everywhere (though always in the neatest way), and each framed photograph is dusted to a noble shine. There is even a lace-edged sling above one bed in which the occupant could hang his watch. The study opposite is masculine (it belonged to Mark Elizarov, Lenin's brother-in-law, who made his money in commercial shipping), but that means only that the walls are brownish, the lace supplanted by chessmen. The clutter is distracting for a while, but then my eye rests on a coconut. 'Elizarov had contacts overseas,' the curator explains. 'He brought this home; it was a treasure.' I shake it, and the desiccated kernel responds with a dull rattle. The wretched thing has been here for over a hundred years. If levity were not so obviously out of place, I might have been tempted to laugh.

From here, we cross into the drawing room. The building where the Elizarovs lived was designed to mimic the prow of a ship, and this is the room that occupies the sharp end. If the muslin curtains were ever lifted, the triangular space would immediately flood with daylight. Instead, there are electric bulbs. Lenin had a special reverence for those. 'Communism', he once said, 'is Soviet power plus the electrification of the whole country.' His sisters cannot have been quite so sure, however, for every lamp is veiled by a shade with a heavily beaded fringe. 'Anna made those', the curator explains, 'because she did not want her brother to be harmed by unhealthy electric rays.'

Lenin loved it here. It is easy to forget that he was respectable and relatively wealthy – a member of the early twentieth-century bourgeoisie; waistcoats, antimacassars and all. His wife's sketchbook is on the dining table. I leaf through it, amazed that she had time to draw at all. The couple were childless, and Krupskaya devoted almost all her energy to the demands of revolution, but she took up this book when she had a few moments to relax. The pages show plump-faced children with ribbons in their curly hair; here little boys with puppies and there a girl with a kitten. We have missed something about the world of the successful revolutionary, it seems. These firebrands came from tranquil, and even stifling, homes. They did not live outside their times; they were almost cocooned by them.

I am still reflecting on this when the curator motions me to sit. She lifts the lid of the inevitable upright piano (candelabra, German case, gothic lettering) and flexes her schoolteacher's arms. And then, as I sit in the drawing room where Lenin used to take his ease, surrounded by his knick-knacks and his sisters' dainty needlework, she starts to play. The piano is out of tune, but I am too entranced to object to that. The street sounds of St Petersburg are banished as my host coaxes the instrument into the famous first movement of Beethoven's Moonlight Sonata. She plays it well, though there is just a hint of saccharine, of smothering pillows.

Lenin loved music, the piano especially. It is a point that all the textbooks used to make, along with tales about his fondness for children and cats. The Lenin I am looking for is not so sweet. I want to find the man with the consuming, merciless cold fire. It was not lace and coconuts that changed the world. I see him now, pacing the room, impatient with the soothing notes. Like chess, which he had also liked to play, music distracted him from revolution. 'I know nothing that is greater than the Appassionata,' he once said. 'I would like to listen to it every day. But I can't listen to music too often. It affects your nerves, makes you want to say stupid, nice things, and stroke the heads of people . . . You mustn't stroke anyone's head – you might get your hand bitten off. You have to hit them on the head without any mercy.'[10]

1. Dark Forces

A minister today, a banker tomorrow; a banker today,
a minister tomorrow. A handful of bankers, who
have the whole world in their grip, are making a
fortune out of the war.

V. I. Lenin

In March 1916, a British officer called Samuel Hoare set out
for Russia. The last thing he was thinking about was revolutionary socialism. If anyone had asked, he would probably
have muttered that he wanted to be soldiering – when war
with Germany had broken out he had been among the first
to sign up with the Norfolk Yeomanry – but his physical
frailty had ruled out active service in combat. Instead, at
thirty-six, he had been recruited by Sir Mansfield Smith-
Cumming, the legendary 'C', to work for the British Secret
Intelligence Service in the Russian capital, Petrograd.[1] While
other members of his class were in the trenches, he mastered
espionage, censorship and ciphering. He probably experi-
mented with disguises, too. His new boss was addicted to
them, and had his own designed at William Berry Clarkson's
theatrical shop in Soho's Wardour Street.[2]

The task that Hoare had been assigned was intricate. He
had to find out if his country's Russian allies were maintaining their side of a wartime anti-German trade embargo. The
British were particularly keen on this; they hoped to move

into the Russian market when the war was won. In the meantime there were also fears that the remaining commercial links between Russia and Germany might serve as cover for spying and possibly for sabotage. As he worked with Russia's haphazard Restriction of Enemy Supplies Committee, Hoare would have to monitor the patterns of Russia's import trade, the merchants, markets and any complaints of shortages.[3] His other mission in the Russian capital was to take a close and critical look at the operation of the British intelligence mission. Though this might feel like military stuff, he was supposed to keep in mind the business angle even here. As Frank Stagg, the man who ran the Russia desk in London, explained to Hoare before he left, 'a firm footing in Russia' might produce 'sufficient information to serve up some tempting dishes not merely to the British Government but to the big financial and commercial interests in the City'.[4]

It was a job that called for tact. For one thing, the French were the people with the real Russian expertise. For decades now, Frenchmen had been established at the tsarist court as trading and investment partners as well as arbiters of fashion and suppliers of champagne. French officers had all the best contacts inside the Russian secret services. To some extent, this was a help, for Britain and France were allies, yoked to each other and to Russia through a treaty system called the Triple Entente, but by 1916 their understanding was no longer quite enough. When the day came for British exporters to move into a post-war tsarist empire, after all, those same Frenchmen would represent the competition.

More immediately, C had a string of problems in Russia. There had been tensions from the first between his agents and Colonel Alfred Knox, the British military attaché, while the officer whom C had initially entrusted with the Russian show, Major Archibald Campbell, had recently been recalled after a storm of complaints.[5] To cap it all, the ambassador, Sir George Buchanan, was old school and stiff upper lip, the kind who disliked covert operations on principle. 'Difficulties had arisen,' as Hoare put it, because of 'interdepartmental disputes as to the exact place the Secret Service should hold in the official hierarchy'.[6] The phrase was English understatement at its best. As a member of Parliament and a baronet, Hoare was the man to sort things out.

The new spy had to make his own way to the posting. Hoare had a berth reserved from Newcastle on a Norwegian steamer called the *Jupiter*. Among the other passengers, huddled in the fog like so many exotic birds, was a party of French dressmakers bound for Russia with their suite of fashion models. Theirs was a risky business, for the seaway was a magnet for German submarines. As the *Jupiter* steamed out of the Tyne, everyone took to scanning the waves. The crossing was uneventful on this occasion, however, and Hoare disembarked safely at the port of Bergen among the grey officials and the businessmen, the smugglers and the mannequins. From here, the journey continued to Christiania (Oslo), the capital of Norway, and on by sleeper to Stockholm.

Hoare had to cross the Scandinavian countries 'in mufti . . . concealing my sword in an umbrella case'.[7] As an officer in the service of a belligerent power, he would have been liable to internment if he had been caught by the police in neutral Sweden. That was the theory, anyway. In fact, he found that Sweden swarmed with spies, although it seemed to welcome only German ones. When he paid a visit to Sir Esmé Howard, the British ambassador in Stockholm, Hoare learned how volatile the mood in Sweden had become. The ban on war-related trade with Germany had hit it hard; food and jobs had come under pressure as British naval ships began to claim the right to control the cargo of neutrals as well as that of belligerents. Children were going without medicines, businessmen without their cheques and traders without markets for their timber, grain and iron. A large section of Sweden's ruling elite was sympathetic to the idea of a pact, even an alliance, with Germany.[8] The Baltic, after all, united the two countries far more than it divided them. When he dropped into Stockholm's Grand Hotel, Hoare hung his fur coat on a peg, and was amused to watch a German agent scuttle out to rifle through the pockets straight away.

He came to need that fur coat more and more as he went north. From Stockholm, he headed into Sweden's remote Norrland, a wilderness that Sami hunters shared with elk and Arctic fox and bear. As the writer Arthur Ransome had put it when he traversed the same route, 'the whole thing promises to be interesting but cold.'[9] Hoare was the MP for Chelsea, however, and he travelled first class for the whole route. 'The ride', he wrote, 'was peaceful and monotonous. At one point the train could not have gone more than five miles an hour, and ample time was allowed for the excellent hot dishes at the appointed stations.'[10] One of those stops, nearly 600 miles north of Stockholm, was the Bothnian port of Luleå, whose docks were used to load the iron ore from mines at Kiruna and Gallivare. The previous autumn, as Hoare knew, the British submarine commander Captain Cromie had sunk a large number of Swedish ships just off this port, all carrying blockade-breaking cargoes of iron for Germany, thousands of tons of it in every hold.[11]

The region was an awkward place for any British officer,

and Hoare was heading for its wildest town. No pre-war timetable would mark his route, for no line had existed here before the summer of 1915. Arthur Ransome, who made his way to Russia when the railway still ended at Karungi, recalled that the last miles in Sweden had involved 'a sledge-journey in the short light of winter, lying flat on a sledge, kept warm by a Lapp driver who kindly sat on my stomach as we hissed over the snow-track and down a frozen river to the Finnish frontier at Tornio'.[12] Fifteen months later, Samuel Hoare could breathe in relative comfort as his train crept forward between walls of blackened snow, the skeletons of trees just visible beyond the steam. The final miles were signalled by the appearance of countless wooden crates, huge piles of them at every stop. Then came the reindeer-sledges and the grizzled men in city coats. Hoare had arrived at Haparanda, the frontier town that controlled the crucial land-route from Europe to Russia and onwards to Shanghai.

He did not pause to see the sights. He could have explored the frozen marshes, where boxed-up freight from the United States and Britain, Denmark, France and Sweden itself had been piled in makeshift streets and courtyards like a second town. He could have dropped into a local bar. There, watching the off-duty fishermen and reindeer-drivers, he could have picked up news from three continents at once. A few months later, a Russian politician called Paul Miliukov, who passed through Haparanda in the opposite direction on an official trip to London, took pictures of the midnight sun there with his Kodak camera.[13] A revolutionary activist called Alexander Shlyapnikov, who crossed the border so often that he knew every safe house for a radius of miles, would marvel at the Northern Lights in winter skies. But

Hoare, a true-born Englishman, was most struck by the weather. 'Everything was dazzling white under the blazing sun,' he recalled. 'The snow had not a stain upon it, and the white sheepskin caps of the Swedish garrison looked yellow in the glare.'[14]

The Russian border post at Tornio felt bleak after Haparanda. Most new arrivals spent a long time sitting in the huts that served as checkpoints for the tsarist border guards. Hoare was travelling to Russia on official business, and an undercover agent of British intelligence was almost certainly on hand, but C's new spy could not afford to draw attention to himself by pulling rank. After several trying encounters of his own, Arthur Ransome had learned to flourish a letter on heavily embossed paper, and though it was in fact a demand for the return of overdue books to the London Library, the signature of the librarian, Dr Charles Theodore Hagberg Wright, was so flamboyant that it reduced even the sternest bureaucrat to unctuous servility.[15] Lacking Ransome's resourcefulness, most other travellers recalled the inside of the border buildings with a shudder. Hoare's wait was so long that a group of Russian soldiers broke into a dance, hoping to screw some small change from their audience. It felt like a whole season of his life had passed before the papers were finally stamped, the baggage clumsily repacked, and Hoare could climb aboard the southbound Finnish train.[16]

The line was once again a single track. Progress was slow and dirty, for since the war began the engines on this route had run on wood rather than coal. Clouds of ash blew through any window that was left open. Grey smoke and steam concealed the view of Finland's famous lakes. The days were growing longer fast, but it was dark when his train finally arrived at the border station of Beloostrov. Here, crossing into Russia proper from its province of Finland, he faced another round of paper-checking and incomprehensible commands. As crumpled and bewildered as a peasant, he reached Petrograd's main northern terminus, the Finland Station, at midnight. The platforms and arrival hall were barely lit and almost deserted.[17] There was a moment of exhausted panic before he made out a familiar British uniform; it was the official driver at last. In minutes, and with all his luggage safely stowed, Samuel Hoare was settled in a car, secure again after his short brush with barbarity.

It did not take long to speed through the working-class district behind the station. Crossing the river (wide and still half frozen), Hoare headed for the palace quarter and a hotel bed. A diplomat was wisest to avoid the streets where ordinary people lived and worked. It was a lesson he would learn in the coming days along with the rules of court etiquette and the problems of finding a reliable maid. The MP had arrived in Petrograd, and he was about to begin his work for the 'new, secret, and very indefinite' British intelligence service.

In 1916, Petrograd had a population of more than two million, swelled since the war began by huddled lines of migrant workers and refugees.[18] Built on the Neva river delta, the city lent itself to social subdivisions. The poor tended to live in the factory quarters that had sprung up round the vast new metal-working and armaments works. The streets behind the Finland Station led to narrow yards and blind windows, for this was the Vyborg district, home to the Erikson metal- and machine-works, the Nobel and New Lessner factories (both specializing in weapons and explosives), the Old

Sampson spinning and weaving factory and several large steel mills. South of the river, to the east, the Okhta district boasted a state-run explosives plant and a gunpowder factory, while to the south-west loomed the massive Putilov works, employing a workforce of tens of thousands and turning out rail track and rolling stock as well as artillery. Manufacturing had been a goldmine for speculators in the years before the war, but housing for the men and women it employed had seemed a less attractive investment.[19] Whatever the hardships, however, recruits continued to flock from the villages in search of work.

The other citizens of Petrograd, the types who kept a carriage and took boxes at the theatre, settled on the south edge of Vasilievsky Island, along the waterfront of the Petrograd Side and in the better districts near the Winter Palace. Tall houses by the city's network of canals afforded spacious first-floor flats for wealthy clients, although the basements and attics were available, at lower rents, for anyone from tradespeople to failing writers. In general, however, the main contact that moneyed people had with the city's grittier side was through their servants, drivers and doormen. The magnificent Nevsky Prospect, Petrograd's main street, was a place where the poor and unenfranchised seldom stepped. At times of stress (and there had been a revolution in 1905), the city governor could order that the bridges should be raised, turning the Neva into a huge moat and blocking access from almost all the most notorious suburbs. It was a pity that there had to be a mainline railway station near Nevsky Prospect and it was unfortunate that factories were visible behind the palaces. But troublemakers could always be packed into the cells of prisons like the Peter-Paul Fortress and Kresty, both of them landmarks on a dazzling waterfront.

The British embassy occupied a large part of the Saltykov Palace, a building otherwise known as No. 4 Palace Embankment. The location was magnificent, just a short walk along the river from the Winter Palace and commanding views across the water to the Peter-Paul Fortress and its golden spire. The embassy 'was an enormous building, spacious and solidly comfortable, though not in the least beautiful', the ambassador's daughter, Meriel Buchanan, would later write.[20] Its most remarkable features were the grand staircase and the ballroom, both of which had windows facing the river. But the offices were inconvenient, and the building was shared with an ancient princess, Anna Sergeyevna Saltykova, who still lived in the back with her servants and a loquacious geriatric parrot.[21]

Hoare would soon need to meet his own men, but the diplomatic part of his mission, the interdepartmental peace-making, demanded that he pay an early call on the ambassador. Sir George Buchanan had been London's man in Russia since 1910 and had built a reputation as Petrograd's most reliable and experienced diplomat. Hoare would soon fall under his spell. 'If I had to draw a picture of a British Ambassador,' recalled the spy, 'I should have drawn Sir George Buchanan. Distinguished, detached, rather shy in manner, and good-looking in the style that was most admired twenty years before.'[22] Robert Bruce Lockhart, who supported Sir George from an office in Moscow, agreed, observing that 'his monocle, his finely-chiselled features, and his beautiful silver-grey hair gave him something of the appearance of a stage diplomat.'[23] In *Ashenden*, the collection of stories that he based on his own wartime spy-missions, Somerset Maugham turned Sir George into Sir Herbert Witherspoon and had him presiding over dinner like the baronet in one of England's grandest country houses. A less kindly visitor, however, remembered a 'frigidity that would have sent a shiver down the spine of a polar bear'.[24]

Buchanan's view of spies might have been dim, but he was determined that Russia should go on fighting for an allied victory in the Great War.[25] To ensure that it did, he was prepared to sup with almost any devil London sent, and Hoare became a regular guest at the embassy. He was entertained by Lady Georgina, the ambassador's wife, by his daughter Meriel and by at least one bad-tempered Siamese cat. Hoare also dined with some of Europe's diplomatic stars, including Maurice Paléologue, the French ambassador, and the Marquis André Carlotti di Riparbella from Italy. The man from the United States, David Francis, preferred his poker to Buchanan's linen and claret, but that still left an assortment of interesting British staff for Hoare to meet.[26] The place to find them was the chancery department on the first landing of the embassy stairs. There young men in their worsted suits devoted the best hours of every day to typing, encoding or deciphering reports. No Russian secretary was on hand, for secrecy was paramount, even between allies. 'My impression', Lockhart recollected, 'was of a typing and telegraph bureau conducted by Old Etonians.'[27]

Hoare's own office was a brisk walk west along Palace Embankment. You turned left at the Winter Palace, a vast ensemble of 1,500 rooms whose stucco had been painted in a melancholy ox-blood red. Behind it, across Palace Square, stretched the parade of well-matched buildings, also painted like beefsteak, that housed the main government departments, including the Military General Staff. Here, crammed into some upper rooms, was the office of British Military Intelligence, an afterthought to that of France, which was next door. It might have been convenient, but it was not a place Hoare grew to love. 'True to Russian type,' he complained, 'the façade was the best part of the building. At the back of the General Staff was a network of smelly yards and muddy passages that made entrance difficult and health precarious.'[28]

But Hoare was not in town to admire the Rastrelli palaces. As he set to work in that stuffy room, he had to come to terms with Russia's extraordinary foreignness. Despite his straitlaced English background, the sheer amount of ceremony in the capital oppressed him. It was a good thing that the Swedes had never found his sword, for now he was expected to wear it at work. Another unwelcome surprise was the discovery that the Russians did not have a unified secret service of their own that he could work beside. The General Staff, the head of each army group and the ministry of marine each had their own intelligence agents, but the competition between them was so fierce that none could spare much energy for him. A more efficient network was operated by the interior ministry, and another by the Holy Synod, but neither was prepared to share its information with a foreigner. 'No-one else was fighting the war as we were fighting it,' the disappointed Englishman observed. 'The people in London ... projected Whitehall into the Square of the Winter Palace,' but Russia's war effort was as chaotic as it was unpopular.[29]

He might have learned more if he had been more attentive to the staff already working in that cramped room over the Moika canal. The acting head of intelligence at the time was Major Cudbert Thornhill, an old India hand and 'a good shot with rifle, catapult, shot-gun and blow-pipe'.[30] In the summer of 1916, however, when Hoare took over the British secret intelligence mission himself, Thornhill was moved into the role of assistant military attaché. The transfer left a small and dedicated staff for Hoare, theoretically, to command. Lieutenants Stephen Alley and Oswald Rayner were both fluent Russian-speakers with good contacts in the capital. Captain Leo Steveni, who worked with Thornhill, helped collect battle intelligence, including information about German naval strategy.[31]

Clashes with the military attaché, Colonel Alfred Knox, were inescapable from the first. In one embassy official's view, after all, Knox constituted Britain's 'real link with the country'.[32] It was an opinion that Knox himself fully endorsed, and he always behaved as if he knew Russia better than the rest of the British colony put together. As an Ulsterman, however, he was deemed to have come from the wrong class, so he could not be assigned to the tsar's military headquarters, the Stavka, a job reserved for an incompetent called Sir John Hanbury-Williams.[33] The tension could be almost tangible, but all the same this small group of men had been able to set their differences apart for long enough to gather a good deal of vital information in the months before Hoare arrived, including (Steveni later affirmed) the intelligence that had enabled British ships to intercept part of the German High Seas Fleet off Dogger Bank in 1915.[34]

As Hoare would discover, the rest of the British colony in Petrograd had all the makings of an Oxford college inadvertently displaced. There was a scattering of academics and a more voluble cluster of writers, many of whom were earning their keep by sending columns to the British press. Arthur Ransome was one of these, but the most colourful was Harold Williams, a linguist, essayist and correspondent for three newspapers who had married a prominent liberal activist. Through his wife, Ariadna Tyrkova ('a woman of advanced views', pronounced Buchanan), Williams knew almost every political figure in Petrograd. 'He was a very quiet man,' Arthur Ransome remembered, 'and extraordinarily kind. I do not think it possible that he can ever have had an enemy.'[35] If Knox was the embassy's link with the country, and especially with the army, Williams connected it to Petrograd's emerging political class, the critics and reformers who yearned to introduce a modern constitutional government.

It was not long before the gloom began to get to him. While Alley and his friends continued with their secret work, Hoare was approached by a representative of the Orthodox Church, who wanted him to help resolve a candlewax shortage. Before the wartime trade blockade, a German firm called Stumpf had supplied 13.5 tons of the stuff to Russia's churches every year; the politicians might have cut the supply but the faithful still needed to light their prayers. The blockade (and, indirectly, Britain) was also blamed for other kinds of darkness in day-to-day Russian life. In time, Hoare arranged for wax imports to come in through the port of Archangel, but he could not brighten up a whole society. Petrograd's theatres were half empty, the shops were grey, and conversation focused on bad news and worse prospects. 'Most of the men and women who had made the Russian capital so brilliant in pre-war days were at the front,' Hoare remarked, 'and for those whose households and fortunes were limited, entertaining had become almost impossible.'[36]

He had problems enough himself, for rents had soared in recent months. Even Sir George Buchanan was worried by the fact that several of his staff, including married ones with families, had taken hotel rooms because they could not keep up the inflated payments on their erstwhile homes. The prices of basic commodities had risen so fast that diplomatic salaries were stretched; in September 1916, Maurice Paléologue observed in his diary that wood and eggs now cost four times what they had done two years before and butter five times more.[37] How Russian workers were supposed to cope remained a mystery. The long queues – Hoare observed 'grey women' – outside food shops had become a fixture by 1916; so hostile was the general mood that there were rumours that the anti-war feeling in the crowds was being fanned by German agents.[38] Everyone had to make do. Hoare employed an English servant who worked for him every day, but the man kept two changes of livery handy so that he could help out, on alternate nights, at functions for the British and French embassies.

All countries suffered in the war, of course, but Russia seemed to suffer most. While London imagined that the difficulties could be solved by sending extra guns and offering a bit more credit to the Russian Bourse, it did not take anyone in Petrograd long to see that goodwill and imports were not enough. Nothing was working as it should, from transport to the army General Staff and from the Russian police to the delivery of coal supplies. The political machinery had completely stalled, sabotaged by the tsar, his empress and what some now saw as a complex German plot to undermine Russia itself. 'There was no directing will,' observed one leading politician from the time, 'no plan, no system, and there could not be any ... The supreme authority ... was imprisoned by harmful influences.'[39]

Hoare would have got the story from the clubbable liberals and wealthy industrialists who made up Russia's political class. Where his ambassador was too fastidious to interfere, he met these through Harold Williams, who knew everyone from Mikhail Rodzianko, the chairman of the Russian parliament, the Duma, to reformers like Paul Miliukov and Alexander Guchkov.[40] All told the same basic tale. Russia was heading for disaster like a car speeding towards a cliff. It might have needed two brandies to get any Russian to say it openly, but the fundamental problem was the tsar.

Since he had taken personal command of the army in August 1915, spending more and more time at his headquarters near the front, Nicholas II had lost whatever knack he ever had for leadership. He ignored or actively spurned the Duma while stuffing the upper house, the Council of Ministers, with people so talentless that they were almost comical.[41] Hoare knew about the Council at first hand, having recently attended a reception in its chambers at the Mariinsky Palace. The place had smelled of mothballs and despair, and he had been cornered over tea by an official who was so deaf that he mistook the British officer for a German and began loudly to denounce English perfidy and English democratic ways.[42]

The catalogue of Nicholas' errors was growing fast. In January 1916, the tsar had dismissed his seventy-six-year-old Premier, Ivan Goremykin. But Goremykin's replacement, Boris Stürmer, was almost as reactionary and even less effectual. No one liked Stürmer, including Harold Williams, who threw down a gauntlet with the remark that 'a more corrupt, cynical, incompetent and lying functionary it would be hard to find in the Russian empire.'[43] 'He was totally ignorant of everything he undertook,' remembered Paul Miliukov.[44] Untroubled by this opposition (or by the suspicions that the German sound of Stürmer's name inevitably roused), the tsar added the foreign and interior ministries to Stürmer's portfolio in the summer of 1916. The only qualification the man appeared to have for any of these vital tasks was his experience of fawning on the imperial family during their tour of Russia for the Romanov tercentenary a few years earlier.

The Duma met at the other end of town, in the notoriously draughty Tauride Palace. Created as a concession after the upheavals of 1905, it still felt like the dress rehearsal for a parliament. A portrait of the tsar stared over its chamber, showing him on a trip to Italy (not even Russia) and apparently smirking in contempt at the vulgar notion of democracy. Hoare found the Duma's members 'obviously disillusioned and embittered by the hopelessness of their situation'.[45] They took their politics very seriously, but the tsar prorogued their house whenever he detected challenge or dissent. The last round of elections, held in 1912, had returned a few Marxists, mainly members of the Menshevik Party, but most of these had promptly been arrested or exiled. Apart from them, the only real radicals were members of the Kadet Party, all devoted to reform but none so wild that he would not sit on a committee. 'Ours was a party of lawyers, doctors and professors,' remembered Paul Miliukov, one of the most distinguished of the Kadets.[46] His views, according to Professor Bernard Pares (an academic who had come to town, as C's nephew, to do a little spying on the side), 'never seemed to me to diverge much from what one could hear at any time in the National Liberal Club in London'. Miliukov's aim was to steer Russia into constitutional monarchy. In 1916 Petrograd, that made him a red firebrand.

The Duma's list of demands had grown during the war.[47] In 1915, a group of its members, including the Kadets, had formed a Progressive Bloc to defend Russia's military honour and its people's fragile constitutional rights.[48] On the left wing of the coalition, Miliukov believed that Russia could not continue to force its rule on subject nations like the Balts and Poles. Autonomy and equal rights, rather than full independence, might offer an acceptable compromise, while inside Russia there should be an end to discrimination against religious minorities, including Jews. Other Kadets were keen to talk about trade unions and labour rights, a political amnesty and an end to the censorship by which even speeches in the Duma were not always reported.

As a whole, however, the Bloc was there to win the war and foster trade, courting the European markets and proposing smoother regulation of a system that was choking on red tape. It was to promote his country's industry and commerce that Miliukov, who had always taken a special interest in the Balkans, came to advocate Russian control of Constantinople and the Straits that connected the Black Sea to the Mediterranean. His hopes in that direction inspired an obsessive commitment to the war, but Miliukov knew all too well that victory came at a price: a year before, his younger son had died in fighting on the Austrian front.

It was not liberal reform, however, and it was not even the army's terrible record of casualties that Petrograd was talking about as the first snow blew lightly on the Neva in the autumn of 1916. The city was gripped by the fear of what were simply called 'Dark Forces'. The Germans, it was whispered, had a foothold at court. Their goal was to persuade Russia to withdraw from the war. If that happened, Berlin could focus all its troops along a single front, crushing the French and British like so many gnats. The enticements for Russia included an end to the heartbreaking deaths, but extreme right-wingers also hoped that Prussian officers, as paragons of discipline and hierarchy, might help them to restore a fitting (and reactionary) government. The talks went on quietly, sometimes in Stockholm or in Copenhagen.[49] A British businessman called Stinton Jones suggested that the game was darker than Russians themselves could see. The plotters, he explained, would engineer a popular revolt to make Russia seem ungovernable. As planned, the emergency would serve as an excuse to sign a separate peace with Germany. Thereafter, however, Russia would become 'a nation despicable in the eyes of the world' and 'when the time arrived for Germany to rend Russia there would be none to help her, so Germany would progress a step further in her scheme of world domination.'[50]

The trail of rumour led directly to the empress. Alexandra had been born with a different title, Alix of Hesse and by Rhine, and many believed that she remained Germany's agent. Sir George Buchanan dismissed the idea. 'She is not', he wrote in February 1917, 'a German working in Germany's interests, but a reactionary, who wishes to hand down the autocracy intact to her son.' Her interference in ministerial appointments, however, had turned her into what Buchanan called 'the unconscious tool of others, who really are German agents'.[51] Liberal critics believed that she was behind Stürmer's appointment, for nothing else could explain it. When the ingratiating Alexander Protopopov, another of Alexandra's favourites, was appointed to the interior ministry in September 1916, suspicion seemed to be confirmed. Protopopov, who was rumoured to be insane (he suffered from a degenerative nervous disorder linked to advanced syphilis), had been spotted talking to a German agent on a recent visit to Stockholm.[52]

In reality, Protopopov was more likely to see a vision of the Crucifixion than to hatch a plot, but there were other agents of the kaiser in the Empress Alexandra's suite. Maurice Paléologue believed the shadowy movement to include representatives of the Holy Synod, members of the Baltic nobility, big financiers and pro-German industrialists. 'The predominant motive', he wrote, 'is fear, the fear to which the reactionary party is inspired on seeing Russia in so close and prolonged an association with the democratic powers of the West.'[53] In October the French ambassador spent an evening with a 'court functionary' who gave more details of the cabal that was snaking its way about the court. 'That gang will stop at nothing,' he warned. 'They'll foment strikes, riots, pogroms; they'll try to produce social distress and famine and make everyone so thoroughly wretched and despondent that the continuation of the war will become impossible.'[54] The informant had been so terrified that he had refused to confide in Paléologue at all until the servants had gone home.

The spies seemed to be everywhere. It was almost a reflex to blame the Jews, a prejudice that the British indulged at least as often as the Russians. As George Buchanan put it, 'Jews as a class are pro-German, and rumours aimed at spreading dissatisfaction or mistrust in Russia herself and in her allies are traceable to them.'[55] But there was nothing else about the continual plotting that was routine. As Samuel Hoare reported to Military Intelligence in December 1916: 'The outstanding feature, unique in the history of Russia, is that all sections of society are united against the small group, half Court, half bureaucracy, that is attempting to keep the complete control of government in its hands.'[56] 'A palace coup was openly spoken of,' Buchanan recollected, 'and at dinner at the Embassy a Russian friend of mine . . . declared that it was a mere question whether both the Emperor and Empress or only the latter would be killed.'[57]

Buchanan's sole priority was keeping Russia in the war. Every move in the critical weeks ahead was judged by what it meant for the next spring's campaign, every new minister or public strike assessed in terms of military morale. And the picture was changing very fast indeed. First came the Duma's new session, which opened on 1 November 1916. The mood was tense already, but the opening speeches would have been sensational at any time. Although it could not be reported (the newspapers, in protest, carried blank spaces where the words should have been), Miliukov's attack on the tsarist administration was soon being quoted everywhere. He had listed the many misdeeds of the past few months, pausing after each to ask, with theatrical repetition, whether the house considered it to be a case of 'stupidity or treason'.[58] The answer was damning ('the consequences are the same,' concluded Miliukov), and the speech led to Stürmer's dismissal. As the imperial secret police, the Okhrana, reported grudgingly, 'the hero of the hour is Miliukov.'[59]

Heroics in the Duma notwithstanding, the mass of the population was struggling, increasingly resentful of both government and war. The winter of 1916–17 was hungrier than any since the war began. Factory workers, forced to queue for basic goods and work in bitter cold, grew anxious and then angry, blaming the empress and the war. At a time of inflation, some found their wages dwindling as the labour-force was augmented with unskilled women from the villages, a group who did not think of bargaining as cadre workers had. Although a striker could face deportation to the front (or years of hard labour in penal camps), the number of strikes increased as prices rose, and many included direct political demands. In October, during a strike at the Renault works, some of the troops who had been called to disperse the protesters changed sides and fired on their officers. The atmosphere was so poisonous that many cavalry officers, reluctant to shoot their own people, began asking to be sent to the front to avoid a posting in the Petrograd garrison.[60]

On Boxing Day 1916, Hoare cabled a sombre message back to London. 'It is probably correct to say that a very great majority of the civilian population of Russia is in favour of peace,' it read. 'The conditions of life have become so intolerable, the Russian casualties have been so heavy, the ages and classes subject to military service have been so widely extended, the disorganization and untrustworthiness of the Government have become so notorious that it is not a matter of surprise if the majority of ordinary people reach at any peace straw.' His last sentence was conveyed with special emphasis: *'Personally, I am convinced that Russia will never fight through another winter.'*[61]

Within a week, however, these thoughts were interrupted by the murder of a notorious monk. Rasputin shared the public's hatred more or less equally with his patron and admirer, the Empress Alexandra. He was widely believed to sympathize with the German cause, to favour tyranny and to have allowed German agents to get close to the empress. He was also dissolute, dirty, manipulative and rude. His murder at the hands of a small group of titled patriots, therefore, was enough to divert attention from almost any hardship of the New Year holiday. Hoare prefaced his own ten-page report with a disclaimer. 'If it is written in the style of the Daily Mail,' he began, 'my answer is that the whole question is so sensational that one cannot describe it as one would if it were an ordinary episode of the war.'[62] These things would not have happened to a clergyman in Chelsea, certainly.

At first light on the first day of 1917, the Petrograd police had found a man's overshoe, in a large size, in snow on the bank of a branch of the Neva. The trail led them to search the frozen river, and thence to the discovery of a mutilated corpse. As it was hacked out of the ice, the body, huge and difficult to move, was unmistakably Rasputin's. He had been poisoned with cyanide, beaten and shot with at least two guns before his body had been bound in heavy chains and pushed under the ice. A devastated Alexandra went into mourning as soon as she was told the news. The rest of Petrograd, by all accounts, was delighted. 'There was great rejoicing among the public when it heard of the death of Rasputin,' wrote Paléologue. 'People kissed each other in the street and many went to burn candles in Our Lady of Kazan.'[63] 'If one cannot say good about the deed,' reported Hoare, 'one can at least say about the death "nothing but good".'[64]

What Hoare seemed not to want to say was that his own men may have helped to plan and execute the crime. It could even have been Oswald Rayner who fired the fatal shot, killing Rasputin after torturing him for hours to find out what he knew of German influence within the tsarist court. A cover-story was prepared, and the murder came to be seen as a purely Russian patriotic act, but even Hoare had noticed recently that members of his team had started using the word 'liquidate' with an alarming frequency.[65] As Hoare conceded, the murder showed what could be done, though what it had achieved was questionable.

The capital soon returned to its accustomed mode of bleak

despair. In an act of pure spite, an unrepentant clutch of
ministers outlawed a conference of local government and
charitable organizations that had been planned for the new
year. A round of elections to Moscow's city council was blatantly rigged. Visiting Petrograd in January 1917, Robert
Bruce Lockhart 'found the atmosphere more depressing
than ever. Champagne flowed like water. The Astoria and
the Europe – the two best hotels in the capital – were
thronged with officers who should have been at the front . . .
Even in the Embassy hope had sunk to a low ebb. Sir George
himself looked tired and ill.'[66]

After a struggle with his conscience and the regulations,
Buchanan broke with protocol and tried to warn the tsar. On
12 January, the Russian New Year, he called at the palace at
Tsarskoe Selo. Perhaps anticipating some bad news, the tsar
received him without the customary warmth. Both men
remained standing as Sir George said his piece. 'I explained',
he wrote, 'that the co-ordination of our efforts would not
suffice unless there was in each of the Allied countries
complete solidarity between all classes of the population.'
Nicholas heard him out, said almost nothing in reply and
dismissed his visitor before he let himself give way to angry
trembling.[67] The empress may have hurried to console him,
for Paléologue learned that she had been listening to everything through a half-open door.

Russia remained an ally, however, and allies always had to
talk. Back in December, the British, French and Italian general staffs had met at Chantilly to plan the new season's
campaigns. The logistics of the journey had kept the Russians away, so it was agreed that a delegation from all three
western powers should travel to Petrograd for talks.[68] Lord
Kitchener, the Secretary of State for War, would normally

have run the show, and had set out to visit Russia the summer before, but he was killed on the way when his armoured cruiser hit a mine off Scapa Flow. His leadership was missed as a team assembled under Lord Milner and General de Castelnau, neither of whom knew Russia at all. What Hoare would call 'the allied Noah's ark' set out by sea for the port of Romanov (now Murmansk) in January 1917. Passing safely through the submarines, the members of the delegation were among the first to trundle down the Murman railway to Petrograd, a journey that required four days.

Lockhart despaired. 'Rarely in the history of great wars', he wrote, 'can so many important ministers and generals have left their respective countries on so useless an errand.' [69] To avoid the possibility that Milner's mission might do harm, Hoare wrote, the Russians decided to prevent it from doing anything at all, a tactic that involved a succession of dinners, lunches, concerts and dances. 'Court carriages with beautifully groomed horses and the crimson and gold of the Imperial liveries passed up and down the streets,' Meriel Buchanan recalled. 'An endless stream of motors stood at all hours of the day before the Hotel d'Europe, where the missions had been lodged.' Hoare persuaded the governor of Petrograd to permit a restaurant called The Bear to stay open all night so that the delegates might entertain their favourite stars from the ballet and opera: 'The Russians were prepared to keep up their hospitality as long as the vodka and caviar lasted.' [70] Though talks took place about finance, supplies and plans for the next spring's campaign, Lord Milner did not think much was achieved. The parties were too large, the noise too loud, and every meeting room was watched by far too many spies.

In February, they were gone. Their leaving was so secret

that the delegates were asked to sacrifice their shoes, leaving the pairs as usual outside their hotel rooms so that the staff (or German assassins) would think the occupants still there.[71] Perhaps conceding that events had overtaken him, Sir Samuel Hoare had also packed his bags. He claimed to have put the spy mission on its feet – it had a staff of seventeen by the time he left – but yet again he decided to invoke his own ill-health to get him out of an uncomfortable fix.[72] He joined the Milner delegation on the train, heading for Port Romanov and a British warship named *Kildonan Castle*. The journey home was sobering, the nights were haunted by phantom explosions, and many of the travellers chose to distract themselves by preparing reports. By the time Orkney's cliffs came into view most of them had completed at least one draft. On 6 March, Lord Milner told the British Cabinet that the Russians were 'in fact, orientals to a large extent – very suspicious and sometimes stuffy, but willing to be led by capable leadership'.[73] That leadership might be a problem, but as Milner had assured Lockhart, 'the general consensus of informed opinion, both Allied and Russian, as far as I can gather, is that there will be no revolution until after the war.'[74]

For Meriel Buchanan, who had remained in Petrograd, it seemed as if the frost set hard after the mission left. Without the distraction (and the champagne) there was no avoiding the evidence of social tension. It was said that Protopopov, perhaps after one of his religious visions, had ordered that machine-guns should be placed on the roofs of the city's large buildings in readiness for popular unrest.[75] The queues were growing longer, and the number of strikes seemed to increase from week to week. Two hundred and forty-three political strikes had been recorded in Russian cities in 1916, but the number exceeded a thousand in the months of January and February 1917 alone.[76] From Moscow, Lockhart reported that a large factory producing hand grenades had found its orders cancelled 'nominally on the ground that no more hand grenades were required but in reality because the government were afraid of allowing the public organizations to have any control of such dangerous articles for revolution as hand grenades'.[77] For now, however, the bitter cold, exceptional even for Russia, seemed to have paralysed all life. With the mercury at 38 degrees below, no one was throwing anything.

In balmy London, as the daffodils began to bud, the MP Major David Davies, another member of the Milner team, delivered his report to the British Cabinet. 'It is not believed', Davies declared, 'that a popular rising would have any chance of success. What may happen is a Palace Revolution, ending in the removal of the Emperor and Empress.' Russia's war effort would not be harmed, for it was 'probable that a fait accompli will be accepted quietly by the country'. That meant that the allies would win; what mattered now was the next step. As Davies warned, 'After the war there is no doubt that the Germans will make strenuous efforts to regain the ascendancy in Russian trade which they have temporarily lost, and it will be our business to make provision in time for the development of our own trade, and to exercise sufficient influence over the internal affairs of the country . . . The progress of the world in a large measure depends upon the planting of British ideas on Russian soil.'[78]

2. Black Markets

Sometimes a scoundrel is useful to our party
precisely because he is a scoundrel.

V. I. Lenin

The Germans had their own plans for a network in Russia. They had a lot of damage to repair first, however, for with the outbreak of the war their diplomats had been expelled and many of their businessmen and engineers had been deported. The German foreign ministry had watched its list of Russian contacts shrink, and the few that remained had almost no real friends at court. 'Can we send a pigeon . . . with a discreet olive branch?' the German Chancellor Bethmann-Hollweg enquired at Christmas 1914.[1] He thought that an industrialist called Albert Ballin might still approach his old friend Sergei Witte, who had been Russia's finance minister some years before. It was a measure of the depth of Bethmann-Hollweg's desperation that the only sympathetic Russian he could think of was a dying man whose influence had long predeceased him.

Since German nationals were all suspect in Russian eyes, the next best option was to find a neutral with the right idea. Sweden remained a fruitful source of volunteers. Denmark turned out to be another. Copenhagen's ambassador in Petrograd was Harald Scavenius, a man who was to use the diplomatic bag to forward information to Berlin on several occasions during the war.[2] German diplomats also courted the Danish king, Christian X, whose family connections gave him access to the tsar.[3] The official who handled most of those approaches was Berlin's minister in Copenhagen, Count von Brockdorff-Rantzau, who also happened to have an ancestral link to Denmark's royal house. It was all very tentative and secret (German leaders did not wish to be thought cowardly or battle-shy), but in the first two years of war Rantzau's office was used to broker several peace initiatives, all unsuccessful, with the Russian empire.[4]

At one point, as Petrograd's liberals suspected, there had also been moves to exploit the family loyalties of the Empress Alexandra. The kaiser's son, Crown Prince Wilhelm of Prussia, appealed for help to the Grand Duke of Hesse, Alexandra's brother, in February 1915. Two months later, the German foreign minister Gottlieb von Jagow added a note of his own. He suggested that the grand duke should remind his sister of the overwhelming force of German arms, and also of the needless suffering that simple Russian soldiers might so easily be spared.[5] Jagow was correct to choose the sentimental route to Alexandra's heart, but he had underestimated the extent of her loyalty to Russia. She was genuinely sad about the bloodshed, but she made no move to stop the war. By the end of 1916, the Russian army had sustained more than five million casualties – killed, missing or wounded – but the tsar remained a pillar of the Triple Entente.[6] Even the Romanian campaign of 1916, which almost crushed one of Russia's smaller allies, failed to force Nicholas to think again. The murder of Rasputin was a further blow to German interests, closing a door into the court and giving comfort to the anti-Berlin faction there.

The chances of a German-inspired palace coup had never

been particularly strong, however, and as they weighed the options for disrupting Russia's military campaign, the experts in the foreign ministry on Berlin's Wilhelmstrasse were prepared to consider an alternative: fomenting social discontent. It was a risky policy that called for accurate advice. The ministry kept thoughtful experts like Kurt Riezler and Carl-Ludwig Diego von Bergen on its staff, both of whom knew something about Russia, but its general strategy was also shaped by characters like Theodor Schiemann, an ageing and disgruntled member of the Baltic aristocracy with a particular interest in the future of small nations.[7] Schiemann pointed out that nationalist movements had been simmering on the fringes of the Russian empire for decades. There were plenty of secret clubs and underground societies from which to choose; the problem was to avoid wasting scarce resources on romantic fools. The Germans began building links to nationalist groups in the Caucasus, Finland, Ukraine and the Polish lands, but there was always more groundwork to do. As a critic later remarked, 'They did not seem to realize that it was not possible to foster a holy Muslim war in the Caucasus and at the same time give effective support to [Christian] Georgian separatist tendencies.'[8]

The best results came from their work in the Grand Duchy of Finland, a region that had preserved a good deal of its autonomy (and its historic legal code) inside the Russian empire. Anti-tsarist revolutionary groups had been active there for generations, but seldom had hope soared so high. In the winter of 1915–16, some 2,000 Finns were smuggled out of the country for training in Jaeger Battalion 27, eventually graduating to fight beside the Germans on the eastern front.[9] Further south, the brutality of Russia's occupying troops pushed locals in another borderland grudgingly to accept a German puppet state, the Kingdom of Poland, created in 1915. But Ukraine, much of whose population lived directly under Russian rule, was far more difficult to second guess. Germany could not stop its ally, Austria-Hungary, from encouraging a so-called Union for the Liberation of Ukraine (based partly in Constantinople). Among its German advocates was Gisbert von Romberg, the minister in Bern, whose base in neutral Switzerland was a centre for covert talks. Back in Berlin, however, the sceptics doubted that a revolution in the name of such a diffuse population could ever be more than a fantasy. Diego von Bergen's opinion was especially patronizing. 'The Ukrainians would only rise', he decided, 'in the event that we moved in.'[10]

The nationalist camp did not give up. This was a time when Germany's image in the world had been tarnished by its reputation for aggressive militarism. If it could act as sponsor to some small countries (which could be dominated when the war was done), the balance might shift and Germany acquire the mantle of a liberator – romantic, visionary and energetic – in contrast with the tyranny of Russia to the east and what Riezler called the 'empty and meaningless Anglo-American dullness' to the west.[11] Tsarist Russia, moreover, was not the only empire that the Germans thought of melting down. Because of its unwieldy size, the British one was much more vulnerable. Indeed, it was the succession of German plans to subvert the British empire that carried this world war so far across the globe.

Even before hostilities began, German provocateurs had been hard at work from Ireland to Afghanistan.[12] The narrow streets of Cairo hummed with rumours of a rebellious Muslim brotherhood. A German mission reached Kabul in 1915, and there were many plots to unleash holy war. An even more outlandish plan involved training an Irish republican legion for deployment against the British in Egypt.[13] Although that never really worked, the fear of insurrection forced London to station tens of thousands of troops near Suez, a distraction that German strategists could count as a success in its own right. At times during the First World War, nationalism appeared so deadly a threat to the British empire that the War Cabinet all but forgot Russia, palace coups and all.[14]

Four main centres were recognized by the footsoldiers of this global shadow war. Constantinople was the most exotic, the capital of the Ottoman empire and a gateway to the Middle East. The steady collapse of Ottoman rule had fascinated Europe for a century; as the last sinews of the empire snapped, almost every European power began to have designs on fragments of its territory. Britain's focus was on Suez and the Arab lands. For Russia, Constantinople itself was the objective, for the pre-war economic boom in Ukraine and the Russian south had been possible only because of the shipping lane along the Bosphorus and Dardanelles. In the short term, however, what was left of Turkey had aligned itself with Germany and Austria. Constantinople was awash with military advisers, and the magnificent Pera Palace Hotel became a kind of German club. Across the water in the narrow streets of old Stamboul, spies on their way to Medina or Aleppo delivered tiny scraps of information between furtive sips of sweet mint tea.[15]

The other rings on every secret agent's map were all round cities in Europe. As a neutral country with a German border, Switzerland had looked promising enough for the British Secret Intelligence Service to try running a permanent base there in 1914. The 'firm of shippers' was a disappointment, but freelancers continued to operate in Geneva, Lausanne and Bern. In 1915 the British recruited Somerset Maugham to work with these; he was sent first to Lucerne and then to Geneva under the cover of writing plays.[16] For several months he sat in a hotel room, occasionally making the journey across Lake Léman to report to his handlers in France, but the lakeside air damaged his lungs and the vigil turned out to be tedious. Like Leon Trotsky, who spent some time in Switzerland in 1914 and concluded that the locals 'worried chiefly over the surplus of cheese and the shortage of potatoes',[17] Maugham thought that Switzerland was dull. He seems entirely to have missed the troublemaking potential of its Russian colony, let alone the fellow agents who had flocked to Switzerland to spy on them.[18] In Bern, a peacetime diplomatic corps of seventy-one had swelled to more than 200 by the end of the war, and many of the extras specialized in semi-secret work.[19]

If he had been presented with a choice, Maugham might have found Copenhagen more interesting. Like Switzerland, neutral Denmark was a relatively cheap place to live during the war, a fact that had attracted profiteers from far and wide. The port was also full of displaced former prisoners and exiles from the war zones on the Russian front. The Bolshevik activist Alexander Shlyapnikov arrived in 1914 and later remembered Copenhagen as a place 'teeming with spies and reporters from all countries. It was from here that all the worldly gossip, fabrications and ballons d'essai originated during the war . . . It was generally a nasty scene.'[20] The spy networks followed smuggling routes from here into Norway and Sweden, and some of the characters who turned up in the restaurants of Stockholm's picturesque old town, claiming to be purchasing agents and gulping vintage champagne by the case, were actually members of the tsarist secret police.[21]

The least sinister outcome of all this listening and note-taking was the development of propaganda for use in enemy states. The Germans took the lead in this, for three decades before it had been the Iron Chancellor, Otto von Bismarck himself, who provided the resources for something that he called 'the reptile fund'.[22] By the spring of 1917, the German foreign ministry is said to have spent 382 million marks on peace propaganda aimed at its enemies. Its efforts in Romania and Italy had failed (both had entered the war on the opposing side), but secret German funding continued for four newspapers in France.[23] In Russia, the goal was to encourage weariness and doubt, especially since people were already grumbling that 'Britain will fight on to the last drop of Russian blood.' An intellectual arms race had begun, as a result of which the British were forced to set up a propaganda bureau of their own to keep the Russians in the war. Its staff was headed by a novelist, Hugh Walpole, assisted from Moscow by the Anglophile secretary of the Arts Theatre, 'Lyki' Lykiardopoulos. Captain Bromhead, the future manager of Gaumont Cinemas, took charge of mobile movie-screenings for the masses. In a single month, April–May 1916, his team showed films about the British war effort to 3,000 Russian officers and 100,000 of their men.[24]

The problem was that propaganda could be slow. As Berlin weighed the Russian case, a few officials started to consider something more dramatic. For years, as even the most innocent of junior clerks would have known, there had been revolutionary parties in Russia (the ideas that inspired them, after all, had begun life in Germany). The uprising of 1905 had shown what havoc Russia's working class could wreak. The strikes and rioting had forced the tsar to end a war on that occasion, too – in that instance against Japan. Although fomenting revolution was a dangerous idea (Germany had socialists of its own), the prospect of a bit of inconclusive civil chaos certainly appealed. Russia had a network of home-grown revolutionaries, known troublemakers who would do the job. The trick would be to contact them, making sure to distinguish carefully between obliging Russian criminals and the tsarist informers who shadowed them.

With the aid of local sympathizers and strategic double-agents (several of them nationalists from the Baltic and Ukraine), officials at the German foreign ministry began to assemble a picture of the Russian revolutionary movement, and especially of its émigré wing, the exiles who had fled the tsarist empire in the pre-war years. Among the latter, the group that was most promising was based in Switzerland. It helped that Berlin's minister in Bern, Gisbert von Romberg, had a long-standing interest in Russia and the Slavs. Romberg was wary of the socialists (he preferred to work with aristocrats) and devoted most of his energy to his network of nationalists. For all that, however, he knew far more about the Russian revolutionary underground than his British or French counterparts, who seemed to think that every Russian exile they met must be a German agent.[25] As Romberg realized, most exiled socialists would be content to sit in Switzerland indefinitely, continuing their arguments about the character of bourgeois government and the moral value of religion. He knew there was supposed to be a hard-line group somewhere, but it could well turn out to be a gang of posturing thugs.[26]

Such scepticism held him back, but Romberg was prepared to set his doubts aside for the good of the German cause. More serious was the fact that the Russians in question were all marooned in western Europe. If the idea was to exploit their hostility to tsarism, moreover, they could not be allowed to guess how much the Germans might be helping them. A revolutionary might have thought himself the enemy of all empires, but he was still susceptible to the nationalist prejudice of the times. Even for an internationalist, for someone who wanted to see the dissolution of every nation-state, an open acceptance of help from a government whose armies were slaughtering Russians might have been political suicide.

The difficulty crystallized in the case of Victor Chernov, a former Duma deputy and the leader of the largest of Russia's revolutionary parties, the Socialist Revolutionaries. Like all his Russian counterparts, Chernov had tried to run a party newspaper, in his case basing it in France. When pressure from the French censors (and lack of cash) threatened to close it in 1915, an agent of the Germans with the code-name Weis (a Russian double-agent really called Zivin)[27] was cleared to make his first approach. As far as Chernov was concerned, Weis was a fellow pacifist who wanted a partner for a new publishing venture, so the talks proceeded warmly. But Chernov was in Italy, trapped by wartime geography, and Weis had proposed that the paper should be based in Norway, from where copies could easily be smuggled into Russia via Tornio. For poor Chernov, the office might as well have been located on the moon. The British would not allow a Russian revolutionary to travel to Scandinavia through Newcastle or Scotland, and it was obvious to any honest person that Russian citizens would get no travel visas out of Germany.

The German foreign ministry weighed the options. They would have been delighted to give Chernov his visa (they would have sent him first-class on the train), but he could not be allowed to suspect their involvement. Weis was asked to consider whether the revolutionary leader would accept a visa if he were told that the Germans had been tricked into offering it on humanitarian grounds, permitting him an exceptional three-week journey to the north for the sake of his lungs. Since even Chernov was not endlessly naive, that idea was eventually dropped. Instead, months passed while the secret agent persuaded him to use a doctored Swiss passport, calming his fears by promising that German border guards were known to ignore Swiss travellers and wave them through. Chernov made his way to Norway in January 1916, but funding for the project disappeared, and a forlorn Weis was relegated to collecting gossip from Russian refugees.[28]

Berlin could not afford false starts like this; it did not have the time. So it was with some relief that its officials stepped up their efforts in another direction. The first ray of hope came in January 1915 when the German foreign ministry received a telegram from Ambassador Hans von Wangenheim in Constantinople. Apparently, a businessman called Alexander Helphand had a plan for the destruction of tsarism. As he had explained to Wangenheim, 'the interests of the German government are identical with those of the Russian revolutionaries.' Helphand believed in acting fast, 'contaminating' Russian troops with anti-tsarist propaganda before they were sent to the front. He also proposed to call a congress of the Russian revolutionaries in exile, the aim of which would be to get them acting as a group. 'He was prepared to take the necessary first steps to this end,' Wangenheim wrote to the foreign ministry, 'but would need considerable sums of money for the purpose.'[29]

If Wangenheim had only known, considerable sums of money were something of a habit with Helphand. The man was a magician of finance. If any actor could have played him, it would have been the mature Orson Welles. Like the Third Man, Helphand belonged in the smoke and shadows of war, and also like his film counterpart he combined a visionary charisma with bottomless personal greed. Born in 1867, he had begun life as the hungry, impatient son of a Jewish artisan who had fled Belarus for the port city of Odessa. By the time he was twenty, the boy had become a socialist, a choice that forced him to take to the road. His first home, as a student, was in Switzerland (which he did not like); he then worked as a revolutionary journalist in the German cities of Stuttgart and Munich. Germany was a country that he adored from the start, and it was there that he would find his feet. Even the great Karl Kautsky, the leader of the German socialist movement, accepted and then came to admire him. So fat that he was more like seal than man, Helphand adopted the pen-name of Parvus ('small') in 1894. Kautsky's children called him 'Dr Elephant', but Parvus was the name that stuck.[30]

Helphand-Parvus was excellent company, and many travel-weary Russian exiles used his Munich flat as a cultural decompression-chamber, a space in which to get accustomed to the world of European politics. Almost everyone turned up at his door sooner or later, including Lenin, who made his first visit in 1899. 'Parvus was unquestionably one of the most important of the Marxists at the turn of the century,' Trotsky would later write, crediting him with 'fearless thinking . . . wide vision . . . and a virile muscular style'.[31] These qualities marked Parvus out among the dull pen-pushers of the day, but it was not merely his words that counted. As a business-man, he also knew how newspapers were made; eight issues of the illegal Russian revolutionary journal *Iskra* were pro-duced in a locked room in his residence and he played host to its editorial board until the spring of 1902. Even at this early stage, some German comrades found him crude, but Lenin and his friends admired the hard edge that his voice took on whenever conversation turned to strikes and bombs.[32]

Trotsky arrived at Parvus' flat in January 1905. In St Peters-burg, the massacre that would launch Russia's first revolution had taken place on Palace Square just days before.[33] As they prepared to join the workers' cause, Trotsky and his wife became unofficial lodgers at the big man's place, sharing all the latest news and imbibing Parvus' theories of revolution along with his strong coffee and delicious late-night wine. The two men talked about the revolutionary potential of the general strike, they honed their idea of a world revolution (for Russia was only ever meant to be a starting-point) and they dared each other to get tickets for the next train east. In the spring of 1905, Trotsky crossed into Ukraine. Parvus fol-lowed in October, heading for St Petersburg. For a few months that winter, the two men took the platform almost nightly at meetings of the workers' Soviet, or council, in St Petersburg's magnificent Technological Institute. They also helped to produce and promote the revolutionary newspaper *Russkaya Gazeta*. Parvus tended to be more spectacular than effective, but no one could accuse him of armchair politics.

The hopes raised in the spring of 1905 were largely dashed within a year. Parvus was arrested in April 1906 and ended up pacing a gloomy cell in the Peter-Paul Fortress. 'The fat one has lost weight,' commented the Polish left-wing socialist Rosa Luxemburg, who visited him in the fortress on the eve of his journey into penal exile. True to form, however, Parvus managed to evade his guards at one of the remoter stations on the eastward trail. He was armed with a false passport and quantities of hidden cash, and he also had the addresses of several local party agents who could help him.[34] Heading west into the freezing mud, he crossed the Russian border in November 1906. He would never return. In future, whatever his theoretical position, his hatred of tsarism would be personal.

'The exact details of the way in which Helphand became a rich man', write his biographers, 'must remain a matter of conjecture.'[35] At least some of the cash was stolen from fellow revolutionaries. Parvus began to publish books, exploiting Russia's lax copyright laws to put out Russian writers' works in German translation. The most profitable of these was Maxim Gorky's play, *The Lower Depths*, the rights to which he had obtained on condition that some of the proceeds went to socialist party funds. Instead, however, Parvus spent the lion's share on a trip to Italy with a female companion ('it must have been a pleasant holiday,' observed Gorky).[36] The money had gone, and soon Parvus would vanish with it, abandoning his fellow publisher in Munich with a pile of debts. He had tired of the stifling correctness of German social-democracy and he had tired of scandal. He disappeared into the Balkans, making contacts in Sofia and Bucharest before surfacing in Constantinople in November 1910. He was so poor at that point that he had to hide the holes in his shoes, but in two or three years, by trading and by making deals with Turkish and then German agents, he had turned himself into a tycoon.[37]

*

Reviewing all he knew about the case, the under state secretary at the German foreign ministry, Arthur Zimmermann, advised his master that it would be wise to summon Parvus to Berlin.[38] In March 1915 the big man met Kurt Riezler, and at the same time he drafted a report, 'Preparations for a political mass-strike in Russia', which amounted to a blueprint for revolution. As a pitch, it was magnificent, promising everything from separatist uprisings (in Ukraine and Finland especially) to a strike wave among Russian sailors that was to be launched from Constantinople. The 'mass-strike' itself, an epic undertaking that would paralyse the war effort, would be organized with the slogan 'Freedom and Peace'. As Parvus explained, using a language that German romantics loved, the goal was nothing less than to 'shatter the colossal political centralization which is the embodiment of the tsarist empire and which will be a danger to world peace for as long as it is allowed to survive'.[39]

The price he had in mind was 'one million marks, exclusive of losses incurred in exchange ... together with any other expenses'. On 11 March 1915 the German imperial treasury duly approved a grant of two million marks 'for the support of Russian revolutionary propaganda'.[40] It was a monumental sum, and the largesse continued with a grant of five million marks in July. But Wilhelmstrasse kept an eye on Parvus. The magnate had wound up his affairs in Constantinople, relocating to Denmark, where Brockdorff-Rantzau, as German minister in Copenhagen, could meet and then report on him. On 14 August, Rantzau told Berlin that Parvus was 'an extraordinarily important man whose unusual powers I feel we *must* employ for the duration of the war ... whether we personally agree with his convictions or not'.[41]

The promised campaign to unite the Russian underground

began in March 1915. As ever, Parvus worked in style. When he booked a suite at Zurich's Baur au Lac, it was clear that he intended to enjoy himself. War or no war, he had chosen the best hotel in town. Among its many claims to glory, the Baur au Lac had gained a sort of immortality in October 1856 when Richard Wagner performed the world premiere of the Annunciation of Death scene from *Die Walküre* in the dining room, accompanied on the piano by an admiring Franz Liszt.[42] By the time that Parvus came to sign the guest book, it had also hosted both the kaiser and the Russian royal entourage. 'Helphand did not just move into the Baur au Lac,' wrote his biographers, 'he set up court there. He lived like an oriental potentate, surrounded by an ostentatious show of wealth. There was usually a retinue of rather well-endowed blondes about; his liking for enormous cigars was matched by his indulgence in champagne: preferably a whole bottle for breakfast.'[43] From this absurd base by the lake, the big man hoped to reach out to fellow exiles. It may not have occurred to him that most were penniless.

His plan for uniting the factions was also optimistic. In 1903, the Russian Marxist party, still only in its sixth year, had split, ostensibly over a point of organization. The disputes had dragged on for days, and though the majority of the delegates supported the affable Yuly Martov and his allies, it was Lenin, the relentless revolutionary, who seized one of the rare moments when he commanded a majority to give his faction the title of Bolsheviks ('men of the majority'). The rest, the Mensheviks (or 'men of the minority', though they had in fact been the larger group at almost every turn), were left to carry the stigma of inferiority. Few suffered more than Martov, a charming, easy-going journalist whose background – activism, prison, penal exile – had been similar to Lenin's. Martov was appalled by his old ally's calculated verbal violence. The days of witty, spacious comradeship were done; it was hard to see how the two men could ever reconcile. The war had trapped them both in Switzerland, and as Marxist revolutionaries they had more in common than either would admit, but the sparring continued, often falling only inches short of real violence.

Still, Parvus had convinced himself that they would talk. 'So far it has been mainly the radicals who have prevented unification,' he advised the Germans in March 1915. 'However, two weeks ago their leader, Lenin, himself threw open the question of unification with the minority.'[44] He had almost no grounds for saying this, but Parvus was not one to spoil a lifetime's dream for mere details. He tracked his quarry to a modest restaurant in May that year. When Lenin had finished his lunch, he and his wife took Parvus back to their rented rooms. The story goes that they then perched their visitor's enormous bulk on an inadequate item of furniture and subjected him to a shower of invective: there could be no deal with social-chauvinists, there could be no compromises, Parvus had shown himself to be a renegade, a trickster, no better than that German bourgeois guttersnipe Kautsky. That, at least, is one version of what occurred.[45] Official records from the Soviet era, by which time Lenin was almost a god and Parvus a forgotten chancer, do not mention the meeting at all. The Soviet chronicle of the leader's activities for that May observes that Lenin borrowed a book from the public library in Bern (called *The Influence of High Mountain Climate and Mountain Excursions on Man*), but Parvus does not figure anywhere.[46] In November, the Bolshevik leader attacked his erstwhile visitor in print, describing the socialist journal that Parvus was now publishing, *Die*

Glocke, as 'a cesspool of German chauvinism' and its editor as a 'petty coward'.[47]

The truth, however, was that Parvus had become too big for Lenin to ignore. No revolutionary of the time would have risked losing track of him. His journal did quite well – *Die Glocke* turned out to be very popular with schoolteachers – but Parvus had much larger plans. He was especially busy in the summer of 1915, for that was when he returned to Copenhagen to set up a research institute, dedicating it to the study of the social effects of war. The institute employed numerous Russian exiles, driving the Danish police into a frenzy of suspicion, but no one could prove that it did anything other than collate statistics and write papers. In August, a man called Max Zimmer, who had known Parvus from his Turkish days, reported to Berlin on the big man's progress. The dinner that the two had shared must have been excellent, for Parvus had convinced his guest that his scheme for revolution was maturing splendidly. Zimmer concluded that Parvus was managing his German budget 'thriftily' and running secret operations through his research outfit with such discretion 'that not even the gentlemen who work for [it] have realized that our government is behind it all'. Parvus had even managed to persuade his visitor that he was close to uniting the disparate wings of the Russian revolutionary movement.[48]

Meanwhile, there was more money to be made. With German help, Parvus turned his hand to coal imports, pocketing another fortune while running a sideline in agitation among Danish dockworkers.[49] But he also supported a fledgling import–export company, the Handels og-Eksport Kompagniet, founded in the summer of 1915. Its business was conveying goods through Denmark and Sweden to

Russia, and it was managed in Copenhagen by a Lithuanian-Polish exile called Yakov Fürstenberg, also known to the revolutionary underground as Hanecki. Few of this man's associates seem to have warmed to him. His principal attractions were an inexhaustible capacity for work and an extensive address book. But within a few months he had become Parvus' chief acolyte, and though he had the handshake of a salamander he started to look every inch the businessman, from his hand-made leather shoes and tailored suit to his white gloves and the flower in his buttonhole.[50]

The Handels og-Eksport Kompagniet operated on a simple business model. As everyone in Europe knew, it was Germany that had supplied the bulk of Russia's import needs before the war. Hoare's candlewax was just the start of it. The Empress Alexandra drove a Daimler, and the same company had the contract to supply St Petersburg with prison vans.[51] From sewing-machines and bicycles to electrical switches and tinned food, the shops in Russian cities all relied on German brands, as a result of which the wartime embargo had hit the Russian market hard. By 1915, when Fürstenberg set up his Danish firm, the lack of certain goods was desperate. In particular, Russia was critically short of the commodities that people need in times of war, especially pharmaceutical products and dressings, thermometers, syringes and contraceptives. It was this shortfall that Fürstenberg's firm made good, building up a network of contacts along the northern transport route and fulfilling every order to the last detail (the contraceptives for Russian consumption were always supplied, the records specify, 'with teat end').[52]

The Russian Restriction of Enemy Supplies Committee was powerless to control the underworld trade on which Fürstenberg thrived. Using a string of black-market contacts, his company imported consignments from Germany into neutral Denmark (which was legal), and then repackaged them for re-export with Danish labels (which was not). The police caught up with the racket in January 1917, after raiding the Danish port of Frederikshaven to search a shipment bound for Sweden. Inside three of the suspect crates, their officers found 1,150 clinical thermometers, 114 hypodermic syringes and 40 kilograms of clinical drugs, all ultimately bound for Russia. None had the necessary export papers, and while the goods originated in Germany, most packages had been through several sets of hands before they reached Fürstenberg's warehouse.[53]

The police threw their businessman into a cell. They questioned him for several days, but his answers always confounded them. It was concluded that the Handels og-Eksport Kompagniet's business was illegal, and Fürstenberg was fined and deported in January 1917. He settled in Sweden almost at once, resuming his lucrative activities. By now, the company had acquired a new co-owner, Georg Sklarz, who was also a German agent working with Parvus.[54] But Fürstenberg, on the surface, was nothing other than an ordinary, if conspicuously successful, black-market trader.

If the Danes had been more ambitious, however, they could have looked more closely at Fürstenberg's friends. He and Parvus had lived close to each other in Copenhagen's fashionable Vodroffsvej, so it would have been easy to keep an eye on both. Fürstenberg's business contacts included a German agent, 'K', whose network specialized in smuggling rubber into Germany with the help of Scandinavian companies.[55] An Austro-Hungarian diplomat called Grebing, who was based in Copenhagen at the time, later explained what he had heard about these deals. 'Parvus and Fürstenberg-Hanecki carried on trade between Scandinavia and Russia with German help,' he wrote.[56] Parvus received the German shipments and Fürstenberg forwarded them, managing the business through trusted contacts in Petrograd and keeping an account with a respected Swedish bank. Contact with Berlin, some said, was maintained through a secret department code-named 'Stockholm'.[57] But the money that Fürstenberg's business made from the trade was not repaid to the German suppliers, or so Grebing alleged. The final link in the chain may have led to Zurich. As well as being Parvus' friend and business partner, after all, Fürstenberg-Hanecki happened to be one of Lenin's most trusted aides.[58]

The gentlemen who ran the German foreign ministry might not have recognized who Lenin was before 1917. The idea of fomenting revolution was a tricky one in any case, but if Russia was indeed heading for revolt, then Parvus was the man their experts had agreed to put in charge. Meanwhile, as the big man prepared his promised wave of strikes, those same experts had other clients on their list. The Irish republicans, for instance, had a rising planned for the spring of 1916 that looked set to undermine the enemy just as capably and at considerably lower cost. That project ended in disappointment, as did Parvus' romantic scheme. By June, support for covert operations was flagging in Berlin, allowing the military to take over with a renewed U-boat campaign and plans to deploy mustard gas. By September, the idea of using socialist insurgents as a weapon of war had virtually been dropped, and even the most devious of strategists was trying to broker a peace deal with the tsar.[59] For all that, however, a filing clerk who kept alert might have noticed that Lenin's name had cropped up on several confidential documents. Parvus was not the only agent who had mentioned him.

Just days after war had been declared in 1914, an Estonian called Alexander Keskula had turned up at the German legation in Bern.[60] Like Parvus, he loathed the Russian empire. As a nationalist, his dream was to put his native country on the European map, enlarging it by adding the territory around Pskov and possibly the whole of Petrograd.[61] Keskula also had credentials as a revolutionary socialist, having joined the Bolsheviks for a short time in 1905. He quickly built a set of contacts in the underground, and met Lenin for the first time in September 1914.[62] Alexander Shlyapnikov, who was one of Lenin's most practical agents, remembered having his suspicions. Keskula 'offered to supply funds, arms, and everything necessary for revolutionary work in Russia', he wrote, and 'all this was offered through such individuals that their origin might have seemed reliable. But I managed to establish that behind these figures lay a strategic manoeuvre by militarism.'[63]

In the guise of a Marxist comrade, however, Keskula hung around the fringes of the Russian exile colony. Like every other outsider, he found its divisions bewildering. A powerful group (whom he called the 'social patriots') had ruled out any opposition to their government while it was still fighting a war. These people suspected that Russia was not ready for socialism, a conclusion that allowed them to forget about action and pass the evenings in talk. Other Russian socialists appeared to think that the kaiser was no better than the tsar, a verdict that also left them at liberty to smoke and doze. Only one group, Keskula reported to Romberg in September 1915, was willing, capable and ready to bring down

Russian imperial rule. 'In Keskül's opinion,' Romberg wrote to Berlin, 'it is essential that we should spring to the help of Lenin's movement in Russia at once. He will report on this matter in person in Berlin. According to his informants, the present moment should be favourable for overthrowing the government . . . but . . . we should have to act quickly, before the Social Patriots gain the upper hand.'[64]

Keskülä claimed to have discussed with Lenin the terms on which, if the Russian revolution were successful, a new government might make peace with Germany. Romberg was sceptical about everything, from Keskül's inflated claims to the capacities of the Bolsheviks themselves, but as he read the passage about the terms for a separate peace, he understood that in its own right it could be a propaganda tool. 'If skilfully distributed,' he wrote, the document 'could be especially effective in France, in view of the monstrous ignorance of the French in foreign, and particularly Russian affairs . . . I shall give it to various French confidential agents for distribution among the ranks of the opposition . . . I feel that it should be put out in an aura of great secrecy, so that it creates a belief that an agreement with powerful Russian circles is already in preparation.' British opinion was not discussed. If Keskül's notes had found their way to London, however, there really would have been alarm at the revelation that Lenin was supposed to have agreed, in the event of a successful Russian revolution, to raise an army and fight alongside the Germans to help bring an end to the empire in India.[65]

Four months after all of that, with revolution still a longed-for prize, Keskülä was in Sweden. 'I now have a new collaborator,' he wrote to an agent of the German General Staff in January 1916, 'and through him, the possibility of working on the whole of Scandinavia as well as the whole of

Russia . . . At the end of this week my confidential agent will be travelling to Russia (for about four weeks) to discuss financial support from Western Europe with the revolutionary centres inside Russia.' The Estonian claimed to be financing several projects, including a secret press. 'Today, or in the next few days,' he continued, 'some highly interesting revolutionary documents from Russia are being sent to Lenin. I read them through yesterday, but had no chance to make copies of them. Could you please be so kind as to return them to me . . . and to handle the papers with all possible care, as I do not want Lenin's joy at his Russian Christmas present to be decreased in any way.'[66]

Like Parvus, Kesküla was rewarded generously. In total, he received over 200,000 marks for his information and the propaganda work that he proposed.[67] Like Parvus, too, and like almost everybody, he eventually argued with Lenin (allegedly about his beloved nationalities question), and from the autumn of 1916 the two men had no more contact. Shlyapnikov would have it that no one ever trusted Kesküla, and that he was excluded from the Bolsheviks' inner circle almost from the outset. But at the end of his life, as an old man, the Estonian made an extravagant claim. It might not have been true, but it reflected something of the wartime underworld, its vanity and wild schemes, the envelopes of money and the whispered, unfamiliar names. 'Lenin was my protégé,' he told Michael Futrell. 'It was I who launched Lenin.'[68] This was a hollow boast, of course, but poignant as an epitaph.

3. Red Lake

To the socialist, it is not the horrors of war that are
the hardest to endure . . . but the horrors of the
treachery shown by the leaders of present-day
socialism.

V. I. Lenin

Unlike Parvus, to say nothing of Trotsky or Somerset
Maugham, Lenin was a genuine devotee of Switzerland. He
enjoyed its lakes and mountains and the opportunities they
gave for what he described to his mother as 'walking, swim-
ming and loafing'.[1] Its big cities, especially Zurich, had
districts where a refugee could rent a room. He did not have
a problem with the Swiss cuisine because he did not really
notice what he ate. In any case, while war-torn Europe went
hungry, Switzerland still had its milk and cheese and soft
white bread. On afternoons when his beloved library was
closed, Lenin and his wife could share a bar of cheap nut
chocolate ('about 15 centimes') before they set out for a walk.
Meanwhile, although the doctors' fees were high, there was
no country in the world where he preferred to go if he needed
medical treatment. His first expedition to the mountain
state, when he was only in his twenties, had been to seek
advice for a stomach complaint.

Lenin had settled in Zurich in 1916, partly because it was
cheap. The other attraction was the newly opened public

library, which was housed in spacious quarters near an early medieval church, the Predigerkirche. Here, and preferably at the desk that had become his favourite, he planned to finish the research for a new work. 'He tried to utilize all the time the library was open,' remembered his wife, Nadezhda Krupskaya. 'He got there exactly at 9 o'clock, stayed until 12, came home exactly at ten minutes past 12 (the library was closed from 12 to one), after lunch he returned to the library and stayed there until 6 o'clock.'[2] He toiled in a high-tension frenzy, his stack of books a fortress wall, his pencils sharpened to cruel points. 'We used to say among ourselves', a friend from his old student days recalled, 'that he had such big brains that they pushed his hair out.'[3] During this stint in Zurich, as his notes suggest, he read 148 books and 232 articles in English, French and German, including works by Aristotle and Hegel, Chekhov and Feuerbach. By June 1916 he had drafted the extended essay that was later published as *Imperialism: The Highest Stage of Capitalism*.[4]

Another exile might have gravitated to the Cabaret Voltaire. It met at the bottom of Lenin's street. Not long after the Bolshevik had settled in, a Russian chorus had indeed joined the anarchic show, which was the founding movement of Dada.[5] If dissonance and destruction began to pall, then Zurich offered numerous alternative cultural possibilities. As a refuge from conscription and the privations of war, the city had become a magnet for artists and writers. To the west of Lenin's district, on the Limmatquai, the patrons of the Café Odeon included Stefan Zweig and James Joyce, Albert Einstein, Erich Maria Remarque and the infamous Mata Hari. Lenin was not averse to a glass or two of tea himself, but he never forgot that his life was devoted to causes higher than mere talk. No merriment had ever distracted him; on one occasion in the past, in a café in Paris, he had been so engrossed in a newspaper that Amedeo Modigliani had managed to set fire to it while he was reading.[6] It was not for nothing that the Bolshevik had been known as 'the old man' for years, although in 1916 he was only forty-six.

As the leader of the most intractable of Marxist factions, Lenin was a dangerous exotic in a world of disputatious, haunted Russian exiles. He had not repented of the Bolshevik–Menshevik split that he had forced upon the Russian movement in 1903. Yuly Martov hit back in 1904, accusing his tormentor of 'petty, at times senseless, personal malice, amazing narcissism [and] blind, deaf, unfeeling fury'.[7] But outbursts like that, while making the attacker appear querulous, served only to burnish Lenin's charisma.[8] Wherever Europe's socialists might gather, Lenin was bristling with trademark pugnacity. In 1907, during a keynote lecture by the venerable Marxist Georgy Plekhanov, he fidgeted and scratched, his shoulders shaking with soundless laughter. At a banquet in honour of August Bebel, one of the most distinguished socialists in Germany, he delivered a public snub to the guest of honour.[9] His aggression was certainly a symptom of the importance that he placed upon the struggle and the cause, but it also said a lot about his personality.

In 1916, a Romanian Marxist called Valeriu Marcu, a pacifist and wartime refugee, decided that he had to meet the man he called the 'brigand chief'. The impulse was romantic as well as political, for Marcu was enchanted by a fantasy of Russia, a place that he had never seen but which evoked both revolution and the empty vastness of Siberia. 'What reality', he admitted, 'can be stronger than a preconceived ideal?' His pursuit of the chimera drew him along the narrow streets behind the Limmatquai in search of a restaurant run by a forty-something blonde called Frau Prellog. Thumping up some rickety wooden stairs to its premises on the second floor, he found that the place consisted only of 'a dimly lit corridor, long and narrow with bare walls and a long, unpainted wooden table that took up most of the space'. It smelled 'like a mouldy cellar' and the food turned out to consist of 'thin soups, dried-out roasts and cheap desserts'.[10]

Lenin had not turned up by the time Marcu arrived, so the young man could indulge his preconceived ideals for a few minutes more. At Frau Prellog's, he discovered, Lenin was known by his real name – Mr Ulyanov – and he was respected and generally liked. As he tried to picture the man, Marcu may well have imagined someone tall and handsome, or at least imposing, for that was what most people expected on the basis of the leader's writings. How such a hero could sit down to eat the grease at Frau Prellog's remained unclear, although the other men around the table were 'all young, bold-looking, enigmatic figures'.[11] When Lenin stepped into the room, however, reality displaced Marcu's imaginings. The eagle of the left was short ('a stocky red-headed man of medium height', recalled another fascinated disciple), he was balding, with only wisps of ginger hair around the great dome of his head, and where the younger man had expected a scowl, Lenin's face 'creased instantly into a playful smile'.[12]

Marcu was not unique. Almost everyone found Lenin confusing. Robert Bruce Lockhart, who would meet him later, decided that the world's first and greatest socialist head of state looked 'like a provincial grocer'.[13] Maxim Gorky, who also considered Lenin to be 'somehow ordinary', suggested that 'something was lacking in him. He . . . did not give the impression of being a leader.'[14] A police photograph from 1895 shows a disdainful, unappealing face, a young man powered by loathing. To Ariadna Tyrkova, the wife of the journalist Harold Williams, Lenin 'had the evil eyes of a wolf'.[15] But everyone would end up giving that face another look. There was a vigour in it that no photograph ever conveyed; the closest anyone could get was to fix on the eyes. A fellow Bolshevik, Gleb Krzhizhanovsky, remembered that they 'were unusual, piercing, full of inner strength and energy, dark, dark brown'.[16]

Those eyes would shine with pleasure, after lunch, when Frau Prellog expressed her view that soldiers fighting at the front should shoot their officers and make for home. 'Shoot the officers! A magnificent woman!' Lenin declared. It was the first of many shocks for young Marcu. The next day, at Lenin's invitation, he attended the great man in his rooms at No. 14 Spiegelgasse, another ancient building in the old town's warren of steep lanes. Lenin and his wife were renting from a shoemaker ('an internationalist', to Lenin's evident delight). The place was small and stuffy, but it was impossible to open the windows because of the stench of boiling bratwurst from the butchers' vats in the back yard.[17] Inside, the cramped spaces were gloomy and the furniture austere ('like a prison cell', declared another visitor). As Marcu conversed with the Bolshevik, however, their talk ranging from strikes to European civil war, he did not notice that two hours had passed. The leader's words would burn into his memory for ever. Even his quirks of speech (Lenin did not roll his rs, but almost gargled them, so that the word 'imperialism' – which is the same in Russian as in English – became 'imperrrilism')[18] helped Marcu to remember everything.

'One thing is astonishing to me,' Lenin began. 'You and your friends want to transform this entire world which reeks from every pore with baseness, slavery and war, and yet you renounce the use of violence in advance.' Pacifism had become a common response to the war among young people on the left, but Lenin's line was different. He reached into a drawer for the notes to an article that he had just completed and continued, reading: 'An oppressed class which does not strive to learn the use of weapons [the Russian word, *oruzhiia*, contains another wonderful long r], to practice the use of weapons, to own weapons, deserves to be mistreated . . . The demand for disarmament in the present-day world is nothing but an expression of despair.'[19] The published version of those thoughts, appearing in September 1916, was no less vehement. 'If the present war rouses among the reactionary Christian socialists, among the whimpering petty bourgeoisie, only horror and fright, only aversion to all use of arms, to bloodshed, death, etc.,' Lenin had written, 'then we must say: Capitalist society is and always has been horror without end.'[20] The rumble of artillery was too remote to have been audible in Zurich, but all the same it was a strange response to Europe's blackest agony.

As Marcu was to discover, Lenin's vision for the future was far more apocalyptic than mere fighting. As the Bolshevik outlined it to his guest, both of them sitting in that atmosphere of sausage-fumes and lakeside damp, he predicted a revolution throughout the world, a series of co-ordinated, pitiless and violent campaigns that would annihilate the twin oppressions of capitalism and empire for ever. The bourgeoisie would have to die, the big country estates would burn, and everywhere the slave-owners would face enslavement themselves. 'Lenin did not plan invasions from the outside,' Marcu observed, 'but from the inside . . . Every revolutionist must work for the defeat of his own country . . . The chief task . . . was to coordinate all the moral, physical, geographical and tactical elements of the universal insurrection, to join together all the hatreds aroused by imperialism across the five continents.'[21] As Lenin had put it in 1914, 'The conversion of the present imperialist war into a civil war is the only correct political slogan.'[22]

'He wrote as though thousands awaited his command,' Marcu remembered, 'as though a typesetter was standing outside the door.'[23] This man would not content himself with peace talks or a plan for social ownership of factories: his aim was to destroy the very system that created war. As Pavel Axelrod, a Menshevik and ally of Martov, had put it years before, 'Lenin is the only man for whom revolution is the preoccupation twenty-four hours a day, who has no thoughts but of revolution, and who even in his sleep dreams of nothing but revolution.'[24] 'It was not without significance', Trotsky wrote, 'that the words "irreconcilable" and "relentless" should be among Lenin's favourites.'[25] The veteran revolutionary Vera Zasulich had been getting at the same idea years earlier when she compared the young Lenin with Georgy Plekhanov, who at the time was still the most respected of the Russian Marxists in exile. 'Georgy is a hound,' she had told him, 'he will shake a thing for a while, and then drop it; whereas you are a bulldog – yours is the death-grip.' Lenin savoured the words under his breath several times, his pleasure obvious: 'death-grip'.[26]

Although Lenin liked Switzerland, it was the war that had forced him to settle there. Before hostilities began, he and his wife had been living in Poronin, a peaceful Habsburg-ruled hamlet at the foot of the Tatra mountains in what is now southern Poland. It was about as close as a political exile could get to home, with Russian territory only a little to the north. Yakov Fürstenberg, the man with all the contacts, had helped Lenin and Krupskaya to find their new place there, and he had organized the necessary papers, too. Another obliging comrade, Grigory Zinoviev, had settled close by with Zina, his second wife, which meant that Lenin could declare Poronin to be the headquarters of the Foreign Bureau of the Bolshevik Central Committee. Though Lenin always travelled frequently (a party leader had to attend the key meetings of Europe's socialist elite), he had lived happily in this backwater, working on theoretical questions and amusing himself by taking long walks in the nearby woods to pick mushrooms. The nervous headaches that had troubled him for years began to ease. As for the news from Russia, it was good. The summer of 1914 had been a bitter one for tsarism; there had been strikes in Baku and the barricades had gone up in St Petersburg.[27] On 6 August, however, when Austria declared war on Russia, the idyll ended overnight.

All over Europe, thousands of people found themselves suddenly in the wrong place. As Russians, Lenin and his wife had become hostile aliens in Austria. The gendarmes turned up at their door soon after dawn. Barging inside, they searched the house, turning up a lot of papers in the leader's tight, impatient hand – mostly collections of statistics and notes about the agrarian economy. Then one of them discovered the pistol, a loaded Browning. A Russian in the border zone would always have been suspect in wartime, but now the gendarmes had their proof that Lenin was in Austria to spy. They took him away, and by evening he was sitting in a prison cell in the local town of Novy Targ. Again, it was Fürstenberg who led the campaign to get him out.[28] It took a lot of cabling and negotiation, but the authorities agreed to release their captive once they had become convinced that there was no Austrian alive who hated Russia's government as heartily as he. 'He is not a socialist', Lenin would tell a friend when he arrived in Bern a few days later, 'who does not, in time of imperialist war, desire the defeat of his own country.'[29]

The Lenins had to move, that much was clear. At one point that summer, before the shooting had begun, they had considered relocating to Sweden, but they could not cross Germany to get there now. In any case, Lenin liked Switzerland, he had a good network of contacts there, and though the war was forcing prices up, he could afford the food and rent. His choice had consequences that he could not have predicted at the time. As Krupskaya packed their things, however, the main concern was to make sure of their documents and check the wartime train schedules. In a random and abstract way, Lenin worried about everything, but the detailed arrangements were Krupskaya's domain. The great man was more absorbed by the task of composing his first formal response to the world war.

He had begun to write before their train reached Vienna. By the time they were on their way to Bern, his draft was almost finished. Anxious to hold on to his permit to reside in Switzerland, he hesitated about signing the finished work, and in the end let it be published anonymously, as if 'copied from an appeal issued in Denmark'.[30] But anyone who knew his style would have seen past that artifice. Lenin's verdict on the hostilities was crystal clear. The war amounted to 'a struggle for markets and for the freedom to loot foreign countries'. Europe's leaders had revealed 'a desire to deceive, disunite and slaughter the proletarians of all countries by setting the wage-slaves of one nation against those of another so as to benefit the bourgeoisie'.[31] To be sure, none of that was really a surprise. The scandal, the perfidy, the crime against the working class was that the cowardly turncoats of European social-democracy, the very people who were meant to lead the masses in their fight, had abandoned class politics in favour of 'bourgeois-chauvinist' nationalism. The German socialists, all of them pacifists just days before, had granted the kaiser the money he needed to buy stockpiles of guns. 'From this day,' Lenin was said to have remarked on hearing of the betrayal, 'I am no longer a Social-Democrat; I am a Communist.'[32]

The Social-Democrats who had excited Lenin's rage were members of a Europe-wide network, the Second International, to which all major socialist parties belonged. In theory, their collective opposition to the idea of a general war was meant to be as unyielding as their rejection of imperialism or the taking of slaves. At their Stuttgart Congress in 1907, socialist leaders from a range of European countries had committed their members to an active anti-war campaign; five years later, in 1912, a further resolution threatened the great powers with strikes and even revolutions if they took further steps towards hostilities.[33] But in 1914 the gathering diplomatic tension had turned many of Europe's comrades into unexpected patriots, including a majority of the membership of the huge and influential SPD, the Socialist Party of Germany. Abandoning the language of fraternity and peace, the SPD's parliamentary wing had responded to the summer's military pressures by approving a bill to grant war credits to the government. Though its leader, Karl Kautsky, had opposed the move, he had bowed to the party's choice when the time came to cast his vote. 'Kautsky is now more harmful than all of them,' Lenin wrote to Alexander Shlyapnikov in October 1914. 'No words can describe how dangerous and mean . . .'[34]

To no one else's great surprise, the British left had also abandoned its peacetime ideals. The Lenins had spent time in London years before, and had been shocked then by the spinelessness of local socialists, which Krupskaya took as evidence of 'the whole bottomless inanity of English petty-bourgeois life'.[35] Still, the international section of the Labour Party had organized several anti-war rallies in 1912 and 1913. On 2 August 1914, no less a venue than Trafalgar Square had filled with worthy left-wingers intent on deploring the rush to war. They were addressed by the veteran pacifist Keir Hardie and leading MPs such as Arthur Henderson. Within days, however, the Parliamentary Labour Party, like its German counterpart, had approved a vote for war credits. Keir Hardie died of a stroke the following summer, but Henderson went along with wartime policy, joining the coalition government when it was formed in May 1915 and going on to agree to almost every wartime intervention from price controls to conscription.[36]

The story might have turned out otherwise in France, where the socialist leader Jean Jaurès had led the resistance to militarism. In keeping with the spirit of the Second International, he had attempted to organize general strikes in Germany as well as France in protest against threatened war. But Jaurès had been murdered in July 1914, his assassin a patriot who believed himself to be acting for the honour of France. Without Jaurès, even former sympathizers such as Edouard Vaillant were drawn towards the truce with government that its admirers called the 'Union sacrée'.[37] Public opinion was on their side, for Frenchmen yearned to regain

Alsace and Lorraine, the provinces that they had lost to Germany in a treaty of 1871. As if infected by the mood among their hosts, many of the Russian exiles who lived in France were also tempted to enlist, eager to fight an enemy who menaced their adopted land as well as far-off Russia. Even some of the Paris Bolsheviks wanted to fight, at least until they read Lenin's opinions on the matter.[38]

There were also plenty of jingoists in Russia itself. 'No matter what our attitude towards the government's domestic policy,' Paul Miliukov had written as the cavalry rode off to fight, 'our first duty is to preserve the unity and integrity of our country, and to defend its position as a world power – a position which is now being contested by the enemy.'[39] For a few weeks, the idea of a sacred union deflected everyone's attention from the deficiencies of tsarist government. 'All my hairy Russian friends', wrote Arthur Ransome, 'have shaved their heads and gone into uniform.'[40] Abroad, the great Georgy Plekhanov refused to condemn either French or Russian patriots, arguing that the defence of the nation was enough to justify support for war.[41]

But other Russian socialists stood out against the European trend. The left faction in the Duma was almost the only parliamentary group on the entire continent to oppose war credits from the start (the other was in Serbia).[42] In Paris, Martov agitated for an immediate peace, calling for the renunciation, by all belligerents, of plans for the seizure of territory. When Trotsky joined him from Switzerland, the two used their newspaper, *Nashe Slovo*, to help construct an anti-war faction in France, attracting French leftists like Henri Guilbeaux as well as many dissident Russians.[43]

As people started to grasp the true nature of the war, this tide of opposition to hostilities began to swell. The first steps, it was true, were hesitant. A conference of socialists was scheduled for London in February 1915, but the French refused to attend if German delegates came. Lacking the necessary passport for England, Martov also missed the talks. But by the spring the pressure for a conference of anti-war socialists was mounting from Berlin to Brussels and from Paris to Turin. Only Lenin remained apart, refusing to join anything as bloodless as a peace movement. In February, at the time of the London conference (which he would not have been able to attend), he called a meeting of his own in Bern. 'At the present time,' he told his closest followers, 'the propaganda of peace unaccompanied by revolutionary mass action can only sow illusions . . . for it makes the proletariat believe that the bourgeoisie is humane, and turns it into a plaything in the hands of the secret diplomacy of the belligerent countries. In particular, the idea of a so-called democratic peace being possible without a series of revolutions is profoundly erroneous.'[44]

This was the line Lenin would stress whatever any congress of his fellow socialists might rule. In May 1915, he lambasted the authors of an anti-war essay in *The Economist* ('a journal that speaks for British millionaires') on the grounds that their publication 'stands for peace just because it is afraid of revolution'.[45] In July, as centre-left socialists like Karl Kautsky and Switzerland's Robert Grimm began to press for Europe-wide peace talks, he was calling for bloodshed, for 'We regard civil war . . . as fully legitimate, progressive and necessary.'[46] 'There is nothing more puerile, contemptible and harmful', he added in September, 'than the idea current among revolutionary philistines, namely, that differences should be "forgotten" in view of the immediate common aim.' On the contrary, 'Life is advancing . . .

towards a civil war in Europe.[47] As for Martov and the *Nashe Slovo* gang, their chances of a coalition with him had been dashed in May. 'After two hundred days of propaganda,' Lenin wrote, '*Nashe Slovo* has acknowledged its complete bankruptcy ... These people were talking of uniting the internationalists, only to find that they could unite nobody, not even themselves.'[48]

The dangers Lenin faced during the war were not from guns. Far more deadly (at least from his distinctive point of view) was the risk that the rest of the European left might unite on a peace platform. The movement would be popular, but that was not the worst of it. More seriously still, he might not ever control it, for Kautsky was a more distinguished candidate and there were others, such as Émile Vandervelde in Belgium. As the war dragged into a second summer, the anti-war movement began to attract supporters from almost all Europe's socialist parties. To prevent what he could see only as an impending disaster, Lenin was forced to hammer at the wedge that he was driving between these peacemongers and his own group. Whenever fellow socialists gathered to talk, he seized the chance to emphasize the split. Accordingly, when Robert Grimm called a meeting of leading socialist internationalists in September 1915, its aim to relaunch the International on an anti-war platform, Lenin was ready with a verbal and tactical offensive.

The thirty-eight delegates assembled in the Volkshaus in Bern. Grimm knew the place was full of spies, so his guests had barely tasted their first mouthful of Swiss beer before they were handed their tickets for a horse-drawn coach to take them to the mountains of the Bernese Oberland. So few vehicles were needed (only four) that the occasion struck

Trotsky as a tragi-comic commentary on the feebleness of European internationalism.[49] The cover-story was that this assemblage of Swiss, Germans, Swedes, Russians and assorted eastern Europeans was an ornithological society on its annual outing.[50] The group was bound for the village of Zimmerwald, a settlement of twenty-one squat mountain houses in a sea of fading autumn grass. Throughout their stay, the delegates kept close to their hotel, their entertainment limited to yodelling by Grimm.[51] But this was a noble sacrifice, for most saw the meeting as a chance to refound the International, a fresh start untainted by petty-bourgeois patriots. Up to a point, moreover, they succeeded. On 8 September, a manifesto was agreed and signed by the entire meeting (Lenin included), and for the next three years any socialist who opposed the war or pressed his government for swift peace talks was identified as a Zimmerwaldist.

For Lenin, however, the meeting was an opportunity to stake his claim to be the leader of the real European left. The Swiss left-winger Fritz Platten remembered the great Bolshevik as the most attentive listener at Zimmerwald, but when he spoke his interventions had the impact of a caustic shower. Again and again, Lenin pressed the case for common action to bring down the whole structure of imperialism. While bourgeois governments might weigh their chance of wartime victory or of defeat, the European working class could win only when it had smashed the systems that oppressed it. 'Lenin's strength', concluded Platten, 'consisted in the fact that he saw the laws of historical development with phenomenal clarity.'[52] Lenin's faction was a small minority at every stage (at times he seemed to be its sole member), but it managed to set the tone of most discussions, flaying Grimm and the Mensheviks in the process.[53]

Eight delegates eventually formed a leftist clique, including Fritz Platten, who defied his own party to side with Lenin. The representatives from Sweden, Ture Nerman and Zeth Höglund, were also Lenin's men, as was the ever-faithful Grigory Zinoviev, but Lenin was surprised by the support of a mercurial newcomer called Karl Radek. This louche and garrulous character was a refugee in many senses of the term. As an Austrian citizen (he was born in Lviv), he had fled to the Swiss mountains to avoid conscription. But he was also on the lookout for a new political home, having been ejected from two previous ones in awkward circumstances (there were rumours of substantial missing funds).[54] A fluent and lively stylist, he had been writing for Grimm's newspaper, but he would find his real niche at Zimmerwald with Lenin's hell-raisers. He might have been an ugly man with a notably chequered past, but the simian, bespectacled Radek was always magnetic, his laughter infectious, his greed for books and gossip limitless. He was also a natural contact for Parvus, and beat a path to see him at the institute in Copenhagen at the first opportunity.[55]

The allegiance of this talented maverick (though it would be erratic) proved what the Zimmerwald meeting had done for Lenin. He had transformed himself into a leader on the international stage, the inspiration for a distinct political tendency, the European movement of radical socialists that was to be known as the Zimmerwald Left. In the months to come, he and his network of supporters worked to persuade more socialists to join their cause. In France, the task fell to Lenin's long-time friend (and possibly former lover) Inessa Armand. Despite formidable opposition from Trotsky, who was still Martov's political ally, she spent the winter of 1915–16 kindling enthusiasm for Lenin's views among the socialists of Paris.[56] In April 1916, when the Zimmerwald group reconvened (this time in the Swiss village of Kienthal) the atmosphere was more tense. It was clear that the pro-peace centre had become more vulnerable, and Lenin's confederates, Radek especially, duly attacked it.[57] The left was growing, it was more confident, and Lenin took the whole proceedings as a harbinger of future victory.

He had the socialists in that 'death-grip', but he could not relax. When he was not buried behind his books in the Zurich library, he kept up a relentless campaign to maintain his faction's distinctive line. He had split the Russian party in 1903, now he would split the Swiss. 'A split is always painful,' he conceded, 'but sometimes it turns out to be necessary, and in those circumstances every weakness, every sign of "sentimentality" is a crime.'[58] When news of a possible peace between the tsar and the kaiser reached Zurich at the end of 1916, Marcu recalled him 'roaring like a lion'.[59] If Russia pulled out of the war, after all, his hopes for a Russian uprising would begin to ebb away, and with them his ability to dominate the European left. 'An imperialist war cannot end otherwise than in an imperialist peace', he wrote in November 1916, 'unless it is transformed into a civil war of the proletariat against the bourgeoisie for socialism.'[60] Or, as he put it in another outburst, 'Only when we have overthrown, finally vanquished, and expropriated the bourgeoisie of the whole world, and not merely of one country, will wars become impossible.'[61]

It was one thing to scandalize Europe's pacifists, however, and another to have a following of any kind among workers, peasants and soldiers in the Russian empire itself. However solemn the European meetings, however bilious the prose,

Lenin was still a Russian leader, and Russia was the place where his ideas would need to have their greatest hold. The danger was that he was getting out of touch. Since 1914, he had relied increasingly on Swiss newspapers, getting any news from Petrograd when it was already two days old. The strain told on the leader's health as well as his temper. 'My nerves are no good,' he wrote as he cancelled a public appearance in 1916, 'I'm scared of giving lectures.'[62] He would not have conceded it, but he was becoming an institutionalized exile, cut off from Russian life and barely relevant to it. Valeriu Marcu could have been giving expression to Lenin's own deep fears when he wrote that by 1916 'The whole Bolshevik Party . . . consisted of a few friends who corresponded with [Lenin] from Stockholm, London, New York and Paris.'[63]

Neither Marcu nor Lenin could know for sure how Bolshevism, as opposed to Lenin's personal network, was faring inside Russia. The picture was not as bad as they might have imagined. Although the tsarist secret police, the Okhrana, had battered at the Russian underground for years, most commentators on the spot believed the Bolsheviks to be the best-organized and most determined of the surviving socialist factions.[64] Born in the trade unions and benefit societies, the party had a predominantly young and relatively educated membership. Better still, a network of activists had survived the crackdown after 1906 and continued to recruit new members despite the ever-darkening political atmosphere. Local organizers toiled assiduously among the workforce, and while they knew about Karl Marx they also dealt with practical issues such as sickness pay, insurance and the niceties of employment law.[65] As a result, the Bolsheviks had retained a committed following in heavy industry and among seamen and railway-workers. Petrograd was the party's main stronghold, and by the end of 1916, according to an estimate by Alexander Shlyapnikov, there were 3,000 Bolsheviks among the workers there.[66] The fervour of this rank and file had not evaporated in the heat of patriotic war. But there had been a number of setbacks, the effect of which had been to leave the party cash-strapped and more or less leaderless.

The Okhrana counted on at least twelve well-placed inform-ers among the Bolshevik general staff.[67] One of these, Roman Malinovsky, had been the subject of a three-man party trial while Lenin was in Poronin. The charges had been serious. 'It's a total bacchanalia of arrests, searches and raids,' declared Stalin in 1913, just days before falling victim himself to the informant's wholesale treachery.[68] But Lenin was not yet con-vinced, and brought Zinoviev and Fürstenberg to Poronin to help him weigh the evidence. The trio considered a range of reports from outraged comrades inside Russia, but in the end they decided that Malinovsky must be innocent. He was soon the only senior Bolshevik who remained at liberty in Petro-grad, and the information that he passed to the police wreaked havoc on an epic scale. Keeping the party's address book, a list of key contacts, was one of Krupskaya's responsibilities. In 1916 there were only 130 names on her list, and at best twenty-six of those were political operatives within the Rus-sian empire. By 1917, the number of her active organizers on the ground had dwindled to ten.[69]

The police had been watching everything. Another informer, Miron Chernomazov, had been appointed to the editorial board of the Bolshevik newspaper, *Pravda*, which had been published in Russia since 1912. The paper was suppressed in July 1914 and many of its staff arrested. With its closure, the party lost more than its most popular propaganda tool, for *Pravda* had been earning revenue, and now the Bolsheviks would have to cast about for funds.[70] Worse was to come in December 1914, when the Central Committee of the Bolshevik Party in Russia gathered for a secret meeting on the outskirts of Petrograd. Among those present were the five Bolshevik Duma members, including Lenin's close friend and long-standing aide Lev Kamenev. The police were waiting, and the whole group was arrested.[71] At his trial in February 1915, Kamenev damaged the party further by betraying it, denying publicly that he had ever supported the anti-imperialist and anti-war line that its foreign leaders advocated. Like all the other defendants, nonetheless, he was sentenced to a long Siberian exile.

The arrests continued as the war ground on. When Shlyapnikov went to Petrograd in 1916 he found a Bolshevik political organization that had been weakened, if not quite shattered, by successive police raids. The Central Committee, which was meant to guide the whole movement, had almost been destroyed by the arrests of recent months. Its surviving members now met only rarely. They also feared to maintain written protocols, avoided fixed venues and often held their meetings while strolling around the city's leafy Lesnoi suburb.[72] The situation was unacceptable to Shlyapnikov, whose solution was to convene a new Russian Bureau to oversee the comrades' day-to-day affairs. Its members included a radical young activist who called himself Molotov as well as full-time stalwarts from the local underground. In parallel to that, the Bolsheviks of Petrograd itself had their own organization, the Petersburg Committee (it had refused to adopt the more anti-German name of Petrograd), which was much livelier than the Bureau. It was raided in December 1916. Some of its members were arrested, but the real blow was that it forfeited its precious, costly and strategically vital printing press.[73]

The loss of the press was disastrous. With no local means of printing, the supply of information for the Russian movement dwindled almost to nothing. Papers were handed round in secret – thumbed and dog-eared, out of date. As the Petrograd Bolsheviks found in January 1917, they could not even produce leaflets for the anniversary of Bloody Sunday, the massacre that had unleashed a revolution back in 1905.[74] It had always been hard to keep up the flow of printed news, or even manifestos and strike-calls. The tsarist censorship was fierce, and wartime changes made it even tougher. For years, as an alternative, activists had been smuggling documents from abroad, sewing them into coat-linings, stuffing them into their corsets or piling them beneath their own small crates of books. The war had complicated all of that, and there had been no let-up in border controls at Tornio.

Lenin's answer, as always, was to write more essays himself. His propaganda flagship was a journal, called *Sotsial-Demokrat*, which he had revived, with the help of a Geneva-based librarian called Vyacheslav Karpinsky, as soon as he arrived in Switzerland. The first number of the new run came out in November 1914. Though party members valued it, the journal made no concession to mass appeal, and the principal contributor (and usually the only one) was Lenin. The war put pressure on paper and print, and the Bolsheviks were short of funds, so *Sotsial-Demokrat* came out irregularly and seldom amounted to more than one closely printed sheet.[75] But transport was the real problem. The stuff was sent by post to Scandinavia, where two agents, Alexandra Kollontai and the resourceful Shlyapnikov, were meant to get it to Russia. Shlyapnikov exploited his trade-union contacts with the fishermen along the Baltic coast, sending rolls of paper slowly on their way along a chain of islands to Finland. There was also a shoe-maker in Haparanda who could sew the precious printed sheets into the lining of his leather soles.[76] But the network was fragile, and not infrequently the only people in Petrograd who got a chance to ponder Lenin's outpourings were Okhrana agents.

The very weakness of the party's formal leadership, however, allowed the people in its rank and file to develop ideas of their own. The organization in Petrograd's Vyborg district, with about 500 members, was particularly radical.[77] In August 1914, the Vyborg group had applauded Lenin's theses on the war. They passed the first issues of *Sotsial-Demokrat* from hand to hand until the paper fell apart. As one enthusiast recalled, Lenin's ideas 'gave us fresh spirit, vindicated and inspired us, fired our hearts with an irresistible desire to go further, not stopping at anything'.[78] But though the Vyborg Committee was distinctive and genuinely Leninist, the Bolshevik Party as a whole had yet to convince the mass of Russia's workforce, let alone the army. The most that could be said was that Bolshevism had become identified with a muscular (and masculine) militancy. Meanwhile, the bulk of Lenin's writing – dripping with invective, sometimes donnish, and studded with completely unfamiliar and foreign-sounding names – remained both hard to come by and deeply perplexing.

If anything, the gap between the Bolsheviks in exile and their Russian following was growing wider by the early months of 1917. This was a question that interested the French ambassador in Petrograd, Maurice Paléologue, when he received one of his best-connected informants for a private conversation in December 1916. 'I asked him if the defeatist doctrine of the famous Lenin, who is now a refugee in Geneva, is making any headway in the army,' the ambassador recalled, no doubt thinking of all the Frenchmen who would die if Russia's war effort should buckle. The visitor was quick to reassure him. 'No, he said. The only advocates of that doctrine here are a few lunatics who are supposed to be in the pay of Germany – or the Okhrana. The defeatists ... are only a negligible minority in the social-democratic party.'[79]

It was a view that would have drawn expletives from Lenin himself. Fortunately, however, he was used to rebuilding his faction after a setback; small numbers made for tighter discipline. What would really have troubled him was the evidence of an emerging coalition between the various socialist party cells in Russian cities. Even as Lenin was banging his fist about the differences that ought to separate the Bolsheviks from any other party in the emigration, some of his followers in Russia were moving closer to their fellow socialists, be they Mensheviks or non-aligned.[80] The enemy, for these comrades, was not their fellow socialist but the employer, the police, the hated tsar. If they had understood the details, too, they would have looked on Lenin's vision of a European civil war (the current reason for the party split) as a foretaste of hell. It was exhaustion, low wages and lack of bread that mattered in the kerosene-lit basements where these people gathered, and everyone was bone-weary of fighting. To change all this, to help themselves, demanded a combined effort. In Russia, and especially in Petrograd, it was not Lenin but the Okhrana, with its poisonous false rumours and sporadic mass arrests, that was having most success in keeping the factions apart.[81]

Some Bolsheviks remained determinedly separate, but many in the rank and file were tempted by the idea of a joint campaign. There were internationalists on the left wing of the Menshevik Party, too, as well as a small movement of left-wing Socialist Revolutionaries. In October 1913, a joint operation called the Inter-District Committee, or Mezhraionka, had formed in the Russian capital to bring the local socialists together.[82] Two of its founding members had been Bolsheviks, and although its numbers remained small (about 150 by 1917), it was well organized and very influential. As that young workhorse Stalin had written in *Pravda* in 1912, 'Complete identity of interests can exist only in the graveyard. But this does not mean that points of disagreement will be more significant than points of agreement . . . Peace and co-operation within the movement – that is what *Pravda* will be guided by in its daily work.'[83] Lenin was furious, but he was also far away. The Mezhraionka continued to agitate in industrial districts, armed with a very useful printing press. As a strike wave mounted in the first weeks of 1917, a protest powered by exasperation with the war, the comrades who knew how to turn out leaflets were soon working round the clock.

4. Scarlet Ribbons

The conditions of bourgeois democracy very often
compel us to take a certain stand on a multitude of
small and petty reforms, but we must be able . . . to
take such a position on these reforms that five
minutes of every half-hour speech are devoted to
reforms and twenty-five minutes to the coming
revolution.

V. I. Lenin

On 14 February 1917, after an extended Christmas break, the
Duma assembled for another year. At a time of mounting
popular disturbance, and with several of its members engaged
in covert plots to oust the tsar, the session should have been
a lively one. Instead, as a stalwart of the Progressive Bloc put
it, the deputies seemed to be wandering about 'like emaciated
flies'. 'No-one believes anything . . . All feel and know their
powerlessness. The silence is hopeless.'[1] The Duma's chairman, Mikhail Rodzianko, conceded that the mood was
sluggish and the speeches dull.[2] Progressive, liberal or mon-
archist, the intellectuals vied to find fresh outlets for their
shared despair. They were not alone in feeling powerless.
Outside the pompous meeting hall, the mood was no more
positive among the leaders of the revolutionary underground.
'Not one party was preparing for the great upheaval,' remembered Nikolai Sukhanov, then thirty-five years old and

working semi-legally as a socialist and writer. 'Everyone was dreaming, ruminating, full of foreboding, feeling his way.'[3]

The atmosphere was different across the water where the workers lived. Few people there had time to ponder their foreboding dreams. The food crisis was now acute. The wealthy could still have their fresh white bread in any restaurant, but families in the factory districts had begun to starve. It was not just a question of inflation, although the price of everything from kerosene to eggs had multiplied beyond the reach of the hard-pressed. The real problem in Petrograd, exacerbated by a transport crisis in the provinces, was a shortage of grain. The city's wheat and flour stocks, already depleted, had fallen by more than 30 per cent in January, leaving many without bread at all. Before the war, as an Okhrana agent reported, a bakery could sell 10,000 rolls a morning, but now the 8,000 that it produced on a good day were sold within two hours.[4] It was not uncommon for a woman who managed to procure two loaves to cross herself in prayers of tearful gratitude. 'Resentment is worse in large families,' an agent informed the secret police, 'where children are starving and where no words are heard except "peace, immediate peace, peace at any cost".'[5]

The government's response might have been scripted for a modern Marie Antoinette. To help conserve scarce flour stocks, the commissioner of food supply prohibited the baking and sale of cake, to say nothing of buns, pies and biscuits. There were also new restrictions on the provision of flour to factory kitchens and workers' canteens.[6] The move had little impact on the bread supply, but working people greeted it with rage. Because they had no legal share in government (few even had a vote), the only thing that they could do was join a protest, usually a strike. The atmosphere became so tense (like living on a volcano, decided Paul Miliukov) that some suspected the shortage to have been engineered. The more hysterical imagined an exotic German plot, while others detected a scheme to provoke riots and thus pave the way for mass arrests and tyranny.[7] But there was comfort in the thought that the most obvious discontent was economic. Such strikes as might occur, a telegram from Sir George Buchanan reassured the British War Cabinet on the eve of the Duma's new session, 'would be primarily on account of the shortage of food supplies . . . but it was not considered likely that any serious disorders would take place.'[8]

What Sir George had failed to understand was that bread itself was political. In factories and engine-sheds, in shipyards and workers' barracks, socialist activists were using hunger as a means to start a conversation with the people. Leaflets, speeches and slogans connected the food shortage to the war and the autocracy. Bread might have been their immediate grievance, but once the people joined a strike they were swept on by rousing songs and revolutionary catchphrases. On 9 January 1917, the anniversary of the Bloody Sunday massacre of 1905, the strikes were explicitly political. When the Duma convened on 14 February, the Mezhraionka and its allies called the workers out again, this time with slogans about peace, democracy and even a republic.[9] There had been large-scale strikes before, but these were new, and called for more from government than cake and buns. Even a patrician outsider could pick up the change of mood. 'At a bakery on the Liteiny this morning,' Paléologue wrote in his diary on 6 March (or 21 February by Russia's calendar), 'I was struck by the sinister expression on the faces of the poor folk who had lined up in a queue, most of whom had spent the whole night there.'[10]

The peace of Petrograd depended on its civil governor, Major-General A. P. Balk, on the police (a force of 3,500 in a city of two and a half million), and on the governor of the military district, Major-General S. S. Khabalov. In charge of the co-ordination of them all was Interior Minister Protopopov, whose first resort as crisis loomed was to consult the ghost of Rasputin.[11] His team was riven by mistrust. It was Balk, for instance, who declared Khabalov to be 'incapable of leading his own subordinates'.[12] No one trusted the police chief, A. T. Vasiliev, whose promotion was entirely due to his friendship with Protopopov, and the best that anyone could say for Balk was that he was good at his paperwork.[13]

None of this might have mattered – incompetents were nothing new in Russian government – if the troops Khabalov commanded had been the right men for the job. There were about 200,000 garrison soldiers in Petrograd, quartered in barracks all around the city centre. Most lived in conditions that felt like the serfdom their fathers had escaped.[14] 'The only troops in the capital', remembered Alfred Knox, 'were the depot battalions of the Guard and some depot units of the line . . . most of whom had never been at the front. They were officered by men who had been wounded at the front and who regarded their duty as a sort of convalescent leave from the trenches, or by youths fresh from the military schools.' Paléologue's source was a disaffected Russian general. 'In my opinion,' this man had confided in November 1916, 'the troops guarding the capital ought to have been weeded out long ago . . . If God does not spare us a revolution, it will be started not by the people but by the army!'[15]

The general had got that wrong. The army played a crucial role, but only when the people had already kindled a revolt.

It started with a celebration, albeit an imported and at times half-hearted one. The festival of International Women's Day had been created just before the war by a German socialist called Clara Zetkin. The event was marked in Petrograd on 23 February, a few weeks after the annual commemoration of Bloody Sunday. In its first years, the comrades in the Russian empire had been reluctant to make a special effort over Zetkin's festival, and some continued to dispute its propaganda value as the date approached in 1917. A march was planned, but it risked being small as well as mostly female. 'We need to teach the working class to take to the streets,' Shlyapnikov wrote to Lenin, 'but we have not had time.'[16] He added (several times) that he had also lost his printing press; the Bolsheviks could lead no one without a manifesto and a pile of pamphlets. But other factions saw a propaganda opportunity. A leaflet from the Mezhraionka, copied into Shlyapnikov's memoir, was unequivocal. 'The government is guilty,' it read. 'It started the war and it cannot end it. It is destroying the country and your starving is its fault ... Enough! Down with the criminal government and the gang of thieves and murderers! Long live peace!'[17]

If the weather had remained inhibitingly cold, if the city had received an adequate supply of flour, or even if the workplace toilets had been heated to unfreeze the pipes, the strikes might not have been so large. But on the morning of Thursday 23 February, the women in the Vyborg cotton mills were in no mood for compromise. Their Women's Day meetings resulted in a mass walk-out, and as they headed for the Neva they called on other workers to march with them, including the men of the New Lessner and Erikson factories. By noon, about 50,000 people had joined a protest on Vyborg's main highway, Sampsonievsky Prospect.[18] 'I was extremely indignant at the behaviour of the strikers,' a Bolshevik from the Erikson plant called Kayurov recalled. 'They were blatantly ignoring the instructions of the party district committees . . . yet suddenly here was a strike. There seemed to be no purpose in it and no reason for it.'[19]

A mile away from all of that, at an address on Serdobolskaya Street, Shlyapnikov spent most of the day discussing party work with fellow members of the Bolshevik Russian Bureau. The meeting was not about the strikes, and the members present, still uncertain that the time was ripe for insurrection, were wary of encouraging a women's march. It was not until he attempted to make his way home that Shlyapnikov began to see what he had missed. His no. 20 tram was 'stuffed full of workers' heading for the expensive Liteiny quarter, and when it reached the Liteiny Bridge it was surrounded by police. Barging aboard, they checked every passenger to weed out those whose hands and clothes looked work-worn. The idea was to keep the poor where they belonged and make sure that their wretched protest could not interfere with decent life.[20]

The bridges were supposed to help protect the more expensive parts of town, but this time, thanks to the sub-zero cold, there turned out to be little point in raising them. An enterprising militant could simply walk across the ice. The first groups made their way from Vyborg to the centre as the sun set over Petrograd on that first day. Later that evening, when he met Alfred Knox (who had become a major-general since Milner's visit), the Duma industrialist Alexander Guchkov described the food shortage as the worst catastrophe his government had faced to date, more crippling and more dangerous than any battlefield defeat. He could already sense that trouble lay ahead. 'Questioned regarding the attitude of workmen in the towns towards the war,' Knox wrote, Guchkov conceded 'that from 10 to 20 percent would welcome defeat as likely to strengthen their hands to overthrow the Government.'[21]

The next day was a Friday, dull and foggy with cold rain. But neither the weather nor the appearance on the streets of cossack horsemen, armed and grim, dampened the demonstrators' zeal. For Shlyapnikov, 'events moved at a dizzying pace', not least because he still could not make sense of them.[22] By late morning, nearly 75,000 workers from the Vyborg district (two-thirds of its total workforce) had joined the strike.[23] As marchers approached the Liteiny Bridge, cossacks were arrayed against them. The lines of horses and the glint of steel must have been terrifying, but these agents of government turned out to share the workers' exasperation. For the first time anyone could remember, the cossacks cantered through the workers' lines, refusing to brandish their sabres or their whips. Meanwhile, in the Petrograd district, further demonstrations filled the streets. It was also here that the first bakeries were looted and food shops attacked. Before long, the disturbance had spread west to the dockyards and naval engineering works of Vasilievsky Island. The ministers had yet to respond to events. In the Tauride Palace, however, Duma members demanded to take control of the city's food supply in a last-ditch attempt to address the most immediate economic woes.[24]

On Saturday, a three-day general strike began. Among its leaders were members of the Mezhraionka and rank-and-file activists from the various left-wing groups, including (in defiance of Shlyapnikov's Russian Bureau) the Bolsheviks' own Vyborg Committee. All had worked throughout the night to spread the message and bring people out, and the morning felt like the start of a holiday. Trainloads of people, including families with children, streamed into the city from nearby industrial towns such as Sestroretsk. In Petrograd itself, working-class districts hummed with earnest preparation. The factories were silent, and there were no trams, but by ten o'clock the streets rang with the sound of marching feet and voices singing revolutionary songs.[25] In all, over 200,000 people chose to march through Petrograd that day. White-collar workers, teachers and students joined the rising, and as they passed the wealthy homes the marchers sometimes saw pale hands waving from an upper window. The protest had acquired a following of sorts in most sections of Petrograd society, but it was the workers in their padded sheepskin coats, some armed with knives or bags of nails, who took the lead when the time came to cross the ice.

Their goal was Znamenskaya Square, where huge crowds had assembled by the early afternoon. Red banners stretched above the sea of heads, many with slogans that demanded peace, immediate and longed-for peace. Between the speeches, some enthusiasts began to sing the Marseillaise. In wartime Russia, this was treason and a breach of martial law. A number of demonstrators had prepared for the likely consequences by lining their hats with home-made metal shields and padding their jackets against the cossacks' whips. For most, however, the crowd felt like protection in itself, the sense of justice and community a shield in its own right.

A little after 3 p.m., a mounted police officer called Krylov told his men to prime their weapons and disperse the mob. In the mêlée that followed, the cossack horsemen charged the crowd, but it turned out when they rode back and regrouped that they had used their sabres on the police, not on the demonstrators. Krylov himself lay dead. For an hour or so, at least if they knew what had just happened, the people could believe in a forthcoming victory.[26] But there were other confrontations between crowds and troops that day, and marchers and some bystanders were killed. No one was certain of the facts, for there were neither newspapers nor public telephones.[27] When Sukhanov and his Menshevik friends assembled at Maxim Gorky's flat that night, a rendezvous that they would use until the old regime collapsed, they blamed high-ranking Bolsheviks. 'Their flat-footedness,' Sukhanov wrote, 'or more properly, their incapacity to think their way into the political problem and formulate it, had a depressing effect on us.'[28]

The intellectuals and writers in Sukhanov's circle would find the next day even more distressing. Overnight, Khabalov had issued orders to turn the city into a military camp. At daybreak, the bridges were raised. Armed police and troops had mustered at the main junctions and squares, while Red Cross wagons, hitched to the rheumatic horses that the army did not want, waited to cart the wounded off to makeshift hospitals near by. Khabalov's orders were to fire on any demonstrator who defied his order to disperse.[29] A Bolshevik called Fedor Raskolnikov, who was due to take his examinations as a naval officer at the time, remembered his walk to the barracks in the frost-hard early light. 'Our company's quarters looked like an armed camp,' he wrote. 'Cartridge-pouches were laid on the desks and everywhere stood rifles with bayonets fixed. I found that the commanders of the classes had armed all the cadets.'[30]

It did not take long for the youngsters in Raskolnikov's company to reject their commanders' plans for them. By mid-morning, the young men had joined the crowds heading towards Nevsky Prospect, marching almost joyfully, their red banners held high. The hopes, the sunshine and the comradeship contrasted with the rulers' cruel resolution. Police and members of the elite guards obeyed their officers this time and fired. The worst confrontation occurred on Znamenskaya Square, where at least forty people were gunned down and many more were wounded. Panicked members of the crowd fled north, and by nightfall the square was silent. All that remained was trampled snow, a few alarmingly bright pools of blood, and a scattering of discarded caps, torn ribbons and galoshes.[31]

The leaders of the underground parties were more convinced than ever now that it was time to stop the strikes. Shlyapnikov still took the view that the working class would not win on its own. Without the army, it was powerless. Even the Vyborg Committee, so militant up to this point, agreed at its meeting that night that there was no choice but to bring the workers' movement to an end. Everyone was exhausted, however, and the Vyborg comrades' session dispersed without deciding how their decision was to be implemented.[32] At Gorky's flat, Sukhanov and his friends could make no sense at all of the events. One story in particular, which Gorky heard when he telephoned Fedor Chaliapin, the world-famous operatic bass, left them completely at a loss. Someone had seen an infantry unit firing systematically into the barracks of the elite Pavlovsky Regiment. It was an act that looked like madness, and Gorky put the phone down on Chaliapin with a puzzled scowl.[33]

The truth would have amazed the most extreme of revolutionaries, for what had happened was a mutiny. In the confusion of that afternoon, a group of workers had informed cadets in the Pavlovskys' barracks that some of their fellows had fired on Russian civilians. Disgusted, a small group from Fourth Company decided to revolt. They quickly settled on a slogan ('There is no cause for which we will allow our people's blood to stain the white tunics of the Pavlovskys'), then broke into a store and seized a number of rifles before setting out for the streets. Their mutiny was unsuccessful (when they were captured by the military police, Khabalov took charge of their punishment in person), but it signalled a changing mood in the ranks of the garrison, a taste for rebellion that was entirely independent of the Duma, the educated radicals or any revolutionary cell.[34]

The demonstrations turned into a revolution on 27 February 1917. The Pavlovskys' defection had pointed the way. As Khabalov prepared to organize a second day of armed repression, full-scale rebellion broke out among the troops. The first to rise was the Volhynsky Regiment, one of the units that had been deployed against the crowd the previous day. Sickened by what their comrades had been forced to do, a group of lads turned against their officers and marched out of the barracks yard, soon to be joined by members of the Litovsky and Izmailovsky Regiments. Before long, even the crack Preobrazhensky Regiment was dispersing into the streets; there was no turning back this time, for the rebels had shot some of their officers on the way out. Sukhanov, waiting by the telephone in Gorky's flat, gathered that by midday at least 25,000 garrison troops had joined the revolutionary side. Young men with rifles now patrolled the streets, some lugging looted food across their backs. It also turned out that the workers had not followed their leaders' advice about standing down. Overnight, there had been a raid on the armoury in Lesnoi District, from which rifles, handguns and ammunition had been seized to arm what was becoming an all-out anti-government revolt.[35]

The rising was neither blind nor anarchic. The workers chose their targets logically, storming the Kresty Prison, the law courts and the main artillery depot. When garrison mutineers turned up to liberate the prison, they appeared to be so calm and disciplined that the French military attaché, Colonel Lavergne, assumed they were acting on official orders. But the calmness was not universal. 'In a short time,' wrote a British witness, Stinton Jones, 'the whole of the city was aglow with the glare from burning buildings which, in addition to the heavy firing, made the situation appear far worse that it actually was.' As he continued:

the mobs presented a strange, almost grotesque appearance. Soldiers, workmen, students, hooligans and freed criminals wandered aimlessly about in detached companies, all armed, but with a strange variety of weapons . . . A student with two rifles and a belt of machine-gun bullets round his waist was walking beside another with a bayonet tied to the end of a stick. A drunken soldier had only the barrel of a rifle remaining, the stock having been broken off in forcing entry into some shop.[36]

From his window on an upper floor, General Knox watched as the marchers swept towards the artillery department. 'Craning our necks,' he wrote,

we first saw two soldiers – a sort of advanced guard – who strode along the middle of the street, pointing their rifles at loiterers to clear the road. One of them fired two shots at an unfortunate chauffeur. Then came a great disorderly mass of soldiery, stretching right across the wide street and both pavements. They were led by a diminutive but immensely dignified student. There were no officers. All were armed, and many had red flags tied to their bayonets.[37]

Those red 'flags', mostly rags or scraps of ribbon, were soon blazing from every hat and rifle-butt. 'Without one,' Stinton Jones recalled, 'it was: Policeman, spy, shoot him.'[38] The crowd's fear of police was justified, for through that day and well into the next there were more fatal shootings of protesters. 'As the streets cleared,' wrote Jones, 'little heaps, some very still, some writhing in agony, told of the toll of the machine-guns.'[39]

In working-class Vyborg, the local Bolsheviks began to plan for an armed seizure of state power, the prelude to establishing a caretaker organization that they proposed to call the Provisional Revolutionary Government.[40] Their leaders hoped to establish a headquarters at the Finland Station, Vyborg's obvious strategic heart. While the extreme left kept to Vyborg, however, almost everyone else seemed to be heading for the Tauride Palace, the home of the Duma. It was not clear what anyone expected to accomplish there, but the Tauride was a hub of political authority and an obvious focus for revolutionary ambitions. The tsar, based at his command centre near the front, had been so alarmed by the messages from Petrograd that he had ordered the Duma to be prorogued in the small hours that morning. By the time the soldiers, students and workers were converging on the Tauride, many crammed aboard the cars that they had commandeered, there was no legal institution left to represent the will of their democracy. The only symbol anywhere was this palace, itself a throwback to the days of Prince Potemkin and the Empress Catherine the Great.

*

The intruders made short work of the iron gates. To their surprise, however, as they stepped in from the wind and snow, the Tauride felt deserted. The emptiness was deceptive, an effect of vastness on a scale that none had ever seen before. It took a lot to make this palace, an extravagance by eighteenth-century Russia's richest man, appear crowded. The main ballroom, for instance, had been designed to accommodate 5,000 people, all of them dancing. Other chambers were a little smaller, but that still left space enough for each to have swallowed a circus, elephant and all. Sukhanov arrived in the early evening, and noticed instantly how Tauride staff, in their shirt-fronts or black cassocks, stood out from the newcomers in their greatcoats and fur hats.[41] The palace had two massive wings, joined in the centre by a domed atrium and columned hall, at the back of which (in what had been a winter garden in the time of Catherine the Great) the Duma had its debating chamber. Most Duma officials also used offices in the building's right wing, and it was in one of these, as crowds surged into the main hall, that some of the dissolved parliament's leading members had gathered to talk.

The gentlemen had no idea what they should do. To go on meeting when the Duma had been closed was an act of treason, but the majesty of the constitution was easily forgotten at the sight of that crowd in the ballroom. For hours the politicians wrangled, uncertain even of their right to call for order in a city where a revolution had begun. That afternoon, with a certain reluctance, a group of them declared themselves to be 'the Provisional Committee of members of the State Duma for the restoration of order in the capital and the establishment of relations with public organizations and institutions'.[42] As a right-winger called Vasily Shulgin had put it, after all, if they did not take action, 'the scoundrels in the factories' might well do so.[43] The Duma Committee had no legal status, a fact that worried the lawyers in its ranks, but its members were national public figures and included Mikhail Rodzianko (its chairman), Vasily Shulgin, Paul Miliukov and a socialist called Alexander Kerensky.

At least the office where they sat was quiet. The drama unfolding in the main hall was enough to terrify any monocle-wearing representative of the political elite. Paul Miliukov never forgot the sight of rough outsiders surging towards the ballroom and trampling on the hallowed parquet and the Persian rugs. 'By night time,' he wrote, 'the Tauride had turned into an armed camp. The soldiers brought with themselves boxes of machine-gun cartridge belts and hand grenades; and, I think, they also dragged in a cannon. When shots were heard somewhere around the palace, some of the soldiers began to run, broke the windows of the semi-circular hall, and jumped out.'[44] 'Against the wall all sorts of plunder was stacked up,' explains a classic history of these events. 'On a heap of sacks of barley and flour lay a carcass of a pig. The noise was incredible. The members of the Duma stood appalled at the gigantic crowds that had violated [the] Tauride Palace and who were behaving as though it were the site of a great festival.'[45]

The Tauride had begun to draw the entire city to its gates. 'While the roadway of Shpalernaya Street was occupied by demonstrators,' remembered the naval cadet Raskolnikov, 'its pavement was crowded with members of the intellectual and bourgeois public. In those days every philistine saw it as his duty to decorate his breast with a magnificent bow of red silk or calico.'[46] Some of these characters had come to stare (Raskolnikov recognized a gendarme with 'a red bow of colossal size'), but others, also in white shirts and suits, had been dreaming of revolution all their lives. 'I would do anything at all', Sukhanov vowed as he rushed eastwards in the dusk, 'so long as it was active, as any sort of cog in these events.'[47]

By Monday evening, the Tauride was awash with public figures, including leaders of the workers' movement who had just been freed from Kresty Prison. Most socialists believed their task to be the convocation of a Soviet of Workers' Deputies, a truly democratic body that could represent the revolution and begin to manage city life. Petrograd's hard-pressed population understood exactly what was meant. The original Soviet (in which Parvus and Trotsky had once starred) had been formed by the workers themselves at the height of the revolution in 1905. As they had then, the people started to elect new deputies from their own ranks, and it was established that the first of these should assemble in the Tauride at seven o'clock that night.[48] But someone had to find a meeting room. The Tauride's central halls were packed, the noise impossible, but there were still spare offices in the left wing. Rodzianko was reluctant to let a rabble of this kind gather at all, but Kerensky persuaded him to let them have Room 12, remarking that 'somebody must take charge of the workers.'[49]

The famous Petrograd Soviet was born in Prince Potemkin's absurd barn of a palace that very night, and it immediately set to work. There were endless greetings to accept, and much applause, but there were also problems to be solved. From the food crisis to the uncontrolled dispersal of explosives, this was an emergency that called for practical measures, including the formation of some kind of militia to make the city safe. One of the Soviet's first acts was to elect an Executive Committee to take charge of its day-to-day affairs, a group soon known to everyone as the Ex Com. While workers' delegates filed in to join the crowd, this small group, mainly literary types, began to take command. The new chairman, Nikolai Chkheidze, was a Menshevik lawyer from Georgia and a former Duma man. Not noted for decisiveness, he was a respected but unexciting choice – the best available, someone remarked, since all the real heavyweights were still in exile or abroad. Other lawyers on the team included Matvei Skobelev, another Menshevik, while Sukhanov was elected in his capacity as a journalist. The Bolsheviks were represented on the Ex Com by Alexander Shlyapnikov and another worker-activist called P. A. Zalutsky.

The most flamboyant member of the team, its vice-chairman elect, was none other than Alexander Kerensky, the gentleman already so involved with the Duma Committee in the palace's other wing. A native of Simbirsk (where his father had been one of Lenin's schoolmasters and Protopopov had been a distant neighbour), Kerensky was a lawyer with a florid taste in oratory and personal attire (Sukhanov, who had known him for some years, remembered a particular pair of silk slippers and a long kaftan). In February 1917, he was still pale and weakened after an operation to remove a kidney, but he threw himself into the revolution with impressive verve, accepting all the calls to serve like a diva with an unusually lavish haul of bouquets. Such drama was to be his trademark style. 'He looks as if he were in pain,' remarked Robert Bruce Lockhart, 'but the mouth is firm, and the hair, cropped close and worn en brosse, gives a general impression of energy.'[50] Before the war, when he was an illegal revolutionary, Kerensky's nickname was 'Speedy', a reference to his habit of jumping on and off moving trams to evade the police.[51] That Monday night, however, he did not show his nimble heels in the Soviet. The delegates would have had to make a pilgrimage across the hall to find him, for Kerensky was far less interested in the workers' plans than in his prospects on the Duma Committee.

Events were moving very fast indeed. The Soviet had not even assembled when a student marched into the Tauride's circular hall, leading a little group that consisted of two soldiers and a captured, trembling tsarist minister. The imperial administration was dissolving. Its members had taken refuge in cupboards and cellars when the shooting started, but now they began to give themselves up. All afternoon, the revolutionaries made arrests, escorting one terrified old gentleman after another into the chaos of the Tauride hall. By evening, the only place to keep the prisoners was the Duma's meeting chamber, a choice that had the advantage (from the Duma Committee's point of view) of keeping the socialist masses out of it.[52] But neither inconvenience nor distraction hindered the Ex Com. It began by considering the food crisis, the garrison and how essential services might be restored. In a city deprived of reliable information, it also made plans to produce a newspaper, *Izvestiya*, the first issue of which appeared the next morning.

Across the hall, seated in greater comfort but without the Soviet's obvious zeal, Rodzianko and his colleagues also talked well into the night. The arrest of the ministers had not been their initiative (when the first victim had been ushered in, Rodzianko had made an attempt to rescue him),[53] and now they faced uncertainty and even ruin. 'God knows what's happened to the city,' Rodzianko was to sigh, 'all work has come to a halt – and we are supposed to be fighting a war!'[54] There were thousands of troops at the front, and no one could predict their reaction to the news from Petrograd. The question to be settled – fast – was who was meant to be in ultimate command.

The Soviet's first session finally ended late that night, but Shlyapnikov remembered that the Tauride was still 'buzzing like a hive' at four o'clock in the morning of 28 February.[55] Sukhanov was among those still inside. Picking his way around the unforgiving built-in seats and tables, the tired revolutionary found a quiet corner in the Duma chamber and lay down in his greatcoat. Through the glass roof above his head, he could make out the glow of many fires, and every few moments there rang out a distant shot. He fell asleep to the muffled conversations of groups of soldiers, his breath infused with damp wool and the tinned herring from which his neighbours were making a late supper. As soldiers in the Tauride licked the fish-oil from their knives, the tsar, at his headquarters near the front, was signing an order to crush the revolt at any price. In light of Khabalov's obvious failure, he appointed a new man, General Ivanov, to do the job. No one had the least idea what might happen if this officer succeeded.

Like almost everyone in Petrograd, however, Sukhanov remained euphoric. Stiff and exhausted from a night in his clothes, he woke on Tuesday in what he called 'the free city of the new Russia'. He had barely opened his eyes when he noticed a group of soldiers tugging the hated portrait of Nicholas II from its frame.[56] Later on, as he took a walk in the fresh air, his mind was 'shot through by luminous shafts of acute happiness, triumphant pride, and a sort of wonder before the boundless, radiant, and incomprehensible achievements of those days'.[57] The triumph belonged to the people,

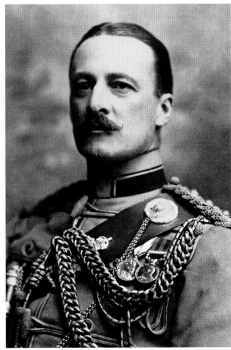

1. (*top left*) Sir Samuel Hoare in 1917.

2. (*top right*) Major-General Sir Alfred William Fortescue Knox.

3. (*bottom left*) Sir George William Buchanan, photographed by Walter Stoneman in 1918. His ordeals in Russia had shocked, aged and exhausted him.

4. (*bottom right*) Ambassador Maurice Paléologue of France.

5. (*top*) Barricades in Petrograd: Liteiny Prospect, 27 February (12 March) 1917.
6. (*bottom*) The Provisional Executive Committee of the State Duma, February 1917.
Mikhail Rodzianko is seated on the right at the desk, with Alexander Guchkov next to
him. Alexander Kerensky appears in the back row second from right and Paul Miliukov
is in the centre.

7. (*above*) Revolutionary crowds in front of the Tauride Palace on 1 (14) March 1917.
8. (*below*) The Tauride Palace as it looks today, with two wings and imposing central hall.

9. (*above*) The Tauride's colonnaded ballroom was built to accommodate 5,000 people, all of them dancing, but it was often packed to bursting in the spring of 1917. Here, soldiers and sailors have gathered to listen to Mikhail Rodzianko.

10. (*below*) Petrograd's solemn funeral for the victims of the revolution on 10 (23) March 1917. The procession is on Nevsky Prospect.

11. (*top left*) Alexander Helphand, better known as Parvus, photographed in 1906.
12. (*top right*) Master of the cunning plot: Arthur Zimmermann, photographed in the last years of peace.
13. (*bottom left*) Fritz Platten, photographed around 1920.
14. (*bottom right*) Karl Radek, photographed in Berlin, December 1919.

15. (*top*) A striding Lenin and his wife, Nadezhda Krupskaya.
16. (*bottom*) Old Zurich: a view of Spiegelgasse from the steps of the building where Lenin was living in February 1917.

Ich bestätige,

1) dass die eingegangenen Bedingungen, die von Platten mit der deutschen Gesandtschaft getroffen wurden, mir bekannt gemacht worden sind;

2) dass ich mich den Anordnungen des Reiseführers Platten unterwerfe;

3) dass mir eine Mitteilung des "Petit Parisien" bekanntgegeben worden ist, wonach die russische provisorische Regierung die durch Deutschland Reisenden als Hochverräter zu behandeln drohe,

4) dass ich die ganze politische Verantwortlichkeit für diese Reise ausschliesslich auf mich nehme;

5) dass mir von Platten die Reise nur bis Stockholm garantiert worden ist.

Bern - Zürich, 9. April 1917.

17. Leaving Zurich: the Russian travellers' final list of conditions, addressed to the General Staff of the German Army, dated 9 April (27 March) 1917. The first to sign, of course, was Lenin himself.

18. (*above*) Lenin in Stockholm, 31 March (13 April) 1917. The leader is in conversation with Ture Nerman; Krupskaya follows in her wide-brimmed hat.

19. (*below*) The Tornionjoki river between Sweden and Finland, photographed by Mia Green in 1915.

but it would be the Sukhanovs and Kerenskys, in the short term, who decided what should come out of it.

The questions were urgent. The people loathed the empress and her gang, but Nicholas was still the tsar. The army at the front had sworn an oath to him, though it was not clear how long the soldiers might honour it. Meanwhile, whatever Ivanov might plan, someone had to make Petrograd safe for its inhabitants. Although the Ex Com was already setting up militias for this purpose, the Duma Committee was determined to take action of its own. On 28 February, Rodzianko issued an order for the troops in the capital to surrender their arms, intending to bring their revolt to an end and get the city on its feet. The move made the disorder worse, for soldiers feared courts martial and the hangman's rope. Tense and hungry, they started planning further armed resistance in the streets. The Soviet backed them, especially as soldiers' deputies now outnumbered delegates from the factories in its plenary gathering. It was not clear which wing of the Tauride had control of the garrison. As a horrified Miliukov put it on 28 February, 'There must be no dual power!'[58]

The Bolshevik Vyborg Committee had its own answer to that. Believing that the bourgeoisie would overturn hard-won new rights, it was still arguing that the people should form a multi-party provisional revolutionary government through the mechanism of their own soviets, or workplace-based councils. Such bodies were already forming all around the city and elsewhere, but the obstacle was the Ex Com, whose leaders refused to take up the reins of state. The Vyborg Committee had a few sympathizers in the Tauride, but in Sukhanov's view 'they merely chattered inaudibly and scribbled a bit . . . they did not even think of engaging in any real struggle for their principles.'[59] It was also clear that the Petrograd Soviet itself did not want power. Its members' hesitation was partly ideological, for most were Marxists who believed that revolutions unfolded in fixed stages. What Petrograd had just begun, they argued, was a process to introduce a sort of parliamentary democracy, a system that they called the bourgeois phase. A workers' government, let alone full socialism, could happen only later, when the people had experience of democratic rule. As Alexander Potresov, a Menshevik, had put it years before, 'at the moment of the bourgeois revolution, the class best prepared, socially and psychologically, to solve national problems is the bourgeoisie.'[60]

Since anyone who thought about it would have dreaded taking power, the theory in this instance was expedient as well as beautiful. The prospect of ministerial office could have no appeal while Ivanov was closing in on Petrograd with his crack troops. The rest of the army – uniformed and armed – might side with anyone. Even the mutineers within it might turn against the revolution they had made, which was why the Soviet encouraged soldiers' deputies to dictate their own terms for restoring order among the capital's garrison troops. As Sukhanov explained, 'It was necessary to treat the garrison with the utmost delicacy, and vital to create at all costs an undeniable authority it would consider its own and therefore obey.'[61] The Soviet's famous Order No. 1, issued in the confusion of 1 March, helped to bring down the rate of random shooting in the streets. Soldiers returned to their barracks, keeping their weapons but observing discipline at work. In the long term, however, Sukhanov and his friends believed that the Soviet had 'to entrust power to the propertied elements, its class enemy', for that was the only way to protect and develop the gains of revolution. For him, 'the gist of the question was whether propertied Russia would consent to take power in such conditions.'[62]

The Duma Committee, however, was as nervous of power as the Soviet. Though almost all its members had long been campaigning for change, they had never dreamed of disorder like this, and disagreed among themselves about the sort of government they hoped to see. Left-wingers like Kerensky imagined a social-democratic outcome, but there were others (including Miliukov) whose ideal was a British-style constitutional monarchy. The only point on which they all concurred was that the current position was illegal as well as dangerous. They had been cornered into shouldering responsibilities, but many ached to set them down. Both sides were trapped, and the only way out of their situation was to look for some kind of deal.

The talks began in earnest on the night of 1 March. As Sukhanov had perceived, the task in hand was really to woo the Duma members into taking power despite themselves. From the Tauride's right wing, Miliukov was the main spokesman for the Duma Committee. It was clear that his principal anxiety was that the Soviet might make it a condition that Russia should cease fighting at once, for peace had always been the workers' most urgent demand. That night, however, much to his relief, that disturbing idea was shelved, at least in the short term. Both parties also agreed that any government would be provisional, for they were all convinced that a permanent solution could be achieved only through free elections and the convocation of a Constituent Assembly, for which they would have to prepare. The Soviet knew that Miliukov was planning to revive the monarchy, but that issue was something that elected constitution-writers could decide. Among the Ex Com's few red lines was a stipulation that none of its members should serve as ministers in the temporary bourgeois government. Instead, they would devote themselves to promoting full workers' rights. The talks dragged on for many hours, and in the end almost everyone, including Chkheidze and Kerensky, was actually lying down.[63]

The two sides might have been debating the conditions for a duel. When an agreement was finally concluded on 2 March, it was largely because the Soviet Ex Com had always wanted an excuse to capitulate. The deal created a Provisional Government with extensive powers, conceived as an assembly of upstanding citizens who could govern till elections could be called and some more permanent regime agreed upon. Its chairman was to be an affable philanthropist from Moscow called Prince Georgy Lvov, known for his fine work as an advocate of education, public health and solid public services. Conveniently enough, the prince was not in Petrograd to consult face to face, but it was established by telegraph that he was ready to accept the role. Paul Miliukov, who was to be the country's foreign minister, was chosen to announce the news to the vast crowd in the ballroom.

Miliukov had prepared a careful speech, but most of it was swallowed up by murmurs from the audience. He told them all that Prince Lvov had been selected as the leader of their government, describing him as a 'representative of Russian society'. When a hostile voice interjected that Lvov represented nothing but 'propertied society', the former history professor bridled. 'Propertied society', Miliukov insisted, 'is the only organized society which can enable other strata of Russian society to organize themselves.'[64] It was the cue for an unfriendly but obvious question: 'Who elected you?' 'I could have written a whole dissertation,' Miliukov's memoir explains, but instead he chose to venture an audacious lie. 'We were chosen', he shouted, 'by the Russian revolution!'[65]

The crowd was not entirely persuaded, and there was more drama to come. Miliukov's group had wanted two members of the Ex Com – Chkheidze and Kerensky – to serve as ministers. Chkheidze had refused straight away, citing the Soviet's judgement that workers' representatives could not be ministers and declaring his intention to devote himself to the Soviet, the revolution's true spearhead. But Kerensky decided to accept the post of justice minister, vowing to serve the people unto his last breath. 'I speak, comrades,' he told a spellbound gathering, 'with all my soul, from the bottom of my heart, and if it is necessary to prove this, if you don't trust me – here and now, before your eyes – I am ready to die.'[66] He was given an ovation, which he took to mean that he could act exactly as he chose. He disappeared into the Duma Committee's chamber, leaving the Ex Com leaders in a state of 'embarrassment, dejection and fury'.[67] As Alfred Knox would later write, Kerensky 'had all the theatrical qualities of a Napoleon, but none of his moral courage'.[68]

A knot of bourgeois monarchists from the Duma Committee had plans, meanwhile, where the tsar was concerned. While all eyes were on the Tauride, the new war minister, Guchkov, accompanied by Shulgin, made a secret approach to Nicholas at his headquarters. The proposal Guchkov was carrying, which had Miliukov's fervent sanction, was that the tsar should abdicate in favour of his younger brother, Mikhail Alexandrovich. In torment, Nicholas agreed, though to protect his only son, a child whose health was always frail, he ruled the boy out of the succession at the same time. On 2 March 1917, the reign of Nicholas II came to an end. If

Mikhail Alexandrovich had not refused the throne (Kerensky called his act 'the highest patriotism'), Russia might have
had to choose between a constitutional monarchy and a
lethal crisis. The revolution had not matured enough by this
stage for anyone to decide exactly what form Russia's government should take, but large numbers of citizens were
clearly finished with all tsars.

The British ambassador applauded Kerensky for attempting to calm the rage of Soviet republicans when the news of
Guchkov's mission eventually leaked out.[69] Conservatives
and monarchists, however, were disgusted. As Paléologue
confided to his diary, not quite understanding what was
going on, 'Fear of the gaolbirds who are in command at the
Finland Station and the Fortress has compelled the representatives of the Duma to give way. The Soviet is now
master.'[70] The more accurate diagnosis was that Miliukov's
nightmare had come to life. The people remained loyal to
their Soviet, while an unelected and reluctant Provisional
Government wielded an untried but theoretically limitless
authority.[71] Russia faced the prospect of long-term dual
power.

The abdication created a republic. The jubilation in Petrograd's streets drowned out the murmured doubts and fears.
But no one knew how the army as a whole was likely to
regard the new regime, nor what might happen in the
empire's many cities and provincial towns. Even the people
who had made the revolution – the factory workers with cal-
loused hands, the women in patched coats and grubby winter
scarves – were not sure who had really won. As Sukhanov
left the Tauride at six o'clock on 2 March, he was seized by
members of the crowd and pressed to make some kind of
speech. 'They wanted news,' he explained, conceding that

the speaker they were really after was Kerensky. 'I was taken by the arms and dragged out into the street. From the steps . . . I saw a crowd the like of which I had never seen before in my whole life. There was no end of faces and heads turned towards me: they completely filled the courtyard, then the street, holding up banners, placards and little flags.' It was snowing and the light had already begun to fade, the people were exhausted and Sukhanov's weary voice was thin, but 'as far as the eye could reach they were all straining towards me in a tense and deathlike silence.'[72]

5. Maps and Plans

Human dignity is something one need not look for
in the world of capitalists.

V. I. Lenin

The pathos was lost on Sir George Buchanan. It did not help that he had missed the drama's crucial opening act. The ambassador had arranged for a short holiday in Finland, and left the country just before the start of the first strikes. He returned to find the whole of Petrograd in chaos. Fires were raging in the law courts and police headquarters, the streets were full of loud young men and rifle-shots, while open cars careened along the embankment under his windows, many packed with drunken youngsters waving flags. When his daughter Meriel's train arrived at the Finland Station, General Knox himself drove over to collect her, for there was no functioning public transport left in the capital. The inconvenience was staggering, the dangers all too clear. Sir George's wife had been alarmed enough to send the members of her sewing-circle home that afternoon while it was light.[1]

On 1 March (14 March by the calendar that London used), Sir George thought it advisable to reassure the public back in England. In one of many telegrams that day, he requested the printing of a notice to the effect that all 2,000 British residents in Petrograd were well. He did not know that London had opted to treat Russian news with a delicacy more usually reserved for unexploded bombs. 'The War Cabinet having decided that events in Petrograd are not to be mentioned in the Press,' reads the neat scribble on the file, 'such an announcement will, if published, require careful "dressing".'[2] The allies saw the uprising as a betrayal. Their problem was not so much that red flags might encourage troublemakers nearer home, for it was high time that the Russians had a sensible democracy.[3] What really worried them was the idea that all those grey-faced workmen in their sheepskin coats, so far away and yet so crucial, suddenly, to Europe's plans, might really mean it when they kept demanding peace.

They could not let the revolution take just any course it chose, but the British were prudent enough to start with a little Anglo-Saxon charm. On 3/16 March, when it was clear that tsarism had collapsed, Buchanan received a copy of the greeting that the leaders of the patriotic British labour movement had prepared, with foreign office help, for 'Messieurs Kerensky and Chkheidze'. 'Organized Labour in Great Britain is watching with deepest sympathy the efforts of the Russian people to deliver themselves from . . . reactionary elements which are impeding their advance to victory,' it began.

> Labour in England and France has long realized that despotism of Germany must be overthrown if way is to be opened for free and peaceful development of European nations. This conviction has inspired them to make unprecedented efforts and sacrifices and we confidently look forward to assistance of Russian labour in achieving the object to which we have devoted ourselves. Earnestly trust you will impress on your followers that any remission of effort means disaster.[4]

The message could not have been clearer: whatever rhetoric they cared to use, the Russians were expected to keep fighting on until the other members of their team agreed to stop. In private, too, the foreign office mandarins had doubts about a people's government of any kind. The Soviet, advised Buchanan, 'is for peace at any price and . . . its advent to power will mean disaster from the military point of view.' His instructions from London, received on 4/17 March, were unequivocal. In deciding whether the British were to recognize the new regime, he should be guided solely by 'the attitude of the new government towards the war. All your influence should be thrown into the scale against any Administration which is not resolved to fight to a finish.'[5] 'The real difficulty here', Frank Lindley, the British embassy counsellor, wrote from Petrograd on 7/20 March, 'is that we have two governments: the real one under Prince Lvov, and a Committee of workmen's and soldiers' delegates without whose orders none of the men will do anything. The British Colony are naturally rather nervous, as all Russians agree that a terrible class hatred exists under the surface and that, if it once broke loose, the consequences would be awful.'[6]

The best that could be said was that the 'real' government looked businesslike, composed entirely of the sort of men who knew what honourable service meant. On 9/22 March, and with a wishful thinking that took little cognizance of facts, the chancellor of the exchequer, Andrew Bonar Law, saluted Russia's new administration on behalf of Parliament. 'This House sends the Duma its fraternal greetings,' he declaimed (though what he should have greeted was the Provisional Government), 'and tenders to the Russian people its heartiest congratulations upon the establishment among them of free institutions.'[7] He must have imagined a chamber full of gentlemen exactly like himself. The academic and Slavonic expert Bernard Pares was certainly a fan. 'These were my friends,' he later wrote. 'Of the twelve new ministers, seven were actually collaborators of my *Russian Review* in Liverpool.'[8] Better still, Miliukov had met George V, and though a Marxist in his youth, he had recently declared (in London) that he 'belonged to His Majesty's Opposition, not to the Opposition to His Majesty'.[9]

To London's evident relief, this Miliukov appeared to be the driving force behind the brand-new government, although officially he was no more than foreign minister. The nominated premier, Prince Georgy Lvov, took a few days to get to Petrograd from his home in Moscow. 'At last we felt ourselves *au complet*,' wrote Miliukov upon Lvov's arrival in the Tauride. Unfortunately, it turned out that Lvov's talents did not run to decisive national leadership. 'The Prince was evasive and cautious,' Miliukov reported, 'he reacted to events in a gentle, defensive manner and talked his way out with gentle phrases.' 'He sat in the driver's box,' Vladimir Nabokov (the father of the famous novelist) conceded, 'but he didn't even try to pick up the reins.'[10] Watching from Britain, Samuel Hoare concluded that Lvov was 'a man better qualified to be Chairman of the London County Council than to be the chief of an unstable government in the midst of a great revolution'.[11]

In Petrograd, Buchanan was dubious about the new regime from the first. 'If only the present Government could get the situation well in hand,' he reported on 5/18 March 1917, 'the best solution would be that it should continue to act as a provisional government for as long as the war lasted.'[12] Privately, however, Sir George considered that the ministers were 'not such as to inspire me with great confidence for the future. Most of them already showed signs of strain and struck me as having undertaken a task beyond their strength.'[13] The French ambassador was more forthright, and judged the revolutionary state with the discernment of a connoisseur. His verdict was that Russia really needed a Danton (if not a Robespierre); instead, it seemed to have been saddled with a committee that would have had trouble managing a private dining club.[14] 'We shall now be faced with economic, social, religious and ethical problems,' Paléologue wrote to the French prime minister, Alexandre Ribot. 'These problems are very formidable from the point of view of the war; for the Slav imagination, far from being constructive like that of the Latin or Anglo-Saxon, is essentially anarchical and dispersive.' His prediction was very dark: 'In the present phase of the revolution Russia cannot make peace or war.'[15]

The one bright spot, as all outsiders soon agreed, was Alexander ('Speedy') Kerensky. 'He is obviously the most original figure in the Provisional Government,' observed Paléologue, 'and seems bound to become its main spring.' Buchanan thought him the 'only man to whom we could look to keep Russia in the war'.[16] The justice minister was everywhere, tripping between appointments with the British ambassador and the Petrograd military governor, the Tauride and his own Masonic lodge.[17] Though he retained his foothold in the Soviet, his sympathies were all with bourgeois government. In mid-March, he reassured Alfred Knox that 'the present position with two governments was impossible' and that 'the sovyet [sic] was losing ground.'[18] The Ulsterman duly recorded that 'There is only one man who can save the country, and that is Kerensky . . . for he still has the confidence of the over-articulate Petrograd mob . . . The Provisional Government could not exist in Petrograd if it were not for Kerensky.'[19] Kerensky himself later looked back upon those first exciting weeks as 'among the happiest of my political career'.[20]

However happy a newly promoted minister might be, however, the Soviet continued to exist. As the ambassadors of Britain, France and Italy gave formal recognition to the Provisional Government on 11/24 March (the US ambassador, the flamboyant David R. Francis, having done so two days earlier), the Soviet's presence loomed beyond the lighted windows like a monster from the Baltic swamp. The new war minister, Alexander Guchkov, might have appeared composed enough in monocle and hand-made suit, but only a few days before he had expressed his nervous doubts to the army's Chief of Staff. 'The Provisional Government does not possess any real power,' he had complained, 'and its directives are carried out only to the extent that it is permitted by the Soviet of Workers' and Soldiers' Deputies, which enjoys all the essential elements of real power, since the troops, the railroads, the post and telegraph are all in its hands. One can say flatly that the Provisional Government exists only so long as it is permitted by the Soviet.'[21]

That idea alone was enough to sour the ministerial champagne. As Guchkov would confide to General Knox, however, even larger problems had begun to intrude. 'I saw Minister of War for a few minutes today,' the attaché informed London just two weeks later.

> He is . . . worried over fall in production in dockyards. Factories in Petrograd only produced 30 to 60 per cent of what they did before revolution . . . Even Council of Workmen and Soldier deputies was powerless to contend with extreme element which consists of Jews and imbeciles. He agreed

that it would come sooner or later to a trial of strength with Extremists but he said Government had not yet physical power on which it could depend and he asked me to keep this very secret. Council have the keys to all Government cyphers and control of wireless stations.[22]

The last thing Guchkov and his friends required was a flood of even worse extremists from abroad. It was the Soviet, armed with all that telegraph and wireless, that appeared determined to summon every last troublemaker back to Petrograd from provincial Russia and beyond. The first internal exiles began arriving that very week, travelling from the villages where they had languished under tsarist rule. With them came a reminder of a smouldering, all-encompassing problem beyond the capital, that of the peasants and their age-long hunger for the land. The land question was the ultimate challenge to any government that believed in property rights, for it could not be addressed without stripping landlords of their estates. Worse, it cast a shadow over Petrograd, for the army was the key to any revolutionary settlement and the army, like the population as a whole, was primarily composed of peasants.

Compared with worries on that scale, the allies and their day-to-day demands may have appeared as pettily troubling to the new government as a swarm of gnats, but they could not be ignored. It turned out that the old regime had bound itself to France and Britain with multiple hidden treaties and wheedling promises. The most important secret deals dated to 1915, when Miliukov's predecessors at the foreign ministry had signed away their country's remaining interests along the Adriatic coast (a volatile member of the

Provisional Government leaped from his chair when he heard this, declaring that 'we can never, never accept those treaties').[23] The equally secret quid pro quo, however, at least in the case of victory, was that Russia was to have Constantinople and the Dardanelles.

With his long-standing interest in the Balkans, that bait meant everything to Miliukov. He may even have been imagining a Russian city on the Golden Horn as he prepared an official declaration on foreign policy, published on 7/20 March 1917. 'The Government', he announced, 'will sacredly observe the alliances which bind us to other powers and will unswervingly carry out the agreement entered into with the Allies.'[24] When that statement was first issued, few knew exactly what those 'sacred' undertakings were. When they were told, sitting around a table in their new office at the Mariinsky Palace, even Miliukov's close colleagues were sceptical. 'I dragged out the "treaties" from the ministry's archives,' the foreign minister remembered, 'and illustrated my report with detailed maps.' To his dismay, Lvov himself described the annexation of the Straits as 'plunder' and demanded that Russia repudiate the 'swindling' provision.[25]

The uproar in the Ex Com was worse still. The Soviet had grown, and by mid-March it numbered about 3,000 deputies, most of them from soldiers' groups. Even the Tauride could not cope (Kerensky thought the palace 'seemed to groan and sway under the pressure of the mighty human waves'),[26] and eventually the entire show would move, first to the Michael Theatre and then to the Naval Academy on Vasilievsky Island. Wherever it convened, however, the Soviet appeared to be engaged in one extended session, stormy and verbose, with intervals for sleep that never seemed to come in time. For anyone who lived through it, the memory of that first month would float, like some chaotic seasick dream, on cheap tobacco fumes and unrequited longing for a good night's rest.

The main fault line in the Soviet no longer ran between the far left and the rest. New tensions and a new agenda had been created by the mass influx of soldiers' deputies, many from units close to the front. Though Petrograd still yearned for peace, these serving soldiers did not want their comrades' sacrifices at the front – the strain and suffering, the deaths – to be sold short. While the Soviet was still in the Tauride, indeed, a woman agitator (whom Sukhanov judged to be a Bolshevik) had been 'practically torn to pieces' for saying 'Down with the war'.[27] The army was a force of over seven million men drawn from the length and breadth of the empire. Its mood remained unfathomable.

The Ex Com (which remained in the Tauride, eventually necessitating the use of a fleet of cars to shuttle back and forth to the Soviet) was alarmed by the threat of a fatal breach within the revolutionary movement. Aside from a brief session on 3/16 March, its members had avoided much discussion of the war; their goals had been more local and immediate in the first days. The workers, as Sukhanov put it (really meaning his own group), 'instinctively felt' that the whole question 'might turn out to be extremely complicated and teeming with submerged rocks'.[28] But by the second week of March, it was becoming clear that someone would have to speak for the Soviet. Miliukov and the right-wing press could not be left with a free hand. As if to concentrate everyone's minds, on 12/25 March the Volhynsky Regiment, which just two weeks before had been among the first to join the revolution, appeared in the Tauride in full formation, with all its officers, urging Soviet deputies to remember their brothers in the trenches and support a war to final victory.[29]

The Ex Com wrestled over forms of words. For its social-ist members, the goals of revolution had always included peace in Europe. At the very least, the majority knew the formula agreed at Zimmerwald, which the Swiss leader Robert Grimm reiterated in mid-March. 'The most important and absolutely right task of the Russian revolution in the present moment', he declared, 'is the struggle for peace without annexations or indemnities on the basis of national self-determination.'[30] No annexations meant no Dardanelles. It meant no Russian adventures in the divided territories of Ukraine, it meant resisting French demands for their lost provinces of Alsace and Lorraine. If it were going to take such an explosive line, the Ex Com had to square it with the soldiers first.

The Soviet's answer, a manifesto that it described proudly as an 'Appeal to the Peoples of the World', was issued on 14/27 March. As well as clarifying the ideas of the revolutionaries themselves, its purpose was to shame the governments of Europe into opening peace talks. 'The Russian democracy has shattered in the dust the age-long despotism of the Tsar,' it announced to all fraternal populations, 'and enters your family of nations as an equal, and as a mighty force in the struggle for our common liberation.'[31] That much was enough to disgust the French ambassador, who noted in his diary that he 'awaited the reply of the Teutonic proletariat'.[32] But the manifesto did not venture any timetable for peace negotiations, nor did it call on Russian soldiers to disarm. The Soviet condemned the war, and called for 'a decisive struggle against the grasping ambitions of the governments of all countries', but Russia's guns still pointed westwards and its bayonets were fixed.

'The time has come to start a decisive struggle,' the Soviet volunteered. 'The time has come for the people to take into their own hands the decision of the question of war or peace.' Unless the allies revised their war aims, however, the most immediate struggle would be inside Russia's government itself. Meanwhile, despite the people's weariness of war, the Soviet could promise only to 'resist the policy of conquest of its ruling classes'. It did not have the power to make peace, and it could not betray the army or its own soldier-deputies. Appeasing them, it offered an assurance that 'the Russian revolution will not retreat before the bayonets of conquerors, and it will not allow itself to be crushed by foreign military force'. The Soviet's chairman, Nikolai Chkheidze, emphasized the same idea in an editorial in *Izvestiya* on 16 March, informing readers that 'in addressing the Germans, we do not let the rifles out of our hands.'[33]

'It's simply shit!' Lenin spluttered after reading a report of recent speeches in the Soviet. 'I repeat: shit.'[34] Whenever he picked up a pen that March, he might as well have drawn the pin from a grenade. Before the news of revolution broke, his wife had likened him to the white wolf in London zoo, the one creature among the tigers and the bears that never grew accustomed to its confinement. But now his frustration was intolerable. It had been a Polish revolutionary called Bronsky who first brought him the news of insurrection in Petrograd, stopping by as Lenin and his wife were leaving for the library. The effect had been like an electric current: the leader paced and coloured, shouted, punched the air. 'Staggering!' he exclaimed to Krupskaya. 'Such a surprise! We must go home. It's so incredibly unexpected.'[35] But the only journey he could make in the short term was down the steep lane to the shore of Zurich's lake, where there were kiosks with a good range of the latest Swiss and foreign newspapers.[36]

The comrade he suddenly missed was his old friend Inessa Armand. 'There is a telegram in the Züricher Post ... of 15 March that in Russia the revolution was victorious after three days of struggle,' he wrote to her that day. 'If the Germans are not lying, then it has happened.'[37] At this point Inessa was living in Baugy-sur-Clarens, another centre for the Russian exiles in Switzerland, so Lenin's intention, in part, was to keep her informed. The real issue, however, was that he needed her help. 'I would very much like you to find out discreetly for me in England if I would be granted passage,' coaxed Lenin on 18 March. He was 'certain' that she would 'rush off to England' right away, but she showed no inclination to comply. When that became clear, he hoped she might at least look into other options, which included attempting to get a Russian or Swiss national to hand over his passport 'without saying it is for me'.[38]

The news from Petrograd had shaken the entire Russian colony in Switzerland. The Russian consul in Davos held a reception to greet the new age of liberty (somewhat half-heartedly, since he was not the revolutionary type), and many of the small foundations that supported refugees began to talk of imminent repatriation.[39] There were 7,000 Russian nationals in Switzerland, and their welcome was wearing thin, but still there was no easy way to get back home.[40] The British saw no particular virtue in helping subversives to travel via the North Sea, while the Provisional Government was horrified, as Guchkov had observed, by anyone who might belong to the camp of extremists, Jews and imbeciles. Caught between these unresponsive authorities, Lenin and his friends were tormented by the newspaper reports of Russians who were starting to return to Petrograd from their exile in Scandinavia, a safe and submarine-free journey through neutral cities with good rail links. The happy fortune of that lot must have made Switzerland seem more than ever like the white wolf's wretched cage.

The newspapers followed the drama of the revolution day by day. Kerensky had remained the star of Russia's dazzling new show. Indeed, the dapper hero had only to appear in a theatre or take the public stage for the crowd to rise in a collective rapture. Lenin called him 'the little braggart', but Kerensky was taking credit for a string of important reforms. Russia became the freest country in the world as the new government granted an amnesty for political prisoners, abolished the death penalty and dissolved what was left of the detested secret police.[41] Inspired by the soldiers' response to the liberal promises of the Soviet's Order No. 1, it set up a committee to examine the case for army reform.[42] Lenin refused to celebrate, deploring the fact that the bourgeoisie had 'managed to get its arse on to all the ministerial seats'.[43] Kerensky he dismissed in yet another snappy line, describing him as 'a balalaika on which they play to deceive the workers and peasants'.[44]

His irritation prompted curt instructions to the Russians who were returning through Tornio. On 6/19 March, Lenin sent a telegram to a group of lucky Bolsheviks as they prepared to board their train. 'No trust in and no support for the provisional government,' it read. 'Kerensky especially suspect; arming the proletariat is the only guarantee . . . no rapprochement with other parties. Telegraph this to Petrograd.'[45] A few days later, he was beginning to consider how workers' soviets might actually take power. 'We need a state,' he wrote on 11/24 March, 'but not the kind the bourgeoisie needs, with organs of government in the shape of a police force, an army and a bureaucracy . . . The proletariat must smash this "ready-made state machine" and substitute a new one [of] . . . the entire armed people.'[46]

The trouble was that he remained the comrade who was watching (as he put it) 'from afar'. 'You can imagine what torture it is for all of us to be stuck here at a time like this,' he complained in one of many tetchy letters to Yakov Fürstenberg in Sweden. 'We have to go by some means, even if it is through Hell.'[47] Imagining himself to be on an English black-list ('England won't *let* us,' he raged to Inessa),[48] he tried repeatedly to organize a false passport so as to sneak back into Russia unobserved. 'Please procure in your name papers for travelling to France and England,' he ordered a Geneva-based comrade called Vyacheslav Karpinsky on 6/19 March. 'I will use them when passing through England and Holland to Russia. I can wear a wig.'[49] His most desperate plan was to acquire the passport of some deaf-mute Swede (though where or how remained unclear). That idea crumpled when his wife reminded him that he would give the game away on any crowded train because he shouted in his sleep. He would have woken an entire carriage, she was certain, with his outbursts, in vernacular but unmistakable Russian, about the perfidies of Kerensky and Miliukov.[50]

That left one option, but it was absurd. The Swiss exiles could travel across Germany to the Baltic coast and on from there to Sweden, Tornio and home. Radek floated the idea, perhaps because he knew that some of the Russians who worked for Parvus in Copenhagen had received transit visas from the authorities in Berlin. Years later, Radek also claimed that it was he who had persuaded a journalist, Dr Deinhard, to sound out the German plenipotentiary in Bern.[51] Whoever it was who first thought of it, however, Lenin's initial response to the idea was dismissive. To accept the assistance of an enemy in time of war would have been to expose himself to charges of treason. That would not do for any self-respecting revolutionary. His business, after all, was not mere perfidy but global civil war.

The strains of war were telling on the German government as well. That bastion of protocol, the foreign ministry, had acquired an unconventional new master, for Jagow had gone and Arthur Zimmermann had been promoted to replace him. Zimmermann was a Prussian and a career diplomat, but he was also a wild card, a devotee of Mosel wine (a quart of which he was accustomed to consuming with his lunch) and a covert-operations addict.[52] Soon after his promotion, he took an initiative involving Mexico, for he was conscious of a growing risk that the United States might join the war on the opposing side. In a telegram of January 1917, he suggested that Germany might reward Mexico for any wartime support in the western Atlantic by helping it to recover the lost states of Nevada, New Mexico and Arizona.[53] The British intercepted this 'Zimmermann telegram' and could not quite believe their luck. There was a pause while they worked out exactly how to leak its contents, for their practice of decoding the classified diplomatic correspondence of friendly powers was not entirely to their credit. They waited until early March to break the scandal, exploiting it to push the US government towards the brink of war. Washington's formal declaration was issued on 4 April.

With the Americans arming at last, the pressure on Berlin could only grow, but Germany's military strategists had been aware for some months that their time was short. The war was straining the home front to breaking point. The Royal Navy's maritime blockade had resulted in the fractious 'turnip winter' of 1916–17, when civilians in some German towns came close to suffering the sort of hunger that would push the Russians to revolt. Protests in German cities stopped well short of revolution, but many witnessed violent unrest.[54] The news from Russia, coming in the darkest month before the spring, could hardly have been more explosive for public morale. Germany's monarchy was bigoted and visibly preposterous. The messages from Petrograd would have been dangerous for any unreformed regime, but in this case there was a well-established left-wing socialist party to amplify them straight away.

One or two trump cards, however, still nestled in the German army's hand. The Royal Navy's very dominance had pushed the High Command to approve a campaign of unrestricted submarine warfare. The plan was to sink any ship that came in sight after 1 February 1917. The resulting mayhem was almost certain to bring the United States into the war (which prospect had prompted Zimmermann to approach the Mexicans in the first place), but there would be an interval while Congress considered its options and then a month or two while the United States prepared an expeditionary force. That window, it was hoped, would be just wide enough for German troops to crush the French. As for the routing of Russia, the most recent campaigning season, with its victories in Romania, had been magnificent. If that went on, the German High Command could hope for a separate peace in eastern Europe that might free its forces for a death-blow in the west.

Before the news of Russia's revolution broke, however, in

November 1916 the chance of any deal with Nicholas II had been destroyed by yet another German Imperial Manifesto on the future state of Poland (large parts of which the Russian empire thought it ruled). Since it would probably have taken a revolution to bring the tsar to the negotiating table after that, the news of Petrograd's uprising was like a gift from providence. According to one colourful account, German intelligence first learned what was happening when a listening-post in the Finnish city of Helsingfors (now Helsinki) intercepted several messages from military units who wanted to know which civil authority they were supposed to be obeying.[55] A flurry of encrypted messages followed on the German side, all proposing a different plan for taking advantage of Russia's plight. But the intervention of Baron Helmut Lucius von Staden, the man in Stockholm, was decisive. As he advised Berlin, Russia's new rulers were divided among themselves. If Germany could resist the temptation to attack, the advocates of peace in Petrograd would almost certainly prevail. Among Lucius' most useful informants in this matter had been a German socialist, Wilhelm Janson, a man with great potential to be useful to Berlin. He knew some of the Russian comrades personally. It looked as if it might be time to send him off to talk to them.[56]

The first thing to get right, meanwhile, was propaganda. It took an effort for Germany's agents to abandon their long-standing strategy of painting Britain as the villain in a Russian peasants' war. For months, they had been dropping information leaflets over lines of puzzled Russian troops in an attempt to convince them that the only real winners in the current conflict were London's bankers. When it was clear that Nicholas had gone, the Germans blamed the British for forcing Russia's 'heaven-sent Tsar' to 'resign'. New leaflets urged the anxious men to go home and 'rescue their people and Mother Russia'. After a day or two, when it emerged that this approach was also doomed, the propagandists' focus shifted to the yearning for peace (which was genuine), a message they presented with a string of genuflections to the soldiers' cherished Orthodox faith. 'Germany is ready to make peace,' read one leaflet that Knox acquired, 'though peace is not necessary for her. She will wait patiently to see if the new and free Russia will start peace negotiations with us in the holy holidays of Christ's resurrection.'[57]

While Berlin waited to see what would come of that, the minister in Copenhagen, Brockdorff-Rantzau (who was also a friend of Zimmermann's), busied himself among the spies. It was not long before he found himself ushering Parvus through his office door. The big man still had good contacts in Petrograd. As a socialist, he had plans for Russia of his own (including armed uprisings and a mass redistribution of the land), but as a supporter of Germany he was at Rantzau's disposal. As usual, he wanted money for himself (he asked for an advance of five million marks to finance revolutionary propaganda). His message, however, was that Rantzau should back the Bolsheviks. In a series of meetings in Copenhagen, he convinced the German envoy that finance for 'extremist elements' would hasten Russia's disintegration and end the war on the eastern front in no more than three months.[58] The only way for Lenin to get back to Russia, however, would be for him to go through Germany.

Foreign Minister Zimmermann's appetite for a plot was still as keen as it had ever been. 'Since it is in our interests that the influence of the radical wing of the Russian revolutionaries should prevail,' he wrote to Lersner, the liaison officer at military headquarters, on 10/23 March, 'it would seem to me advisable to allow transit to the revolutionaries.'[59] The military men agreed, but it was entirely another matter to convince Lenin. Like almost everyone who needed help, Parvus began to talk to Fürstenberg, sounding him out about an approach to the Bolshevik leader. By now, as Parvus must have known, Fürstenberg was also in daily telegraphic contact with Lenin, who regarded him as his right-hand man in Scandinavia. The only person to whom he was writing more frequently at this point was Inessa Armand.[60]

Fürstenberg's credentials as a travel agent were formidable. As soon as the news of the revolution had reached Sweden, he had joined some other Stockholm Russians to form a committee for the repatriation of political exiles.[61] When Lenin despaired of finding legal routes to Tornio, it was to Fürstenberg that he sent his photograph (concealed inside the binding of a book) in the hope that the businessman could get a false passport arranged.[62] It was natural, then, that the first agent Parvus and his colleagues sent to Lenin, Georg Sklarz (who was also a business partner in the Handels og-Eksport Kompagniet), came as a representative of Fürstenberg. The trouble was that Lenin was no fool. When Sklarz made the mistake of offering to pay for Lenin's journey, the leader threw him out, rightly suspecting German subterfuge. As Gisbert von Romberg, the German envoy in Bern, wrote to Berlin on 3 April (21 March), 'Although I have made our willingness to co-operate known to the *emigrés* . . . nobody has yet contacted me, apparently because the *emigrés* are afraid of compromising themselves in Petrograd . . . I do not think that we can do anything but wait.'[63]

Two weeks had passed since the fall of the tsar. The Russian exiles argued with each other and their local hosts, several of whom were offering to negotiate for German help on their behalf. The Menshevik faction under Martov was holding out for a formal invitation from the Provisional Government, the Bolsheviks refused to work with Martov's group, and Lenin had dreamed up a sort of lawyer's list of conditions before he would agree to anything. In France, *Le Petit Parisien* ran a short piece reporting Miliukov's announcement that any Russian exile who accepted German help to return home would be arrested at the border. But there were no alternative routes. At the end of March, Lenin met a representative of the German embassy (in the company of witnesses such as the French journalist Henri Guilbeaux). He also accepted the mediation of the Swiss socialist leader Robert Grimm.[64] Between 29 March and 2 April 1917 (or 16 and 20 March, Russian style), Grimm held four meetings with Romberg, but the Swiss leader was no admirer of Lenin and he was exasperated by the other Russians' endless wrangling. Grimm gave up trying on 2 April. The next day Lenin's Swiss acolyte Fritz Platten, a loyal veteran of Zimmerwald, was deputed to take over the trilateral talks.

An exhausted Romberg submitted Lenin's full list of terms to Berlin on 5 April.[65] The most striking of these was that any carriage in which the Russians crossed Germany should have the status of an extra-territorial entity.[66] Fritz Platten, as a neutral, would act as the contact between the passengers and their German guards, and no one would enter the exiles' carriage without permission. As far as possible, the carriage was to travel without stops, and it was minuted that no passenger could be ordered to leave. There would be no control of passports and no discrimination against potential passengers on the grounds of their political views.

The German negotiators were bending over backwards to assist a group whose leaders they regarded as the vilest criminals, but the gamble was also evidence of German confidence. The beauty of the Bolsheviks was that they looked set to dismember Russia for all time, but their efforts might need months to bear real fruit. A safer bet, albeit one that promised a much lesser prize, would simply have been to start talking with Lvov, Guchkov or Kerensky. As Rantzau had put it on 2 April, 'If we are not in a position to continue the war until the end of this year with any likelihood of success, then we should try to achieve a rapprochement with the moderate parties now in power.'[67] By backing Lenin, Zimmermann was putting some of his chips on the more risky option, confident that it was worth a try. The gamble might result in any one of an ungovernable range of results (including very little at all), but there was still a hope that it would end by disabling the Russian colossus for ever.

News of Lenin's negotiations spread through Zurich's cafés within hours. James Joyce, who heard the story over a drink, thought the proposed safe-passage was proof that the Germans 'must be pretty desperate'.[68] The French novelist Romain Rolland dismissed Lenin and his aspiring fellow passengers as nothing more than instruments of Europe's enemy.[69] The 8th of April was Easter Sunday in Switzerland, and the authorities had hoped to have the Russians packed on to their train before the holiday began. Instead, that weekend was the most frantic of all. To make the whole business more difficult, a chorus of abuse accompanied the travellers' every move. With plenty of time on their hands, the émigrés who were still waiting for a formal invitation from Miliukov joined forces with centre-left Swiss in calling Lenin a traitor.

The greatest strain fell on Romberg and Platten. Both had to deal with endless small details, both disliked the idea of even speaking to the other side, and both knew that exacting masters might destroy their work. For the Germans, it was important that the military should approve the precise route from the Swiss border. Russian-speaking German guards had also (discreetly) to be appointed to travel inside the carriage 'for security'. At one stage, it was also suggested that the amenable Wilhelm Janson, as a representative of the German trades unions, should join the Russians for the German leg of their journey. Romberg put a stop to that, interrupting his Easter Sunday devotions to explain to Berlin that 'The *emigrés* expect to encounter extreme difficulties, even legal persecution, from Russian government because of travel through enemy territory. It is therefore essential to their interests that they be able to guarantee not to have spoken with any German in Germany. Platten will explain this to Janson.'[70]

While the wires from Bern to Berlin ran hot, Lenin commuted almost daily between Zurich and the Swiss capital. Many of his potential followers were too poor to pay for a trans-continental journey, but he refused to let the Germans simply bankroll them. The long-suffering Robert Grimm agreed to organize a committee to raise some cash from local socialists. At the last moment, Platten was detailed to secure permission for the group to bring its own food. There were appeals from unsuitable hangers-on who wanted to join the party and problems with the final list of conditions to put to the Germans.[71] In spare moments, Lenin continued to devour every scrap of Russian news, and he was always writing, drafting, marshalling his thoughts. On the morning before his departure, in one last desperate attempt to secure the allies' blessing, he telephoned the US embassy in Bern. The young man who picked up the phone recognized the caller's name, but it was Easter Sunday and he was on his way to a tennis match. 'Call back on Monday,' he advised, and thought no more of it. When that official, whose name was Allen Dulles, became one of the most influential heads of the CIA, it was a story he would go on telling to recruits for years.

On Easter Monday, 9 April, the travellers finally gathered in the Zähringerhof, the hotel on the square outside Zurich's faux-classical railway station. Thirty-two adults were to travel, including Nadezhda Krupskaya and Inessa Armand. There must have been a lot of surreptitious studying of fellow travellers' packed baskets, stolen glances to size up the bread rolls and the chocolate bars. Zinoviev had turned up with his wife and nine-year-old son, but at the last moment, and no doubt to his exasperation, his flamboyant first wife, Olga Ravich (otherwise known as Sara Savvich), had also joined the party. Two Georgians were on the list: a young writer called David Souliashvili and the veteran activist Mikha Tskhakaya, whose moustache and outlandish sheepskin cap, retained through years of exile in Paris, made him look like a music-hall bandit. It turned out that Tskhakaya had brought no baggage for the journey at all.[72] But no one could object to him. Lenin regarded another passenger, Grigory Usievich, who was travelling with his wife Elena, as a 'spineless . . . dolt', while Elena's father, Feliks Kon, who was also in the party, was 'an old fool' whom Lenin 'could not stand'.[73] It may have been as well that there were also several lawyers in the group, two children and at least one dentist.

The last thing to be done was to eat lunch, a noisy banquet in the Zähringerhof that was accompanied by speeches of farewell. It was Lenin's final chance to win over the many critics who were still attempting to prevent the trip. Instead, he opted for frontal attack. Dismissing Grimm in the same breath as he condemned the right-wing social patriots, he predicted a worldwide revolution that would sweep away 'the filthy froth on the surface of the world labour movement'. 'The objective circumstances of the imperialist war', he declared, 'make it certain that the revolution will not be limited to the first stage of the Russian revolution, that the revolution will not be limited to Russia . . . Transformation of the imperialist war into civil war is becoming a fact.'[74] He was not going home to strike some deal with Russia's bourgeoisie or haggle over tactics in the back of an official car. He was already planning to take the revolution forward to its second stage and set fire to the European left.

At the end of the meeting the Bolshevik leader read aloud a statement (in French and German) on behalf of his whole group. They were returning to their homeland, it announced, despite Miliukov's threat of gaol.[75] Every passenger had signed the formal conditions, which included an acceptance of the risks.[76] Shouts and hisses followed them across the square as the travellers made for their first train. It was merely a local Swiss service bound for Schaffhausen and the border post of Gottmadingen, but the Russians approached it as if walking the plank. Lenin may have preferred Fritz Platten's simile: he suggested that they should imagine themselves to be like gladiators squaring up before their greatest, and final, contest.[77] The pugilistic image was exactly right, for as the engine finally began to move, Lenin noticed a stranger on the train (whose presence was, in fact, legitimate, since this was not a special service, let alone a sealed carriage). A German socialist called Oscar Blum had decided to take his chance. Assuming him to be a spy, the Bolshevik leader seized the intruder by the collar and physically threw him out on to the track.[78]

6. The Sealed Train

The war experience, like the experience of every
crisis in history, every calamity and every turning-
point in a man's life, dulls the minds and breaks the
spirit of some *but enlightens and tempers others.*
V. I. Lenin (emphasis in original)

The first two hours of the ride were almost jolly after that, at
least by Bolshevik standards. From Zurich, the local train
rattled along a valley studded with the chilly stumps of vines.
Most of the passengers relaxed; dun-coloured farms and distant slopes had been home territory for years. As the train
slowed, just outside Neuhausen am Rheinfall, there was a
momentary gasp as everyone looked to the right; the tracks
here curved above the largest waterfall in Europe. But those
short minutes of romance were forgotten as the station at
Neuhausen came into view, for it was one of the last before
the border. A posse of Swiss customs men was waiting for
the Russian group a few miles up at Schaffhausen. The Germans might have promised a free passage to this foreign
exile band, but now the Swiss were making clear that they
had never signed the deal.

Lenin's group was shepherded off the train. As they waited
(on Platform 3), officials of the Swiss police rummaged
through the baskets of blankets, books and provisions that
they had brought for their journey. It turned out that there

was a wartime rule about exporting food from Switzerland. The cheese and sausage were too much, the hard-boiled eggs would have to go. It was a shock to watch as an entire week's supply of sustenance was snatched away, and the process itself (which left a few bread rolls, precisely counted, and a docketed receipt) was enough to set anyone's nerves on edge. At Thayngen, not far up the line, a fresh squad of uniformed men demanded to go through everything again. When the Swiss train came to its final stop at Gottmadingen, with Germany just yards away, the passengers were close to panic. To their despair, as they scanned the platform outside, they spotted two unsmiling figures in grey uniform, the hard-faced types that people send when they are planning a surprise arrest.

Those German officers were hand-picked men. Lieutenant von Bühring was the younger of the two. The travellers were not to be informed, but he had been selected for the job because he understood Russian. Along with his superior, Captain von der Planitz, he had been briefed for the mission by the director of German military operations, General Erich Ludendorff, in person.[1] After the sterile bureaucrats of Switzerland, Bühring and Planitz made a terrifying pair, all gleaming boots and razor-sharp salutes, and now, like cartoon baddies in a wartime film, they ordered the Russians to form two lines inside the third-class waiting room, the men on one side and the women (and two children) on the other. Instinctively, the men surrounded Lenin like so many ants around their hypertrophic queen.[2] Several minutes passed, and although no one dared to speak, most wondered privately how they had fallen for this German trap.

The pause may have given the Germans time to count their guests, to watch them or merely to organize their bags.

It may have been a calculated move to show the Russians who was boss. When the officers were satisfied, they ushered their small party from the station building without volunteering an explanation. Outside, the engine awaited, already spewing out white steam. Berlin had honoured its agreement to the letter. This was a journey that would cost so much, in resources and precious time on railway tracks, that the Germans might as well have thrown in feather beds and free champagne, but the exiles had asked for cheap seats and those were now exactly what they got. The single wooden carriage, painted green, consisted of three second-class compartments and five third-class ones, two toilets and a baggage room for the émigrés' baskets. This was to be the famous sealed train, though what the security amounted to was merely that three of the four doors on the platform side were locked after the passengers had all been counted on board.[3]

There was an awkward moment as the Russians debated who might sit where. After a token protest, Lenin and his wife agreed to take the first of the three second-class compartments at the front. The other two were offered to families with women and children, starting with Georgy Safarov and his wife Valentina, Inessa Armand and Olga Ravich. These settled down with Radek in the compartment behind Lenin's, while the Zinovievs joined two other couples in the next one. The rest took their places in third class, resigned to stiff limbs and a drowsy fug. The German guards sat in the back. To preserve the illusion that the Russians would have no contact with the enemy, a chalk line had been drawn on the carriage floor between their territory and the rest. The only person who could cross it was the Swiss Fritz Platten, who had become the entire company's official middleman.

As the train slowly headed north, Lenin stood at his dark

window, a modest figure in a dusty suit, thumbs locked into his waistcoat pockets. Beyond his own reflection in the glass, he could see that the alder woods were turning green. Despite the lengthening shadows, it was still possible to make out yellow celandines and white anemones, the first wild flowers of a spring to come. The valley broadened, opening to fields. Switzerland vanished into the trail of steam, the rhythmic rattle of the train encouraging a feeling of momentum, purposeful and progressive. The mood was soothing, hypnotic, but before Lenin really yielded to it, the brakes engaged and his momentary trance evaporated. Though the last light had gone, the train seemed to have stopped under a monstrous crag, the Hohentwiel, an extinct volcano that rose 2,000 feet, like an outsized pyramid, against the paler darkness of the night. Topped by the ruins of a tenth-century border fortress, it was the only attraction of the town of Singen, which was where the Russians were about to spend the night. Looming above them near the track, a factory stood witness to the epic powers of the capitalist mode of production. As vast and brutal as any fortress, the point of this particular colossus was to turn out never-ending streams of Maggi's celebrated powdered soup.

The Russians' carriage was parked in a siding and the German crew went home to bed. The factory had closed up for the night, the meadows and the woods beyond were silent and the small town slept. As if to compensate, however, some of the travellers were making a great deal of noise. The background clatter of the moving train had masked the fact, but the party in the compartment next to Lenin's was a raucous one. The occupants had been singing verses of the Marseillaise since Switzerland. Now the very walls were rocking as wave upon wave of laughter burst upon the night, interspersed with Radek's baritone and the shrill voice of Olga Ravich. The merriment was fuelled by German beer, which Planitz and Bühring had bought at a shop in town and passed across the chalk line (with a pile of sandwiches) by way of dinner for their guests.[4]

Lenin was not the type to tolerate disturbances of any kind. He muttered, then tried knocking against the compartment wall. Escape was impossible; he could not even disembark and stretch his legs. It was in Singen that first night that he began to formulate his famous in-train rules. The first of these made sleeping at specific hours into a matter of communist discipline; no longer optional, it was redesignated as the comrades' Bolshevik duty. In furtherance of that great task, Lenin also tried to exile Ravich to a compartment towards the back. This rough injustice was too much, not least because it had been Radek who was making most of the noise. Ravich was rescued by her fellow passengers, and Lenin could do nothing but walk to his own compartment and close the door. As the last of the sandwiches was finished, everyone else was reduced to whispering, fidgeting and stifling their giggles.

They also reached for cigarettes. From the first, Lenin had banned smoking in the compartments and corridors. Since no one could step out for a quick puff, that left the single toilet in the Russian zone (the other, at the back of the carriage, was in German territory). An impossible queue formed very fast, as the passengers who needed to use the toilet for its intended purpose were forced to wait for a procession of smokers. The Bolshevik leader's solution (which Radek dubbed his 'organizational party work') was to issue tickets, giving the smokers 'second-class' passes to the toilet which could be trumped by other users' 'first-class' ones. The move reduced the noisy queue outside the leader's door, but Radek and his comrades went on arguing for hours about the relative importance, in philosophical terms, of the two different types of physical imperative.[5] No one got much sleep. Dawn found the Russians sore and strained – red-eyed, aching and sour of breath. When the sound of the engine started up at 5 a.m., drowning the song of blackbirds in a shriek of steam, the rattle and the movement must have come as a relief.

Their route that second morning, Tuesday 10 April (28 March by the Russian calendar), ran up the Neckar valley between the Black Forest and the Swabian Alps. The travellers were dozing as their carriage passed the gothic town of Rottweil and the ancient castle at Horb. These quiet hills were soothing, punctuated only by villages that looked like children's wooden toys, each with its church and neat, shingled steeple. It struck the travellers that there were few people about; the fields were neglected and there were almost no men of working age to tend them. As they consumed the last stale rolls, brushing the crumbs off their plank seats, they also saw how thin and weary everybody seemed. The villagers stared back if the train slowed, and it was only when the Russians learned that almost no German had seen a white bread roll since 1914 that they understood the hungry and intently hostile looks.[6] The German press had prudently reported who the passengers were (here at last was an opportunity for Berlin to appear benevolent), but it was their status as well-nourished human beings, not as socialists or Russians, that drew these peasants' unkind stares.

There was little pleasure to be gained from contemplating German landscapes and grey waterfalls. The adult members of the party knew the country well enough from the conferences of their pre-war days. They knew the railway, too, and recognized the stations: Tuttlingen, Herrenberg, Stuttgart yet to come. Even Lenin stopped hovering at his window, while everyone else dozed or chatted, waiting in the queue to smoke. They tried to suppress the disturbing sense of loss that ravaged Germany evoked in them, for they had known it as a grand and prosperous place, an inspiration for the future of the world.

Whenever the train slowed or halted, the thin, tired faces swam into the Russians' view – pale, haggard and unsmiling after years of war. Even the cities seemed devoid of men, but at some stations angry women crowded round the carriage windows, shaking their fists or blocking the light with pages from the German press that showed cartoons of the dishonoured tsar. Someone told Elena Usievich that the police were trying to keep such people well back from the train, but the sight of those malnourished wraiths went on to haunt her for decades.[7] The more ebullient Russians preferred to interpret the suffering they could see as proof that Germany was on the brink of a revolution of its own. Such good news called for more rounds of the Marseillaise. As the strains of the revolutionary anthem drifted over Baden-Württemberg, the guards called Platten in to point out that the locals might not relish loud French songs. Chastened, the singers settled down again to doze.

There was a bit of entertainment in the middle of the day. It started when the worthy Platten was summoned down the swaying car into the German zone. Captain von der Planitz wanted to know if Lenin might be willing to meet a new guest: Wilhelm Janson was now on the train. The plan to insert him at Gottmadingen 'as a representative of the German trade unions' had been abandoned, but he had been smuggled on board at Karlsruhe in the hope that Lenin's hand might still be forced.

The first thing to do was to hide Radek. As an Austrian citizen, he could hardly claim to be a Russian exile on his way to Petrograd. Unkind outsiders might point out that he was liable for army service at the front, and there were members of the German trade union movement who wanted him questioned on pre-war charges of theft (those books, that overcoat and someone's hat), as well as the embezzlement of party funds. To get him out of Janson's sight, he was bundled into the goods compartment with a large supply of newspapers to keep him quiet. Then Lenin sent his official response to Janson's comradely request. 'Tell him', he instructed Platten, 'that if he enters [our part of] the carriage we will beat him up.'[8]

The single carriage was devoid of comfort, but at least Lenin and his fellow travellers had just about sufficient room. In Russia, where scores of other revolutionaries had been heading westwards to the capital from their exile in Siberia, the luxury of German third-class seats was unimaginable. As soon as the Soviet had granted soldiers permission to use civilian transport, rail journeys had been transformed into brute contests for space. The carriages came close to bursting as the men in greatcoats crammed aboard: troops on their way back to the front, soldiers in training or on leave, and even small packs of deserters, leering hungrily at well-dressed girls.[9] On shorter trips, passengers clung in desperation to the outside doors; protesting carriage-springs began to break under the weight. A British envoy with a coupé reservation for Baku arrived at the station in Petrograd to find that his seats had been taken by a party of soldiers and sailors. 'The station master . . . said it would cause bloodshed to try to expel them,' General Knox reported to London. 'He had to abandon all hope of travelling that night.' In some cities, tram systems had become unusable as every car filled up with soldiers travelling for free.[10]

Ignoring every hardship on the way, the new arrivals continued to flood into Petrograd. No inconvenience of any kind seemed to deter them. Among the first to get back home were two leading Bolsheviks, Lev Kamenev (Lenin's long-serving aide) and Josef Stalin, both of whom arrived in the capital on 12/25 March. The first real star to return to Petrograd, however, arrived a little later, on 18/31 March. He was to play a leading role in Russia's revolutionary politics. Like Lenin's, his return was awaited with something close to reverence, and just like Lenin he had done a lot of thinking as his train made its way home.

Irakli Tsereteli was a Georgian with the bearing of a prince and the tastes of a poet. At thirty-six, his thick moustache still mainly black, he looked as if he had stepped out of a portrait by Pirosmani, for Georgia's famous primitivist would have loved his ashen face and soulful, doe-like, dark-rimmed eyes. Compared with Stalin's pock-marked, wolfish face, Tsereteli's had the austere and fine-tuned appearance of a medieval saint. He also wore a decent suit, which marked him out as a figure to be reckoned with.

The background of this Georgian had been a privileged one, but he had devoted his energies to revolution since his earliest youth. He had been elected to the Duma in 1907, but ended up condemned to prison and a long exile, as a result of which he had acquired a moral authority within the Russian left that few could equal. Unlike Lenin, he had remained in the Russian empire for his entire life. In 1917, the revolution found him in exile in a village not far from Irkutsk. That accident of geography, which placed him twice as far to the east of Petrograd as Lenin was to the south-west, shaped his response to the revolutionary crisis from the outset.

The news of revolution had reached Irkutsk on one of the last tsarist mail trains.[11] A headline in a newspaper that someone had been careless enough to leave on a desk in the governor's office on 2/15 March was enough to start an uproar in the town. The garrison soon joined the revolution and the old regime collapsed. As local people took control (there was no other option), a committee that included Tsereteli arrested the governor, opened the prisons and declared Irkutsk to be free. For a few days the atmosphere was euphoric, not least because the opposition went to ground. But even in remote Irkutsk, 3,000 miles from any front, the revolutionaries had to face the fact that there was still a war to fight. A former Duma member and a pragma-tist, Tsereteli was convinced that Russia could not simply leave the field. Like the members of Chkheidze's Soviet Ex Com, he also feared the Prussian invader as much as he craved a swift peace. 'The revolution would have to find the strength within itself to end it,' he wrote on pondering the war, 'so as not to surrender our freedom . . . If not, it would itself become the victim of an external enemy and internal counter-revolution.'[12]

The chance to test those theories came at once. Irkutsk was an important staging-post for freight. Bullets and rifles, flour, steel, rubber and explosive fuses were all sent through it on the Trans-Siberian route from the Pacific port of Vladi-vostok to the distant Russian front. Tsereteli was no hawk; he had opposed war credits since 1914. But one morning in early March, a message arrived from the railwaymen in town requesting to know what they should do with a consignment of war supplies. To let it proceed meant collaborating with the war, but Tsereteli could not condemn Russian soldiers to die – the sons, perhaps, of women right there in Irkutsk – for any principle relating to a European peace.[13] The Georgian remembered the moment as a psychological turning-point.[14] It was also exhausting, a first exposure to the agonies of rec-onciling Marxist theory with practical power. After ten days of stress like that, Tsereteli's health collapsed. When he boarded his train to Petrograd, he viewed the many hours of travel as an opportunity to rest.

His journey was quicker than Lenin's, but it was neither smooth nor peaceful. While Lenin had no contact with civil-ians in Germany, the homebound exiles on Tsereteli's train were constantly hauled from their seats and asked to address the crowds of villagers that gathered whenever they stopped. Since he had begun coughing blood, Tsereteli himself could only watch, but the audiences his comrades found were bewildered, eager, brimming with half-formed ideas. 'I had the impression that the people were looking for leaders,' Tsereteli remembered. The prestige of the Petrograd Soviet appeared to be enormous everywhere, far outranking that of the Provisional Government, but no one seemed to under-stand exactly how the two were planning to share power. Tsereteli thought he knew. He also thought the people should be told, and told without concession to their political inexpe-rience. As his extensive notes explained, this was a bourgeois revolution, the first stage in a longer process, and workers owed allegiance to the new Provisional Government. The Petrograd Soviet, like all the smaller soviets assembling in provincial towns, 'was not an organ designed to compete with the government for power, but a centre for the unification and political education of the working classes, established to guarantee these classes' influence on the development of the revolution'.[15]

That settled, he sat back to read the newspapers. The shadow of the war grew sharper as his train approached the capital. As far as he could tell from what he read, the Provisional Government's position was hardening. Its bourgeois leaders disagreed about the country's obligation to its allies, but they all seemed to be convinced that a people freed by revolution would have fresh energy to fight and win. Even *Izvestiya* was taking a more patriotic line. A recent number carried the Soviet's Manifesto of 14/27 March, parts of which now made him glow with pride. 'We will defend our freedom steadfastly against all reactionary encroachments from within or without,' he read. 'The Russian revolution will not yield before the bayonets of the aggressors and will not permit itself to bow to external military force.'[16] The next day's issue described a demonstration by the reserve battalion of the Semenovskys, who had been the latest to turn out in ceremonial uniform (and with accompanying military band) to make their case at the Tauride. 'War to a victorious finish', their red banners proclaimed, 'Long Live Free Russia' and 'For the defence of freedom and victory over Wilhelm'.[17] The reportage gave Tsereteli no idea about the wider public mood, but by the time his train began to slow for its last halt, he had been fully reassured about the soldiers' view of any shameful, hasty peace.

Lenin also used his journey to refine some important ideas. He worked non-stop as the train moved, scribbling in a tattered notebook or summoning trusted colleagues to the front compartment for discussions.[18] His strategy demanded that Europe should take a lead, for the Russia to which he was returning was still in his mind backward, lacking, burdened by its peasant masses.[19] As he considered his revolution's future, however, there was little opportunity for assessing the German comrades' readiness to rise. His sole contact with the locals took place by accident. The Russians had stopped at Frankfurt in the early evening of 28 March/10 April. Their carriage might have been a magnet for the rush-hour crowds, but it was pulled into a quiet siding and the German guards (and Platten) once again made off for the night, heading for friends and beer and the freedom to stretch their legs. The single carriage was discovered when there was no one to secure it. A group of German soldiers pushed in through the unsealed trackside doors. 'Every one of them had a beer in each hand,' Radek remembered, 'and they fell on us with an unprecedented eagerness, demanding to know if and when there would be peace.'

The authorities in Germany could not allow a repetition of that outrageous exchange. The Russians had fallen behind schedule at Frankfurt. The next morning, at Halle, the private train of the crown prince himself was held up to let Lenin's pass.[20] By the time it reached Berlin on 29 March/11 April, the sealed train was still running more than a little late, and there was neither jollity nor beer as it was pushed into a siding for another night (the German staff brought in some plates of rissoles). Even Platten was informed that he could not leave the carriage without an escort. Radek reported that the only people he could see on the platform outside were spies.[21]

The Russians were stuck in Berlin for twenty hours, and no one knows exactly what they did to pass the time. There is no evidence in any source, however, to support the later allegation that Lenin had a meeting with staff from the German foreign ministry.[22] The long delay occurred because the travellers had missed the Wednesday ferry to Sweden. By the time their train reached Berlin, they had the choice of staying there or taking the lonely route to the north coast. The port of Sassnitz, from which a ferry steamed to Sweden every afternoon, was not a very secure option, for it was on the tip of Rügen island, a strategically vital but sparsely settled outcrop, densely wooded and with many quiet landing slips and hidden coves. At one point, German diplomatic staff booked a place there, 'in a locked room', to hold the Russians for the night, but Berlin was a safer bet.[23] The government could keep its guests under control more easily. While the Russians cleared up those plates of greyish food, the locked room in Sassnitz was cancelled and a brace of foreign ministry clerks rushed out to buy three dozen tickets for the next day's boat.

It took five hours of slow travel to get to Sassnitz on 12 April. If Lenin had been watching at his window (instead of writing, eyes set firmly on the page), he would have had a view of flat pasture, still khaki after months of snow, and northern forest where birch trees outnumbered the oaks and maples of the German south. The light was paler now, a cooler grey, and boggy channels in the fields reflected a rain-laden sky. There were hooded crows, the Russian kind, and the first flocks of migrating cranes, shaggy, grey and ravenous, had begun to pick their way about the wet meadows. The farms and villages, however, were as empty as the ones they had passed in the south, and their horses had been conscripted along with the men.

It was a melancholy scene, but any brooding ended as the train approached Stralsund, one of the Baltic's fine old

Hanseatic ports. The screams of seagulls were a sign that they had finally reached the coast, though Stralsund was not to be their last stop on German soil. There was no fixed bridge across the Strelasund to Rügen island, so the carriage had to be loaded on to a ferry, off-loaded on the other side and then sent slowly up the rural track to Sassnitz and the Baltic terminal. A day later than he had planned, Lenin led his troupe of Russians on to the steamer *Queen Victoria* for the four-hour voyage to Sweden. Their gamble with the enemy had paid off. Rügen's wooded headlands, spreading into the Baltic like amphibian fingers, were the last that most would ever see of Germany.

From the allied governments' point of view, the timing could hardly have been worse. The week of Lenin's flight from Zurich had been taken up by the United States' declaration of war on Germany. In Paris and London, the final preparations were also in motion for an offensive on the Aisne. Its overall commander, the French General Nivelle, had convinced his British allies that this was the campaign to end the war. The first British part of it, by the Third Army, began on 9 April as Lenin gathered his comrades for their lunch in the Zähringerhof. By the time he was heading north to Stuttgart, a French attack on German observation posts at Saint Quentin was under way. In Flanders and the Rhine basin the spies were certainly observing trains, but what interested them was the movement of troops and matériel, not Russian émigrés. It was to the credit of the British Intelligence Service that the departure of Lenin's group, reported by Agent SW5 in Bern, was logged at all. In the agent's opinion, however, the revolutionaries in question were 'in the minority among the Russians in Switzerland' and held beliefs 'of a fanatical and narrow-minded nature. My own view', SW5 considered, 'is that these people would be absolutely harmless if, which unfortunately is not the case, other Russians had been allowed to return.'[24]

A few British agents were less equivocal, believing that Lenin was dangerous no matter what the circumstances. In view of other officers' purported willingness to kill Rasputin, it is surprising that some member of this latter camp did not reach for his service Webley and follow the advice that Somerset Maugham's fictitious spy-chief R (for which read C) gave to an operative in a similar case: 'Shoot him and shoot him damn' quick.'[25] Overall, however, the striking feature of British diplomatic and intelligence correspondence at this point was its refusal to accept the finality (let alone the legitimacy) of the February Revolution as a whole.

The results of denial like this could sometimes verge on farce. At the end of March, when Leon Trotsky attempted to return to Russia from New York by sea, he was detained by a British officer in the port of Halifax, Nova Scotia. 'For the colonel,' Trotsky recalled, 'the Russian revolution simply did not exist.' Trotsky and five of his associates were taken to a camp at Amherst that was used for German prisoners of war and there 'subjected to an examination the like of which I had never before experienced, even in the Peter-Paul Fortress'. They were strip-searched in front of others, interrogated, and then taken off and locked up with no promise of release.[26] Their gaolers were responding to instructions from a British agent in New York, who had warned London (wrongly) that Leon Trotsky, 'a pretended Russian socialist', was 'in reality a German'.[27]

Lenin's journey provoked similar levels of confusion. In Petrograd, Buchanan discussed the sealed train with Paul

Miliukov, but the new foreign minister believed Lenin to have damned himself completely in Russian eyes when he accepted German help. Buchanan was not satisfied, but there was nothing more that he could do without breaking his private list of diplomatic rules. Sir Esmé Howard, London's man in Stockholm, was more realistic, not least because his office saw so many Russian émigrés and heard a wider range of tales. Howard would have been delighted if he could have found a way of stopping Lenin, ideally before the wretched man set foot on Swedish soil. The most ingenious proposal came from Keskül, who had his eye on British sponsorship for his beloved free Estonia. In a private conversation, he suggested that Lenin might be detained as a quarantine precaution. The Bolshevik group, after all, would have arrived from Germany, a country where, according to the Swedish press, 32,000 cases of smallpox had recently been reported.[28] It was an attractive idea, but no one could be sure that such a clumsy intervention might not make the problem worse.

While Russia's allies weighed the options (and checked the pistols in their desks), imperial Germany was working equally hard on Lenin's behalf. It turned out that no one in the émigré group had thought to ask the Swedes for transit papers. The Germans had to take over again. On 10 April, with Lenin's train heading north-eastwards across Hesse, the foreign ministry exchanged anxious cables with Stockholm. It was only that evening, as lamps were being extinguished and foreheads wiped, that the Swedish government's approval for the Russians' onward journey finally reached Berlin. It had been a delicate afternoon, and for a few hours it had seemed as if the plan for getting Lenin into Russia might need some last-minute revisions. 'In the event of the Russians being refused entry into Sweden,' a memorandum of

12 April conceded, 'the High Command of the Army would be prepared to get them into Russia through the German lines.'[29]

Seasickness was an unexpected blight. According to Radek and Platten, only a handful of the travellers avoided it, including Lenin, Zinoviev, and Radek himself. As the ferry pulled away from Sassnitz, the braver men resolved to stay on deck. They even sang their favourite songs to keep the icy chill at bay (including Lenin's beloved version of 'They didn't marry us in church'). Radek helped to pass the time by arguing, a talent that never deserted him. But any claim that the Bolshevik leader and his friends remained on deck for the whole crossing is a fantasy.[30] The Baltic was rough – though the worst storms had ended a week before – and the cold was relentless. However cramped and unpleasant the saloon might be, and no doubt blue with Russian smoke, it was the only place where anyone could sit out of the wind.

Lenin resigned himself to a few hours of confinement; this was almost the last lap, after all. It was a shock, then, when the ship's tannoy began to squawk his real surname. The Russians had filled in the usual passenger forms when they embarked at Sassnitz. On Lenin's instructions, most had given false names, continuing the anonymity that they had established in Zurich. Now someone was demanding to know if an Ulyanov was on board, and every nerve in Lenin's body tightened like the sinews of an animal at bay. Perhaps the Swedes intended to arrest him here, perhaps the British had a man on board? For a moment, he considered evading the fate that was catching up with him, but with a heavy heart he made his way towards the bridge. He was expecting nemesis or death; what he found was a message from Yakov

Fürstenberg. The Bolshevik leader's friend and fixer had always intended to meet the boat, but he had waited in vain for Lenin's party at Trelleborg the previous evening. Resourceful as ever, he was checking in advance this time, sending a radio message to the ferry itself before he wasted yet another night.[31]

Lenin almost laughed out loud with relief, and he was in a splendid mood by the time Trelleborg came into view. Fürstenberg was somewhere there, and he had organized a small reception where the ship would dock (smaller, sadly, than the one he had made ready for the night before). The seafarers were sure they could make out a few red flags. The original plan had been to include the left-wing socialist politician Fredrik Ström in the welcoming party, but he was busy with his duties in the capital. Instead, a younger comrade, Otto Grimlund, joined Fürstenberg and the mayor of Trelleborg on the twilit quay. It was an icy vigil, and Grimlund remembered how the Swedes' spirits lifted as they made out 'the strapping figure of Platten' on the *Queen Victoria*'s deck.[32] A whey-faced but excited entourage soon surfaced at his side. As the Russians, dizzy and aching from seasickness, searched for their bags, the Swedish mayor made a short speech. He had just fifteen minutes for the entire show. After that, the passengers were herded into yet another train, flags fluttering against the station lights, and then the whole party was off.

Their destination was Malmö, and in the first instance its marvellous Savoy Hotel. This happened to be the nearest place to the railway station, but it was also the best hotel in town. With a commendable instinct for theatre, Fürstenberg had ordered a buffet dinner for the Russian travellers there, a gastronomic entr'acte under art deco chandeliers. The staff – already legendary for their service – stood ready in the dining room around a generous Swedish smorgasbord. After three days and nights in third-class seats, and still weak from their sea-crossing, the Russians were confronted by a feast of salmon and rye bread, ham, smoked elk with berries, dill pickles, pike perch, slivered cheese, sour cream and mounds of gleaming black and coral roe. It took them less than fifteen minutes to devour the lot. The only person who disdained the food was Lenin. He had been quizzing Fürstenberg for news since Trelleborg and had no time to stop talking and merely eat.

The interrogation continued for hours on the night train between Malmö and Stockholm. Grimlund, who shared a coupé with Lenin and Fürstenberg, witnessed it all. The Bolshevik leader, he observed, was interested in everything. In Sweden, there had been exciting news, for the premier, Hjalmar Hammarskjöld, had just been ousted, partly in punishment for his strict line on the trade blockade. His successor was an even more conservative figure; but beyond the upper house of government, and despite the privations of war, Russia's revolutionary triumph had kindled a new atmosphere of hope. As Fürstenberg and Lenin soon agreed, the likely beneficiary was Hjalmar Branting, a socialist, a patriot and one of the shrewdest political figures in Sweden.[33] The problem was that Branting might not help their cause if things came to a real fight. As a parliamentarian, he would always be open to the suspicion (as a German agent would suggest) that he was 'not really a Socialist at all but a bourgeois in disguise, and he has a lot of money, likes to drink champagne, and leads a dissipated life'.[34]

Lenin was avid for the whole story. He was impressed and fascinated by Branting, who had once helped him escape from the tsarist police. But it was vital for him to get a picture of the Swedish left as a whole. The internationalists, with their anti-patriotic stance, had been under attack, he knew, and his friend Zeth Höglund was in prison. Like other Zimmerwald leftists, Fredrik Ström was becoming isolated from Branting's wing of the parliamentary social-democrats. Lenin wanted to know what his allies were planning to do now, and he quizzed Fürstenberg about the trade unions and the resources they might have. Were there youth movements, he pressed, and who led those? What had changed in the past two months? Why were these people, his good friends, unable to see that the revolution must be armed?

After about an hour of this, Grimlund, who was a journalist by trade, could not help reaching for his pen and pad. The Bolshevik leader was in the middle of outlining his plans for a Foreign Bureau of the party, to be based in Stockholm, but as soon as he caught sight of Grimlund's pen he saw a new disciple for his cause. As the train headed north through the Swedish night, Grimlund enjoyed a master-class in politics. 'Lenin did not need a large audience,' he remembered. 'He would talk to anyone about his ideas.'

Showing no sign of tiredness, the leader detailed the theses he had been rehearsing since Zurich. His programme was already worlds away from anything that Tsereteli had imagined as he crossed Russia's countryside a week before. For Lenin, the Soviet was not the Provisional Government's sub-department for workers' education but the future master of the revolution. There could be no collaboration with the bourgeoisie (let alone that worm Kerensky). Power should pass to the workers' soviets. Lenin had no time for the policy that Tsereteli had started to call 'revolutionary defencism'. Far from facing the Germans with fixed bayonets, the people of the entire world should turn their weapons against the oppressor class. The war was the responsibility of imperialists and they should be the ones who paid for it. Meanwhile, the only valid course in the short term was to demand immediate peace. Peace, bread, and land to the peasants.[35] The message sounded like music to Grimlund, an affirmation of the best hopes Russia's February had raised. If there had been a German spy on board, he would have been delighted, too, but there was still a long journey ahead.

7. Leaderless

A statesman – Bismarck if I am not mistaken – once
said that to accept a thing in principle means, in the
language of diplomacy, to reject it in effect.

V. I. Lenin

There was a lot of quick, decisive action in the spring of 1917.
From Berlin and Vienna to Paris, London and Washington,
assistant secretaries laboured through a haze of perspiration.
In Petrograd, after all, 300 years of Romanov autocracy had
just been swept away in a single dizzying week. But some
things were too solemn to be hurried, and one important
ceremony stood out. On 23 March/5 April 1917, the citizens
of Petrograd gathered together to bury their dead. However
they had met their end – shot by police, caught in crossfire or
killed in one of countless accidents with guns – the heroes of
the revolution were now martyrs in a holy cause. Officially,
there were 1,382 of them, 869 of whom were soldiers.[1] Their
deaths had meaning far beyond the everyday. Nothing that a
politician could promise, and certainly no written words,
meant more, to the people of Petrograd, than the grief and
awe that they felt in the face of irrecoverable sacrifice. It was
because the funeral was so portentous that it had taken
almost a month to organize.

The plan at first had been to dig up Palace Square. There
would have been poetry in that, for it had been the scene of

the Bloody Sunday massacre of 1905. 'Some enthusiastic amateur digging was actually begun there,' Frank Lindley wrote in a report to London, 'but the hardness of the frozen ground and the number of water, gas, and electric light mains encountered by the excavators caused a change of plan.'[2] Another theory was that Maxim Gorky intervened; the writer's passion for artistic heritage was even better known than his disdain for loutish elements within the working class. Meanwhile, reported Lindley, Lvov and his liberal ministers hoped that the whole idea might end up being dropped, fearing fresh mayhem in a city that no longer had police. The wrangling and delay went on so long that many people went ahead and buried their loved ones themselves.

The eventual site was an open space (known locally as the 'Petersburg Sahara') close to the Pavlovsky barracks. A century before, it had been a parade-ground for the imperial military, and the name that it had acquired then, Mars Field, had stuck. More recently, there had been plans to build a permanent home for the Duma there, but nothing had been done before the war broke out. It was an empty plot, in other words, one of the last in central Petrograd, and it suited the purpose perfectly. It also happened that the British embassy backed on to it, affording staff the opportunity for a grandstand view.

Petrograd's citizens were their own master of ceremonies. The Soviet did some of the work of co-ordination, using its newspaper, *Izvestiya*, to publicize the order and timing of the procession. But it was the people who painted the banners, comforted the bereaved and set off with determined step towards the field of graves. Each factory and district had its place, each coffin its red flag. The bodies of those who had already been interred elsewhere were represented in the ceremony by wooden planks, each carried with as much respect as any sacred dead. There was no impatience as the procession flowed along the boulevards. The customary hum of the city stopped and the sky, for once, was clear of smoke. Nine hundred thousand people marched, their steps beating a rhythm muffled by their heavy coats. They sang the hymns of revolution, solemn but secular, and though there was no conductor they kept more or less in time. As each coffin was laid in the ground the guns of the Peter-Paul Fortress sounded from across the water, booming like apocalyptic drums. Six naval searchlights illuminated the ceremony as it continued long into the night. As Harold Williams put it, 'No Tsar was ever given a burial like this.'[3]

'It was a magnificent and moving triumphal procession of the revolution and of the masses who had made it,' wrote Sukhanov. Trotsky agreed. 'Everybody went to the funeral,' he wrote. 'Along with workers, soldiers, and the small city people here were students, ministers, ambassadors, the solid bourgeois, journalists, orators, leaders of all the parties.'[4] In his report for London, written with teeth tightly clenched, Sir John Hanbury-Williams attempted a similar generosity. The event, he conceded, 'which had been anticipated with lively dread by many, turned out to be a real triumph for the Russian democracy and a great encouragement to all its friends.' In private, however, the endless repetition of the Marseillaise (the Russians sang their own version, which they knew as the Marsiliuza) had irritated him beyond endurance. It was so monotonous, he wrote in his diary, that the victims of the revolution themselves were likely to 'rise from their graves and ask them to stop if they keep at it all the time. Pleasant for our Embassy, which adjoins.'[5] These Russian mourners, to an English eye, lacked even basic refinement. In the opinion of Buchanan's daughter Meriel, who was never a friend of revolutionaries, the rain-sodden crowd amounted to 'a seething mass of women, children, workmen, and soldiers, all carrying crimson banners at different angles, all singing the Marseillaise at a different time and in a different key'.[6]

It was the people's raw emotion that had made some onlookers nervous. They felt its power – the sound of tramping feet beat out a requiem for the old world – but no one could be sure where it might lead. There were divisions everywhere. 'The absence of any religious ceremony was a feature of the funeral, due to the definitely anti-religious sentiments of the Social Democrats,' Lindley observed, 'and gave rise to a good deal of criticism among the general public.'[7] Paléologue dismissed the evidence of revolutionary consciousness, of new-born, raw, dignified citizenship, by remarking that 'the art of mise en scène is native to the Russians.'[8] Even Tsereteli turned out to have misgivings. Though he sympathized deeply with the people's grief, he regarded the funeral as the last act in the revolution's 'youthful' phase: spontaneous, emotional, but necessarily to be replaced by leadership of the professional kind.[9]

'There was everywhere a passion for speech,' remembered Knox. 'A new verb was coined, "mitingovat", to attend meetings. A man would ask his friend what he was going to do that evening, and the reply would be, "I will attend meetings a little" ("ya nemnogo mitinguyu").'[10] Everyone wanted to thrash things out; all sensed a new responsibility, a pride in their own sovereign state. Doormen, street sweepers and court staff (who were called 'lackeys' in Russian) demanded new job-titles to reflect their status as free human beings.

Respect for their dignity had been one of the first conditions that the Petrograd garrison wrote into Order No. 1.
New names – from comrade rifleman to street sanitation
superintendent – were relatively easily achieved. What was
more difficult, at a time of national danger and economic
collapse, was to find the new republic's way ahead. Perhaps it
was because the problems were so hard that people talked
incessantly of theory or of trivialities.

Apart from peace and bread, the one thing that the people
yearned for most was something new: an end to the old ways,
the lies, the government by strangers in expensive suits. The
February days had inspired a sense of possibility, and everyone, from the oil-spattered machinists of Vyborg to the
peasants on the rich black earth, tasted a moment of empow-
erment. They were not wrong; their world had changed for
ever. In Petrograd, however, it was another set of businessmen and intellectuals, well meaning but abstracted from the
people's real lives, who quickly took to running things. For
just over eight months in 1917, the men who managed the
greatest revolution that the world had ever seen rehearsed
the manners and vocabulary of genteel government. They
debated treaty terms in diplomatic French and brokered
deals behind closed doors. They traded concessions and
massaged words. They could do nothing else, in fact, because
the one thing that kept them awake at night was the spectre
of social unrest, even of anarchy.

One group of them, survivors of the left-wing anti-tsarist
underground, met daily in the apartment of Matvei Skobelev, which was where Tsereteli had been staying since his
return to the capital. Only a handful of Ex Com members
was invited. Sukhanov (whom Tsereteli thought 'dry, cold
and bilious') was not part of the group, and there were

certainly no Bolsheviks. Small though it was, this largely Menshevik caucus, which was soon nicknamed the Star Chamber, had taken control of the Ex Com's work by the end of March.[11] It set the agenda, that is, and it coined a string of catchy terms, but what it refused to do, as the fires of revolution cooled, was to allow the bourgeois government to step aside. Hamstrung by fear of the wrong sort of change, its members were dependent on the goodwill of the likes of Prince Lvov.

The most immediate problems, unsurprisingly, were the same as they had been before the February days, though now there was no tsar available to take the blame. The war (or maybe the question of peace) remained the most controversial. It was majestic, and it made a lot of noise, but the Soviet's Manifesto to the Peoples of the World had settled nothing. Though Tsereteli's group now had firm views, the rest of the Ex Com remained divided, and arguments between the many factions – about armed defence and fraternization, about war production and the details of the coming spring's campaigns – foiled all attempts at unity. Meanwhile, as the Soviet wrestled with its conscience, the Provisional Government, in its new Mariinsky Palace home, debated the same issues, albeit from a subtly different point of view.

With their empire poised to collapse, the issue that the ministers chose to fight over was a land grab. On 23 March/5 April, the very day of Petrograd's great funeral, the pro-government newspaper *Rech* carried an interview with Miliukov that had been timed to coincide with US president Woodrow Wilson's declaration of war. The foreign minister took the opportunity to restate his determination to honour Russia's existing treaties. What he meant (although he did not quite venture the phrase) was that Russia would need to help itself to several portions of foreign-held territory if it were to fulfil its duties as a genuine world power. Miliukov proposed a 'union of the Ukrainian population of the Austrian regions with the populations of our own Ukrainian regions', a cloak for Russian expansion into Galicia. The real prize, however, remained that swathe of Turkey. Miliukov justified the annexation of Constantinople on the grounds that 'the Turkish nation, in spite of five hundred years' domination, has not spread its roots deeply there.' As the Turks would have been shocked to learn, he regarded a move on the Straits as simple housekeeping, a measure to 'protect the doors to Russia's home'.

The foreign minister never doubted that he was right where Turkey was concerned, and he made no attempt to conceal his impatience with the Soviet. 'Peace without annexations', he concluded, amounted to 'a German formula that they endeavour to pass off as an international socialist one'.[12] As Buchanan observed, Miliukov had 'absolutely refused so long as he remained Minister for Foreign Affairs to negotiate with Allies for a modification of agreements already concluded'.[13] In Tsereteli's view, 'it was like throwing down the gauntlet to the whole revolutionary democracy.'[14] But the Ex Com was trapped, for Miliukov (at the Ex Com's own request) had full responsibility for foreign affairs.

It was Kerensky, who could never glimpse fresh moral heights without leaping to claim them, who next began to stir up trouble. Buchanan drafted a late-evening report about the furore on 8 April, the day that he and other Anglicans had celebrated Easter. With eggs and children's stories on his mind, he may unconsciously have thought of Tweedledum and Tweedledee as he began to write. 'One of labour papers published today a statement by Minister of Justice

[Kerensky] to the effect that Minister for Foreign Affairs [Miliukov] in interview . . . had spoken in his own name and not in that of government,' he began. 'As Minister of Justice called on me this evening I asked him why he had published this statement. He replied he had done so because Minister for Foreign Affairs had spoken without consulting his colleagues and that he moreover considered it very tactless on the part of Minister for Foreign Affairs to make a declaration which had placed Government in a very difficult situation.'[15] It was not the detail of the argument alone that was so damaging, clearly, but also the puerile carping. While that continued, there was little chance that the Provisional Government could build a base of public trust or even hold coherent negotiations with its military allies. There was also likely to be opposition from the leftists in the Soviet. As a despairing Buchanan observed the next morning, 'the [Provisional] Government will not be master until it has put Committee which is self-constituted body representing a small minority of Extremists in its proper place.'[16]

With much the same concerns in mind, Tsereteli had been working on the Soviet Ex Com. He remained an internationalist, he said, but he wanted the Soviet to work beside the bourgeoisie, to co-operate if not ally with it and help create a common foreign policy and win the war. Tsereteli's reputation for statesmanship had continued to grow since his return, and on 22 March/4 April the Ex Com agreed to approach Lvov's government for a clear statement of its war aims, intending to use that as the basis for a united campaign of national defence.[17] Sukhanov was sceptical. He had been pressing for 'a nationwide, systematic campaign for peace' and his goal was to expose and then trap the bourgeois ministers, not to work with them.[18] Deals fixed behind the locked doors of a palace, after all, were precisely the sort of thing that the people's revolution had been made to thwart.

His doubts still simmering, his powder dry, Sukhanov nonetheless joined Tsereteli on the Ex Com's negotiating team. The black cars swept them off to the Mariinsky Palace on 24 March/6 April. Their host and chairman was Prince Lvov, and every member of his cabinet was present except Kerensky. 'Tsereteli tried to be convincing to the Ministers,' Sukhanov wrote, 'looking for points of departure that were close to them.' Still, neither side was keen to compromise, and 'a boring, long-winded, futile discussion started.'[19] The knives were out among the ministers as well. There were rumours of a Masonic conspiracy involving Kerensky and the millionaire minister of finance, Mikhail Tereshchenko. Much later, Miliukov claimed to have identified a plot against him by an unlikely gang whose members included Tsereteli, Prince Lvov, Kerensky and Sir George Buchanan.[20] After a taut but gentlemanly exchange of views, the Ex Com members took their leave, giving the ministers a day to formulate a statement of war aims.

On 26 March/8 April Lvov called the Soviet Executive representatives back to the palace to hear the statement that had been prepared. Its wording was a disappointment: pompous, vague and patronizing. 'The defence of our own inheritance at any price, and the liberation of our country from the invading enemy,' it began, 'constitute the foremost task of our fighters defending the nation's liberty.' The declaration insisted that free Russia did not aim to 'dominate other nations, or seize their national possessions', but the ministers had opted not to use the Soviet's phrase, 'peace without annexations or indemnities'. Instead, they sought 'a stable peace based on national self-determination' while promising

(Miliukov must have fought for hours) that 'the obligations undertaken towards our Allies will be fully observed.'[21]

Expansion was a war aim that the Soviet would not condone. The Ex Com group resigned itself to a long night of talks. At one point Tereshchenko bounded from his seat, accusing Sukhanov of comparing the current ministers to the disgraced ex-tsar. He flounced out of the building for a while, only to slink back some time after dark when his outrage had cooled. Later still, and well after midnight, the telephone rang for Chkheidze. It was his wife, and she was calling in despair: their son, who was fifteen or sixteen at the time, had injured himself in an accident with a loaded gun and was not expected to live for more than an hour. Chkheidze opted to stay at the meeting.[22] By the time he got home, his son was dead. The talks collapsed in any case. Lvov seemed to be backing Miliukov. He knew that the Ex Com was trapped.

The leaders of the Soviet were on the verge of giving up. The next morning, however, it was Tsereteli's turn to hurry to the telephone. The voice that squawked into his ear was Prince Lvov's. A packet containing a revised document, the prince explained, was on its way to the Tauride. The Ex Com group, gathering round when it arrived, discovered that six words, underlined in red pencil, had been inserted into the previous day's text. The important new phrase renounced 'any violent seizure of foreign territory'.[23] Tsereteli was triumphant. He had secured his declaration and a new alliance with the bourgeois government. He also knew that he had outmanoeuvred the large group of left-wingers in the Soviet who wanted an immediate peace. Exactly what the wording meant for real soldiers fighting at real frontiers was something they could all leave for another day.

The compromise did nothing to enhance the reputations of its signatories. Tsereteli and his friends had done their best, and as Marxists they regarded revolution as the heart of their entire lives, but the Ex Com team had now appeared for what it was: a group of politicians with a questionable mandate and a poor to hopeless grasp of real life. 'The history of the committee', remembered one of the participants, 'can be divided into two periods: before and after Tsereteli's arrival . . . He led the committee calmly, full of confidence and courage, until suddenly the random hodgepodge of people was transformed into an institution . . . Yet, strangely enough, at the precise moment when the committee became organized . . . it allowed the leadership of the masses, who turned their backs on the committee, to slip out of its hands.'[24]

On 27 March/9 April, the very day when Lenin's train pulled out of Zurich station on its way to Germany, the Provisional Government's declaration on the war, complete with an endorsement in the name of the Soviet, was published in Russia. Attentive readers knew at once that the revolution's promised peace, the peace of people's dearest dreams, had been deferred indefinitely. 'My dear Knox, you must be easy,' a cheerful Rodzianko commented to the British officer the following day. 'Russia is a big country, and can wage a war and manage a revolution at the same time.'[25] When Buchanan asked Prince Lvov for an explanation of the Soviet's cherished 'peace without annexations', the nobleman was equally complacent. 'If the war went well for us,' he suggested, 'those who now spoke of the permanent occupation of Constantinople and Galicia as annexation would regard it as liberation from the enemy yoke.'[26] It was the sort of comment Lenin had in mind when he observed that 'to urge the Provisional Government to conclude a democratic peace is like preaching virtue to brothel-keepers.'[27]

The soldiers were the obstacle that no one wanted to discuss. Whatever Prince Lvov might say, Russia's foreign plans depended on the army, and no one knew exactly what was in its members' minds. Local troops made a poor litmus test, though most people had nothing else from which to judge. 'Petrograd garrison has issued a declaration drawn up by both officers and men emphasizing necessity of continuing war until new won freedom is secured,' Buchanan informed London in a telegram of 28 March/10 April.

> Declaration states that war must be fought to successful end because army considers that peace even restoring Russia's former frontiers would if reached without agreement Allies be shameful . . . Resolution calls on Committee to end all quarrels between workmen and technical staffs of Petrograd Works factories, as these quarrels causing incalculable harm army . . . Finally to increase munitions output eight hour day is to be suspended and work continued unceasingly at highest pressure bearing in mind that army is working night and day . . .[28]

In all, the news was looking good. But anyone who toured the front would have been troubled by the conscripts' fragile mood.

The Provisional Government had been the first to send inspectors out. In March, two former Duma members called Yanushkevich and Filonenko were dispatched to tour the northern front. Their report was almost entirely positive: 'Morale is so gay, joyful and good that it makes you happy.'[29] Elsewhere, other inspectors watched as soldiers lined up on parade to show how good things were supposed to be, though what was really going on behind the fixed smiles and the public prayers remained mysterious. The army chief, General Alexeyev, who knew a good deal more than any politician ever would, complained to Guchkov about the poor conditions, ammunition shortages and lack of food. No one could hide the fact that discipline was ragged at the best of times.[30] A happy mood, meanwhile, was not always ideal. On 1/14 April, Sir William Robertson, the Chief of the Imperial General Staff in London, cabled Knox and Hanbury-Williams with a demand for information about Russia's combat readiness. 'Give me your considered opinion,' Sir William ordered. 'You should divest your mind of claptrap such as determination to win and fighting for freedom and so forth, remembering that without discipline and reasonable administrative efficiency, an army is merely a leaderless mob.'[31]

The information he was getting, at least from Knox, was inconclusive. The attaché had no time for the garrison in Petrograd, while the bureaucrats who ran the army had infuriated him. 'The main idea seems to be to do as little work as possible,' he had reported to London on 18/31 March 1917. 'The General Staff offices are closed after five p.m., and the Artillery Department shuts an hour earlier. The men are children. One of them said to me in the Duma: "We have been slaves for 300 years, you will not grudge us a few weeks' amusement."'[32] 'Naturally,' he wrote home on 2/15 April, 'the troops at Petrograd who have expelled 3/4ths of their officers do nothing and have no sign of discipline ... The Govt. it seems to me have given up all attempt to protect the unfortunate army from political agitators.'[33]

Knox felt a little better, though not much, when he drove out to tour the lines. He visited the Guards depots near

Petrograd towards the end of March, and April found him at the northern front. His findings were biased, because his main task was to push the British cause, but he spoke Russian (badly) and could listen to soldiers' complaints. As he delivered his lecture ('he had one speech,' remembered British academic Bernard Pares, 'which I got to know by heart')[34] and dished out maps and pictures of the western front, he often encountered a wariness about England. But he thought he could deal with that; a brisk talk man to man was all it took. More serious were the soldiers' stories about their officers, some of whom they had driven out or even killed. 'What would happen in England', one group of Russian conscripts had demanded, 'if an officer came on parade and called his men "a lot of pig-faced cattle"?'[35] It was not clear that anyone could stand a long campaign. The pro-war demonstrations in Petrograd might have been organized and paid for by the right-wing press, but front-line soldiers remained sceptical. Those flag-wavers, they said, the people in clean uniforms with their demand for 'war to a final victory', should spend a few weeks in the trenches for themselves. That way, they would find out what fighting really meant, and 'we, who have suffered for nearly three years' could go home for a well-earned rest.[36]

There was still some hope for the front. Most soldiers had welcomed the Soviet's Manifesto of 14/27 March, especially the paragraph about the loaded guns (the ammunition shortage rankled everywhere), and an intensive campaign by pro-war newspapers like *Rech* and *Russkaya Volya* had reinforced the view that fighting should continue in the name of Russia and its military honour. Though officers felt nervous about controlling their troops, the fury of the earliest days had abated. No one could say for certain if the men would obey an order to attack, but at least they claimed to want to fight. Above all, the army's mood continued to be strongly anti-German. 'There is no doubt that the Extreme Socialists with their "Stop the war" programme have lost power,' Knox wrote on 2/15 April. 'The idea found little support among the troops who have practical experience of the Hun.'[37]

What really worried Knox – and everyone who relied on the army to fight on during the spring – was the rate of desertion. No power, and certainly no politician, could stop the steady flow of men returning home. In April, a thousand soldiers were arriving every day at Kiev railway station. According to intelligence passed on to Knox, something like one and a half million men had left their posts by the second week of April.[38] The latest wave of German propaganda, again using leaflets dropped from aeroplanes, was already making things worse.[39] People had started whispering that the Easter holiday was going to see a decree dividing up all Russian land, and many soldiers yearned to get back to their villages and make sure of their share.[40]

It was partly to combat the consequent panic that the Soviet published a statement in *Izvestiya* on 26 March/8 April. The land, it promised, 'the land that has been soaked by the sweat of the people', would certainly be given to the peasants in due course. Meanwhile, however, 'it will not be by means of violence, or fires, or murders or arbitrary measures that the free people will achieve its will, but by the authoritative voice which will be heard from behind the walls of the Constituent Assembly, elected by all the people.'[41] Stay where you are, in other words, and at some point, when Russia had a constitution and, perhaps, a head of state, the whole thing would turn out all right. The trouble was that the men at the sharp end of it all were getting cynical. 'If I'm dead,' one soldier quipped, 'I won't be needing the land anyway.'[42]

The land question could only grow more acute with spring coming, when the fields would have to be sown.[43] In an army drawn almost entirely from the countryside, the men might well dash home at any point. The Provisional Government, which had abolished the death penalty, had almost no means to prevent them. Meanwhile, in Petrograd, the Soviet was preparing to host a gathering for delegates from all over Russia. The first All-Russian Conference of Soviets was scheduled for Easter weekend. Whatever compromises Tsereteli might have made, the people were about to have another chance to indulge their new taste for public meetings.

The Bolsheviks had not played a large part in the events that month. Years later, official communist accounts of 1917 would paint the party as a united, relentless force for change. This was a lie, of course, but not the worst of that regime, for Bolshevism had a solid grass-roots following that other socialist parties could only envy. It was the Bolshevik elite that still could not agree on anything. 'It must be confessed', a comrade from Petrograd was later to write, 'that before [Lenin's] arrival there was rather a lot of confusion in the Party. There was no definite, consistent line. The task of taking state power was depicted by a majority as a sort of distant ideal and not, as a rule, presented as a close, urgent and immediate aim. It was considered sufficient to support the Provisional Government . . . Vacillation and disunity were typical.'[44] In his retirement, Trotsky reached the same conclusion. As he put it: 'One could write an instructive chapter on the leadership of the Leninists without Lenin. The latter towered so high above his nearest disciples that in his presence they felt there was no need of solving theoretical and tactical problems independently. When they happened to be separated from Lenin at a critical moment, they amazed one another by their utter helplessness.'[45]

There had been some notable triumphs. On 4/17 March, two days after the tsar's abdication, an energetic group of activists had relaunched the Bolshevik newspaper, *Pravda*. Although they had no printing press, they knew where to find one. In the small hours of a chill Saturday morning, a group of armed men burst through the door of a house on the bank of the Moika. Barging up the stairs, they made for the premises of *Selsky Vestnik*, a privately owned newspaper with spacious offices and a fine printing press. With encouragement from *Selsky Vestnik*'s print-workers (skilled men and for the most part socialists), the Bolsheviks cleared a space at the big table and pulled up some of the bentwood chairs. From that night on, they forced the sitting tenants to share everything from the huge rotary printing machine to the office kettle.[46]

It was much easier to seize a press, unfortunately, than to settle on an editorial line after an interruption of three years. *Pravda*'s first number, which came out on Sunday 5/18 March, gave star billing to an appeal for membership fees.[47] The paper did not tempt people to pay, however, for its editorial went no further than stating that 'The fundamental problem is to establish a democratic republic.' Beyond that, its editors felt more comfortable printing the words of the Internationale (and doggerel verse, beloved by *Pravda*'s editors for decades to come) than trying to define their party's position on any urgent problem of the day. Observing the newspaper from outside, Sukhanov commented that 'There was no "line" at all, merely a vague, pogromist form.'[48] *Pravda*'s lack of direction reflected divisions in the Bolshevik Party itself, whose Petrograd organizations (local and national) seemed to be fighting long-running internal wars.

The leftist Vyborg Committee was still out of step with the national leaders. In particular, its members continued to believe that, pending the convocation of an assembly to agree on Russia's future constitution, any caretaker government would have to be formed of workers' soviets, not dominated by the bourgeoisie.[49] For some veteran Bolsheviks, who argued on principle that the Soviet should not oppose the Provisional Government unless it actually attacked the working class, this view, initially, was heresy. Even Shlyapnikov believed that it was not possible for the Bolsheviks (or any working-class party) to take on the burden of government that Miliukov and Prince Lvov had been persuaded to assume. By late March, however, some of the party's second-tier leaders in Petrograd had begun to argue that soviets, rather than any form of parliament, should be groomed to take power soon. The process would take time, however, and the people would need to be armed and prepared for the task, which would involve expanding the militia that the Bolsheviks knew as the Red Guards.[50]

It was at this point, on 12/25 March, that Kamenev and Stalin returned to the capital from Siberia. There was the usual welcome at the station (though Sukhanov had pointed out that they would not need a whole regiment for that), but there was a long history between the comrades in Petrograd and this duo. In Kamenev's case, the problem was that treason trial of 1915, at which he had betrayed the movement and showed shameful cowardice. In punishment, according to the current editors of *Pravda*, he should be banned from writing for the paper and from voting on its line. Party members were also wary of Stalin, citing unspecified 'personal characteristics' as a reason for barring him, on his return, from full voting membership of the Central Committee.[51] Before long, however, both men had elbowed their way into *Pravda* and forced the current editors aside. The impact was immediate and radical; Kamenev's first instinct, he confided in private, had been to shut the paper down. Now he was on the hunt for stylish writers with a range of views. *Pravda* 'has a completely unseemly and unsuitable tone', he told Sukhanov, 'so now I'm trying to attract contributors or get hold of a few articles by writers with some reputation'.[52]

Plurality of views and stylish writing had not been Bolshevik priorities before, but like many 'Siberians' (including Tsereteli) Kamenev was sympathetic to the idea that socialists should work together. He argued that they had a short-term duty to support the bourgeoisie as well, though always with an eye to forcing democratic change. Crucially, Kamenev was also convinced that Russia would still have to fight and win its war, albeit mainly to defend the gains of revolution against Prussian tyranny. It was a theme that he explored in his first serious piece, which came out on 15/28 March with the title 'Without Secret Diplomacy'. 'When one army collides with another,' Kamenev wrote, 'the most absurd policy would be to propose that one of them lay down its arms and go home. That would not be a policy of peace but of slavery . . . The free people will stand firmly at their posts, will reply bullet for bullet and shell for shell.'[53]

The party's left-wing group was horrified. 'The day of the first issue of the transformed *Pravda*', Shlyapnikov remembered, 'was a day of rejoicing for the defencists . . . In the

Executive Committee itself they met us with venomous smiles.' There was an angry meeting in the office on the Moika (the kitchen was the only refuge left to *Selsky Vestnik* staff). Kamenev was censured (and Stalin silently abandoned him), but nonetheless the newspaper's line had been pushed to the right.[54] In the next week, *Pravda* published a series of conflicting pieces, appearing to have lost sight of its whole purpose. Wearied by the confused, tetchy debates, activists like Shlyapnikov awaited the return of Lenin 'like the heavy artillery'.[55]

As if on cue, a train with a distinguished passenger from Switzerland steamed into Petrograd. The date was 31 March/13 April, the day on which the Orthodox observed Good Friday. A larger crowd than usual had gathered and the scarlet flags around the Finland Station were more numerous than ever. In keeping with the custom now, there was a regimental band, and as the station clock ticked round to the appointed time a welcoming committee assembled, this time including foreigners. The engine lights approached, the night air filled with steam and in due course the guest of honour stepped down from the train. Dressed in a fur coat and black boots, he was a tall but crumpled figure well past middle age, and while he was delighted by the reception it also wearied him. The journey from Geneva, after all, had been a very arduous one. Turning to his fellow passengers, he hurried into the grand waiting room, and from there (after more speeches) he and his party made their way into the capital.

The new arrival was Georgy Plekhanov. With Britain's blessing and support, the patriarch from Geneva had been permitted to return to Russia. The point was that Plekhanov, though a Marxist, was a sound man on the war, a patriot who could tell other socialists exactly where their duty lay. In gratitude for that, he had been escorted on the sea-route to Bergen instead of suffering the trials of a sealed train, and for good measure six more socialists had made the voyage with him. They were all foreigners this time, and they had been chosen in the hope that they might talk the language of the common working man. That was the theory, anyway. 'Moutet is a barrister,' Paléologue noted in his diary, 'Cachin and Lafont are professors of philosophy; O'Grady is a cabinet-maker, Thorne a plumber. French socialism is thus represented by intellectuals with a classical education, English socialism by manual workers.'[56]

The Frenchman was exaggerating for effect. Will Thorne was not a plumber but a former brick-maker who had been taught to read, in a socialist discussion-group, by Karl Marx's youngest daughter Eleanor. In 1917, as a trade union leader and MP for West Ham South, he joined James O'Grady, an MP from Leeds (although Paléologue was right about the cabinet-making) and William Sanders, the secretary of the Fabian Society, on a mission to talk some sense into the Soviet. The idea of sending them had originated in Paris, though Whitehall took it up at once.[57] They were experienced public speakers, leaders in their world, but nothing had prepared these envoys – 'splendid types', Buchanan thought – for the reception that awaited them.

The speeches at the station had been exhausting enough, especially after a train journey that felt more like a penal sentence than a trip from A to B. Now they discovered, somehow grasping at stray words, that their arrival had coincided with a mass meeting, something important, and they were obliged to attend it. The meeting was the first All-Russian Conference of Soviets, and the socialist elite of Petrograd had taken up position in a giant hall with workers, soldiers and peasants from the four corners of the empire. Plekhanov was bundled on to the stage like a bewildered pedigree bull. According to Sukhanov, he 'stood motionless in his fur coat and didn't say a word'.[58] The foreigners could only watch in silence, longing for their beds.

The next day was not much better. Petrograd's allied diplomats led their tame socialists to the Conference, but no one else engaged with them. 'However honourable and well-meaning they were as citizens', Sukhanov pointed out, they 'were really delegates from the Allied governments and agents of Anglo-French imperialism'.[59] From the first, remembered Robert Bruce Lockhart, 'the result was a farce,' with the British trio and the French 'completely lost in the wilderness of Russian revolutionary phraseology'.[60] Pouring water into his whisky that evening, Thorne told Buchanan that he had not met a deputy from the Soviet who looked as if he had done a day's work with his own hands. The ambassador concluded that 'the extreme Socialists are not very amenable to foreign influence.'[61]

The closing session of the Conference, Easter Sunday for the Russian Orthodox, was the most rewarding. Again, the visitors were herded along to the meeting hall, but Plekhanov, who appeared on stage beside them, had now been fortified by a good night's sleep and a briefing. He opened with a rousing speech that the provincial delegates could all applaud, pointing to his distinguished foreign guests as if they were the very embodiment of international solidarity. When the foreigners actually spoke, however, it was the timbre of their voices that impressed the crowds rather than anything they said. According to the (sympathetic) journalist

Harold Williams, the audience responded to Cachin's dramatic inflexions and gestures before it had the least idea what his words meant, while O'Grady 'raised his voice to Trafalgar Square dimensions', pouring out a stream of 'thunderous sound . . . on the uncomprehending soldiers and workmen'.[62] The rapture continued as Plekhanov took his last bow with the guests, 'presenting a real and thrilling symbol of allied democracy'. Even Sukhanov conceded that 'the atmosphere was festive and friendly.'[63] Perhaps it was as well, for festivity's sake, that no one had really discussed the war at all.

In private sessions later on, when the talk finally turned to guns and treaty obligations, the visitors' luck ran out. Cachin found the Soviet so unwelcoming that he panicked, abandoning his prepared script and telling everyone that France proposed to drop its claim to Alsace and Lorraine.[64] It was a statement that no sane Frenchman could ever possibly have made, and the speech (like Cachin himself) was ridiculed. Neither Thorne nor O'Grady fared better. The wisdom of well-meaning Englishmen (let alone a brace of French theorists) was never likely to inspire a revived Russian war effort. 'If the English . . . would stop giving advice to Russia and the Russians', lamented a translator at the British embassy, 'and would understand that the . . . revolutionaries are not a ragged mob of long-haired, more or less seedy ne'er do wells and flat-chested bespectacled students but consist of all that is best in the country, then we should become more popular. It is a case of save us from our friends.'[65]

8. Lenin in Lapland

> The British Government decided to prevent the emigrant internationalists from returning to their native land and taking part in the struggle against imperialist war.
>
> V. I. Lenin

Lenin had told them to ignore the journalists; as always, he would be the one who took care of the press. The trouble was that there were dozens of new people on the train; they shoved their way inside the Russians' carriages and deluged them with questions. The pack, its cry a chorus of northern European languages, had boarded all at once when the slow service from Malmö had stopped, just after dawn, at a sub-urban station on the outskirts of Stockholm. It was Friday 13 April (the day on which Plekhanov and his friends arrived in Russia), and some of Lenin's fellow passengers were starting to miss the sealed carriage and the silent German plain. They did not want celebrity at this ungodly hour. They were on edge, they had slept badly, their clothes were sticking to their flesh and it was four days since any had enjoyed the benefits of a clean towel, running hot water and five minutes of privacy.

Such was their mood, weary and sour, when they stepped down from the train in Stockholm to find that a reception party had assembled. Though he had been unable to get to

Trelleborg the night before, the left-wing socialist Fredrik Ström was on the platform now. With him stood some other representatives of the Swedish Riksdag and Stockholm's powerful chief magistrate, Carl Lindhagen. A modest crowd had gathered, too, including at least two Swedish secret policemen and several foreign spies.[1] The Russians were to spend most of the day in the Swedish capital. Someone would make a note of everything they did.

Lenin might have preferred to press on, but there were no trains to the high Norrland until the evening. To make the best of the delay, he had set a busy agenda in advance, much of it focused on securing explicit Swedish approval for his decision to cross German territory in that sealed carriage. Apart from that, he wanted to sound out the Swedish comrades' views on war, peace and revolution, he needed money, and he hoped to set up a permanent Bolshevik office – a Foreign Bureau for his international campaign – with a Stockholm address and staff. If there was any time left after all of that, he intended to visit his old Zimmerwald comrade Zeth Höglund in nearby Långholmen prison.

It was a spring morning in Stockholm, grey but calm, and the conditions were perfect for photographers. The picture that one of them took, capturing Lenin in full stride, is one of the most famous images of the entire story. The Bolshevik leader's face is turned away, but he is marching rapidly along, already embarked on the first of his day's missions. His feet are shod in heavy mountain boots, and though respectable enough he wears a scarecrow's choice of city clothes, including an ill-fitting woollen coat. His right hand clasps a rolled umbrella like a sharpened alpenstock, his left is hidden, drawn back from the cold. If he is aware at all of the camera, he shows no sign, for he is deep in conversation (no wasted small talk for this man) with another Swedish Zimmerwaldist, Ture Nerman. Nerman stands a full head taller, and he is certainly more elegantly dressed, but it is Lenin, a coiled mass of energy, who holds the viewer's attention in the picture just as he always did in real life.

Behind him, in a disorderly line, his wife and other comrades followed. Fredrik Ström had to race to keep up with them all. The Swedes had booked six rooms for their visitors at the nearby Hotel Regina on Drottninggatan. 'Warm and cold water in every room', it boasted in its 1913 advertisement in Bradshaw's railway guide. 'Latest improvements, every convenience'.[2] 'Lenin almost ran to the hotel,' remembered Ström. 'His only thought was to get home.' The hobnailed boots, however, which had been made for Lenin by his cobbler-landlord in Zurich, looked out of place on the feet of a would-be world leader. To Ström, more used to Swedish drawing rooms, Lenin might have been 'a workman on a Sunday-afternoon excursion in unsettled weather'.[3] The staff of the Regina took one look, appraising the entire string of crumpled and unsavoury new guests, and refused to let any of them in. It was only when Ström confirmed that the rooms had been paid for in advance that the Russians were allowed to have their keys, to say nothing, at last, of that blissful hot water.

The others may have washed and rested, but Lenin's day had barely started. Before most of his fellow travellers had finished breakfast, he was off in search of the pre-booked hotel conference room. Lindhagen was to give a speech of welcome here (he chose the theme 'The Light from the East'), and short greetings were delivered on behalf of the Swedish trade unions. Lenin listened patiently enough, but he was there to set the record of his journey straight. He had to tell the Swedes that there had been no contact with potential German spies; he had to tell everyone else that it was imperialist Britain, flagrantly blocking all the obvious routes from Switzerland, that bore responsibility for forcing him to go through Germany at all. It was true, he granted, that the Germans hoped to benefit from his return, but they were making a mistake. 'The Bolshevik leadership of the revolution', he concluded, 'is much more dangerous for German imperialist power and capitalism than the leadership of Kerensky and Miliukov.'[4]

In private talks alone with Ström, Lenin said more about his plans. He was concerned about the future of the Swedish left, and worried that Ström, his ally, was no match for Branting ('he is cleverer than you'). Repeatedly, he stressed the need to take up arms, a point on which he always differed with the comrades here. 'You cannot meet the tsarist army with prayers,' Lenin explained. 'You have to have weapons.' When a startled Ström asked what Lenin would do to stave off a take-over by the armed forces (he sketched a vision of Kerensky as a Bonaparte) Lenin answered that the only future freedom lay in something that he called a dictatorship of the proletariat.[5]

The words were stirring, frightening and hard, but Lenin also needed help. He had already asked the Swedish left to endorse his journey through Germany, and Ström had noticed his relief at the news that Branting had agreed to sign. Now he wanted money. 'It costs a lot to travel through your country,' he explained. That afternoon, Ström raised some funds from local trade unions while a Riksdag member called Fabian Monsson approached his fellow politicians for spare cash. The right-wing foreign minister, Arvid Lindman, is said to have paid up on one condition: 'Lenin leaves today.'[6]

While Monsson passed the hat around, Radek took Lenin to the shops. Armed with some cash provided by a charity that worked with local Russian refugees, the leader was propelled into a grand establishment that catered to the bourgeoisie. The PUB department store was famous: three years after Lenin's visit, an even more glamorous career was launched there when an errand-girl called Greta Garbo was asked to model ladies' hats downstairs. For Lenin, it was time to ditch the hobnailed boots. Equipped at last with city shoes, he also chose the suit that he would wear on almost every public occasion until well into 1918. But two items were quite enough. Lenin resisted Radek's suggestion of a new coat (and even clean underwear), remarking that he was going to Russia to make revolution, not to open a gents' outfitters.[7]

The speeches and those shopping chores took up all the time he might have spent with Zeth Höglund. Lenin's busy schedule also ruled out any other social calls, but he was well aware that Parvus was in town. The magnate had been tracking Lenin's journey day by day, not least because he still regarded the whole thing as his idea. Anticipating Lenin's arrival (and with the blessing of his backers in the Berlin foreign ministry) Parvus had made his way to Stockholm in early April.[8] Though the Bolshevik leader would not agree to a meeting, the two men were no more than a few streets apart throughout that day. In public, eschewing contact, Lenin declared that Parvus was an unreliable traitor, an egotist and German pawn. Behind the scenes, however, he had other ways of maintaining a link to Germany's favourite Russian profiteer. Through Fürstenberg, he had kept the lines of communication open for the past two years. This time, the man he chose to send (when he had dispensed with his services in PUB) was Karl Radek.

Lenin had worked up an appetite, and back in the Regina's dining room he tucked into a steak, grinding extra pepper and joking with the Swedish comrades who were paying for his food. But as his master savoured that fresh beef, Radek was meeting Parvus somewhere in the city. The conversation was entirely secret and no record of it was kept, but Lenin would never have allowed it to happen without dictating the agenda. As he had made clear, what his Bolsheviks needed most was the money to sustain a large-scale revolutionary campaign, and that was something that the big man knew exactly how to get. Thanks to his contacts in the German foreign ministry, Parvus, as his biographers conclude, 'was in a position to promise massive support to the Bolsheviks in the forthcoming struggle for political power in Russia.' Radek was empowered to accept the offer. The events of the following months provide sufficient evidence that this was precisely what happened in Stockholm on 13 April.'[9]

Lenin, of course, denied it all, and with a virulence that never eased. What he did acknowledge (for it was true) was that he had asked Radek to remain in Stockholm and work beside Fürstenberg. As an Austrian citizen, Radek could not have hoped to gain entry to Russia anyway, and the chance of setting up in a smart suburb with a wealthy partner was compensation enough for missing some of the revolutionary action. The task the two men would assume, officially at least, was to manage the Bolsheviks' foreign base, a centre for publicity and news-gathering and an embryonic socialist international. The Swedish police were suspicious from the start, however, and before long Fürstenberg's financial affairs were under scrutiny from Russia, too.[10]

Without Radek, then, but rested, fed and dressed in cleaner clothes, the Russians made their way to Stockholm station for the evening train. It was already almost dark, but the news of Lenin's visit had spread and a party of about a hundred well-wishers with flags had gathered on the large concourse. More red flags fluttered from the engine while the stoker loaded coal. The Internationale rang out as Lenin and his fellow passengers were escorted on to the 6.37 sleeper service to Bräcke.[11] Before them lay a 600-mile ride towards the Arctic Circle, the longest single section of their journey. Thanks to the offices of Fürstenberg, to say nothing of the money that their Swedish friends (and enemies) had given them, Lenin's party had been able to afford a series of compartments, each one equipped with four hard bunks (their fares in Sweden, according to their scrupulous accounts, cost the equivalent of 424 rubles and 65 kopeks).[12] Someone handed Lenin a bouquet, and there were more flowers for the ladies. As yet another whistle blew, the leader left the Swedish capital behind, watching one more landscape vanish for ever into clouds of engine smoke.[13]

They were woken just before dawn. At 5.30 a.m., at Bräcke, there was a change of trains. After a bleary breakfast, the Russians boarded a slower service for the far north. All through that Saturday, they watched the hills and forests slipping deeper into winter. The snow grew thicker by the hour. In some places its weight had bent whole rows of saplings to the ground, creating arches and eccentric loops like the ribcages of some long-dead giant beast. The forest was so close that the observant members of the group might have glimpsed deer and Arctic hares, perhaps a red fox slipping home. There were more elk than people here. The sparse towns on the edges of the track shared the unfinished look of all frontier halts. The station buildings in the larger ones appeared too urban for this wilderness, but beyond them were wooden huts and freight depots: Vindeln, Bastuträsk, Jörn. It was well after 10 p.m. when the Russians reached Boden, and they still had one more night in Sweden to go. Loading their bags on to another train just after midnight, they headed out for Haparanda, a slow pull that would take them more than seven hours.

Sunrise came early this far north, and it was some time after it, when they had cleared the remnants of their breakfast sandwiches and tea, that Lenin called his Russian group to order for a meeting. He had not passed the best of nights, but he had certainly found time to read. In Stockholm, he had bought as many Russian newspapers as he could find, and he had spent thirty-six hours perusing them. The news was dominated by the Provisional Government's recent declaration of war aims and the Soviet Ex Com's triumphant endorsement of it. 'The traitors!' Lenin growled into the newsprint. 'Oh, the swine.' His fiercest hatred was directed at the social-democratic appeasers, and especially at Chkheidze, Tsereteli and their friends.[14] His muttered cursing faded as he finally began to doze, but at each stop the leader had awoken in an increasingly pugnacious mood and he was brisk and brittle with the passengers as they sat down.

The meeting was minuted. There were three items on the agenda: behaviour at the Russian border; travel plans for Fritz Platten; and the response the group should take, once it had arrived in Petrograd, if questioned by the agents of the bourgeois Miliukov. The last of these produced a show of Lenin's legal expertise, although his careful statement of the Russians' immigration rights was little comfort to the ones who feared that they might all simply be hanged. In the event of any interrogation, he decided, a committee of five (which he would lead) could represent the entire group; the others were to hold their tongues and refuse to sign anything.

But Petrograd was still more than a day away. The border post at Tornio was the immediate problem. It was unlikely that Fritz Platten, as a Swiss, would be allowed to cross, but it was also far from certain even that the Russians could. The Bolsheviks did not know it, but that very day a Danish social-ist called Borbjerg, who was carrying peace proposals for the Soviet, had been turned back at the Tornio checkpoint. The decision, according to the German agents who were spon-soring him, 'emanated from the Provisional Government in Petrograd as a result of representations from England'.[15]

It looked as if the British were the real enemy in this out-post. But the Russian travellers might also have heard rumours about German officers, who were said to have taken to soaking suspicious cross-border travellers in chemical baths to find out if there might be concealed writing on their skin.[16] The sense that somebody was waiting at the border up ahead, hidden maybe, and even armed, cast a pall over the last few hours of the Russians' journey. They joined the new branch line to Haparanda just after four o'clock on Sunday morning, heading south towards the marshy coast. Three hours later their train crawled up to the buffers at a half-built station perched on a high bluff. Below it stretched a grey expanse of river. Frozen solid, and dusted with snow, the Tornionjoki marked the outer boundary of a world in which, the travellers now realized, they had been safe and more or less at ease. A handsome church rose opposite, its cupola just visible above skeletal trees. A little further on, they could make out a red flag on the Russian station roof in Tornio. It was time to leave the warm cocoon. Outside, in the make-shift terminus, the cold bit straight through to their bones,

while the only facility was a kiosk selling coffee and sandwiches. The food was unappetizing, but as Elena Usievich
remembered, 'we were in no mood to eat.'[17]

If the Russians had taken the time to explore, they would
have concluded that the British were closer than ever. Remote
and basic though it was, this border town was a strategic life-
line. At a time when it was vital for the allies to maintain
(and increase) their influence over Russian politics and the
Russian armed forces, the crossing here remained the only
safe land-bridge.[18] Usievich remembered Haparanda as a
'fishing village', but she was mistaken. It was humming with
business. According to an estimate from 1917, its customs
post had handled twenty-seven million mail items and pack-
ets in just six months.[19] Assuming (very optimistically) that
the border officials worked a twelve-hour day, that was
roughly three items per second, a calculation that did not
allow for bulky goods. The depot on the Swedish side was
heaped with an assortment of cargo, some marked for distant
cities such as Tokyo and Peking. There were barrels, crates,
boxes and incongruously fragrant sacks of oranges. Haparanda's customs house had long since ceased to cope, and so had
the sledges that plied the frozen river in the winter months.
Since there was still no railway bridge, the answer was to
build an overhead cable system. It was based on floating
pylons, a scaffolding of fragile towers that loomed over the
river, and in April 1917 it was in constant use.[20]

Another thought Usievich may have suppressed was that
the Arctic twilight on the river bank provided perfect cover.
A lively trade in smuggled war-related goods already flourished in these forests; a fog that could hide heavy crates could
certainly make people disappear.[21] There were plenty of
strangers about, too, the kind whom no one could identify.

From the first winter of the war, the international Red Cross had used the wooden footbridge at the border to exchange invalid prisoners of war. In summer, the sick and wounded were ferried across the river on a special hospital boat, but in winter the ones who could walk (or even stumble on crutches) were left to hobble over the bridge under the watchful eyes of local guards. How many were involved is hard to establish, but it is likely that at least 75,000 men, mainly Austrians, Hungarians and Turks, made their way through this northern border crossing. It was never the most secure of operations, and at one point, not long before Lenin and his group arrived, there had been an outbreak of typhus. Many wartime travellers would get no further. The dying were still piling up; fresh graves were filled and covered all the time, and one or two more foreigners could vanish without leaving any real trace.

Lenin allowed no doubt to trouble him. In the deep snow, miles from the nearest big city and boxed in by an archipelago of containers and sacks, the Bolshevik leader was thinking only of revolution.[22] His companions were the ones who worried about their safety as the group was ushered down the riverbank and handed, two by two, into fifteen small sledges. These makeshift taxis, pulled by stocky ponies, shuttled to and fro across the mile and a half of ice for months each year. For their passengers, however, reaching for blankets in the Arctic wind, it was barely six days since that farewell lunch in the Zähringerhof, six days since they had gazed on the blue water of a lake. As they drew closer to the Russian side, the risk that they were taking reduced several of them (including Elena Usievich) to something very like panic. Zinoviev's memoir claims that he sat back in his sledge to watch the sky, but most people were thinking of the border and, beyond it, the unknown.

The British had formed a dim view of the Bolsheviks in Petrograd. In the weeks since the revolution, Frank Lindley at the embassy had reported on their rhetoric, their programme and their newspaper. 'The "Pravda" ... has from the first adopted an attitude of uncompromising hostility to the Provisional Government and to the war,' he noted in late March. 'The former it represents as reactionaries of the most dangerous type, and the latter as the outcome of their machinations and those of similar persons abroad ... It is mainly due to this paper that there exists in Petrograd a feeling of great nervousness among the middle class whom it attacks unmercifully.' The only good news was 'the timely discovery by the Government that one of its editors was in the pay of the secret police', but the paper seemed to have survived that.[23] What no one appeared to know, however, were the names of its new editors or where its money had come from.

Such lack of concrete information was a constant problem at this stage. The only politician in the Soviet whose name Lindley could cite (though not quite spell) was Chkheidze. Exactly who was who among the other activists and orators remained unclear, and sceptics entertained the darkest fears about them all. Still, Lindley thought he could be sure that the Provisional Government was sound. It 'leaves nothing to be desired', he wrote from Petrograd in early April.[24] The more astute General Knox was not convinced, however, so London was left wondering whom it could trust. The Bolsheviks (whom it called 'extremists' and 'maximalists') would certainly be something more than an annoyance if they succeeded in turning Russia against the war.

The question of allied solidarity was no longer theoretical
on the Sunday morning when Lenin was due to cross the
border. Nivelle's main onslaught on the western front was
scheduled to begin at first light on Monday. Originally, the
idea had been for Russia to attack at the same time, but
France and Britain were now reconciled to a delay. They
were content for Russian troops to hold the line along the
eastern front, tying up enemy divisions and vital war supplies. The allies could barely ask for less, and yet the enterprise
was still bedevilled by mischief-making civilians in Petrograd. Even Kerensky suddenly seemed bent on pandering to
the hard left.[25] The minister of justice had taken to harping
on about the unacceptability of annexations and indemnities, challenging the allies to renounce their cherished war
aims by reminding them that the Soviet was in the hands of
socialists. The only leverage London or Paris had was economic aid. In April 1917, the British held back a consignment
of heavy artillery, originally destined for Russia, on the
grounds that it could more usefully be deployed elsewhere.
The government of the United States, a recent entrant to this
game, considered withholding a promised war loan of even
greater magnificence if Russia gave in to the pacifists.[26]

In the week leading up to the Nivelle campaign, it had
come as a great relief to every allied Russia-watcher when the
anti-war left seemed to retreat. *Pravda* had modified its tone
(thanks to the influence of Kamenev), and Tsereteli was
working miracles in the Soviet. In Moscow, Lockhart still
considered the Bolsheviks to be 'the most unsatisfactory element', adding that their ranks 'would seem to contain
German provocateurs; and [they] are very possibly supported

by German money'. As he continued, however, 'it would be extremely rash to express any opinion at so early a stage of the revolution, but I am of the opinion that the socialist campaign is rather losing ground. Their newspapers are less read than at first, and once the novelty of their attacks wears off, they may find it hard to obtain the necessary funds for their propaganda. Strong counter-propaganda has already begun, and one result of the socialist campaign has been to unite all the more moderate elements of the population.'[27] In Petrograd, Buchanan tended to agree.[28]

The last thing that the allies needed, then, was the sudden appearance of Lenin himself. Whitehall had no consistent picture of the man (one note lumped him in with the other 'foreign scallywags'), but British files, which dated from the pre-war visits he had made to London, hinted at some of his disturbing talents.[29] More recently, the wildest rumours had begun to build. According to Herr Stenning, a socialist envoy in Copenhagen, Lenin had 'displayed violent animosity towards England' during his day-long stay in Stockholm. His rhetoric had given credence to a new story, now making the rounds in Amsterdam, that 'peace between Russia and Germany would be declared within a fortnight.'[30] For a moment, the British considered retaliating with a Trojan horse of their own. If the Germans could use Lenin, then maybe Britain could dispatch some other Russian activist 'to try to tell Russia what would happen if the war were not vigorously prosecuted'. They had already waved Plekhanov through, but some imagined that they might get better results from an ex-nihilist known to the intelligence services as Alexis Aledin. Without a party of followers, however, Aledin was not only a loose cannon but a dud, and the note on his file, dated 29 March, reads 'let him sleep.'[31]

It was a pity that the wretched Swiss had let the Bolshe-viks get on their train at all. Even the gentle Prince Lvov had informed an official in Bern that the departure of Lenin's party from Zurich had been 'a considerable embarrass-ment'.[32] There was a rumour that Paul Miliukov had compiled a list of names and was attempting to compel his colleagues to ban those on it from entering Russia.[33] If true, then Lenin and his friends would not be making trouble in the east for long. But the allies' best opportunity to stop him lay in Tornio. The British had an officer on duty there. He could work covertly, taking advantage of the bustle and the chaos, to say nothing of the fog. All he would have to do to save the day was make sure that one particular Bolshevik never got home.

The Russians' sledges drew up at the guard post on the Finn-ish side. The landscape here was one the travellers already knew, for border controls – barked orders, little desks and metal grilles – were part of life for every European revolu-tionary. In the past, as Shlyapnikov had found, the guards at Tornio had been unusually vigilant, but the red flag on the roof this time suggested a change of mood, maybe even of personnel. The Germans, too, were counting on the new regime to be more lax. As one of their reports explained: 'Formerly at Tornio there were sixty-five officials who searched all travellers most carefully, now there are only six-teen soldiers who get through the control very quickly.'[34] A group of local people had already gathered round the Finn-ish customs house, eager to bombard the new arrivals with questions. Dragging their cases, holding the two children's hands, Lenin's party filed into the military hut.

Whatever they had expected, it was not to be separated

into male and female groups. The questioning that followed was close and persistent. The minute inspection of their luggage continued for hours – even the children's books were searched – and some of the travellers were asked to strip down to their underwear. In the past, in the days of tsarist repression, a revolutionary might indeed have sewn her corsetry with secret documents, but this was meant to be a free Russia. As everyone had expected, Fritz Platten was turned back at once. The loyal Swiss would spend three fruitless days in Haparanda, hoping for a change of heart that never came.[35] But Russian citizens had different rights. Lenin was questioned for hours, a process that appeared to be intentionally slow. Again and again, he was obliged to repeat the story that he was a journalist on his way home. Hours passed while no one dared to ask what might be going on. Meanwhile, behind another door, the wire to Petrograd had crackled into life. A British officer in Tornio was trying to raise Miliukov.

The story remains shadowy; a lot of people later claimed to have been in that hut. In 1919, in a rambling article in the *New York Times,* an American ex-serviceman called Lieutenant A. W. Kliefoth took responsibility for approving Lenin's passage. The anti-Soviet mood in his country had built to such a point by then that it made sense to write that the Bolshevik group 'travelled in a sealed train so that Lenin's propaganda would not leak out in Germany'. Despite this bleary grasp of facts, Kliefoth claimed to have worked in Tornio as an allied passport officer. 'The first who came were patriots,' he wrote. 'They came singly and in twos or threes, and joined the army to fight the Germans.' It was a different matter when Lenin and his group appeared. Kliefoth reported that his colleague telegraphed Kerensky in Petrograd to find out if an error had been made; he could not quite believe that such a person could be ushered through. The minister of justice had replied (with the pomposity that was his ultimate undoing) that democratic Russia did not refuse entry to its citizens. With that, there was no option but to let the subversives go home.[36]

There is another version of the tale, however, and the villain this time is a British officer. According to Colonel Boris Nikitin, the head of the Provisional Government's makeshift counter-intelligence team, his British counterpart in Russia, Stephen (now Major) Alley, had approached him in early April to ask for help in dealing with 'a list of thirty traitors, headed by Lenin' who were due to cross the border 'in five days'. Nikitin called into the ministry of foreign affairs, hoping to find Miliukov, but the obliging foreign minister was out of town. His deputy, Neratov, would not sign the required warrant.[37] That left only one option to Alley. His man in Tornio, Harold Gruner, known to his comrades as 'the Spy', would have to deal with Lenin at the border, whatever the Russians said.

Gruner did everything he could. He strip-searched Lenin and he questioned him, he rifled through the books and papers in a play for time, but in the end, just before six in the evening, he nodded to the Russian official whose job it was to wield the rubber stamp. His reasoning was that he could do nothing else, for he was a junior adviser and a foreigner on Russian soil. But he never forgot that he had been the man who had, as he put it, 'actually let Lenin into Russia'. 'Were he Japanese', remarked his friend William Gerhardie, Gruner 'would have committed hari-kari'.[38] The other person who did not forget was Lenin himself, who lost no time when he had taken power in Soviet Russia before sentencing

Gruner to death. The penalty was never carried out, however, and the Spy was later free to join the British expedition
against the Bolsheviks in Siberia. Gruner thereby notched
up not one but two heroic failures, for which a grateful
George V awarded him an OBE.[39]

The Bolsheviks were jubilant. Lenin had always breathed
more easily in Finland; now people crowded round to ask
what their Grand Duchy could expect in the new era of
post-tsarist rule. A special session of the Finnish parliament,
the Eduskunta, had opened a few days before. Dominated
by socialists, its debates had raised the Finnish people's hopes,
and even in these northern villages the farmers were hungry
for further news. Tired though he was, Lenin delivered a few
encouraging words on Finnish freedom, no doubt keeping a
tactful silence on the issue of world civil war. That done, he
made his way to the local post office (conveniently open for
business on Easter Sunday) to send a telegram to his sisters
in Petrograd. 'Arriving Monday 11 p.m.,' it read. 'Inform
Pravda. Ulyanov.'

The Russians were so happy that they barely noticed their
rough seats. The carriages were not quite full – at one point
Lenin sat in an entirely empty one – but they were basic,
Russian and hard class. Nothing could have suited the travellers more. To read their stories of the journey down the
Finnish coast is to sense them expanding, breathing out,
almost as if they were getting used to the extra space that
Russia's wide-gauge track afforded them. They rattled south
in darkness for some hours, chatting to fellow countrymen
and snatching a few hours of sleep. By dawn they were clear
of the snow, albeit in a grey-brown landscape yet to feel the
spring. The soothing clatter of the wheels was broken for an

hour or two when they changed trains, just north of Helsingfors, to join the line to Terijoki and onwards to Petrograd.
Lenin barely looked up from his reading. He had talked to a
few soldiers at one point (his peace in that empty carriage
had been short-lived), but he was more interested in the
newspapers in his lap.

Lenin had bought his first issues of *Pravda* as soon as he
arrived in Finland. The paper was still hard to find, especially so far from Petrograd, so these were treasure, and
Lenin had started leafing through while he was still in the
customs house at Tornio. As he began to smooth the pages
flat, he permitted himself a moment's satisfaction at the idea
of his party's paper coming out in free Russia, but then (and
all too soon) he actually read the thing. Like many writers, he
may well have looked for his own contribution first, for he
had sent two pieces (his first 'Letters from Afar') to Russia
in the care of Alexandra Kollontai. However carefully he
searched, however, he could find only one of them. It had
been printed (at the bottom of the inside pages) on 21 and
22 March (3–4 April), but the section calling for a boycott of
the bourgeois government had been removed.[40] His suspicions aroused, he noted more deletions from the piece; the
cuts were evidently systematic and deliberate.

It was also clear (as he read on) that there were Bolsheviks
in Petrograd who were actively contemplating an alliance
with a faction of like-minded Mensheviks. A critical article
by the left-wing Bolshevik Molotov on 28 March/10 April
could not be read in any other way. Lenin had been prepared
for a fight when he got to Russia. It was not as if he had failed
to make his ideas absolutely plain. His telegram of early
March had been explicit: no support for the Provisional
Government, no co-operation with other parties.[41] His

'Letters from Afar' had called for a transfer of power from the bourgeois 'agents of British capital' to a workers' militia or to soviets. The whole line ruled out any coalition with the Mensheviks. The war, he had insisted, was a bloody capitalist adventure, and not what Kamenev was now calling a fight for revolutionary self-defence.

Speaking of Kamenev, of course, he soon came to the article about defending Russia against German guns. He knew his old friend's soft and donnish ways, but never could Lenin concede that the revolutionaries' wartime duty was to help maintain a disciplined front against the Hun. The paper's politics appeared confused, its tone verging on blandness. As he read on, the Bolshevik leader realized how far the party (or at least his own lieutenants) had strayed from the ideas that he had been drumming into it. Lenin was a relentless communicator – the master of the death-grip – and he now planned to outspeak and outwrite his vacillating followers. He would bang tables, strike out words, he would gather the faithful, work on Kamenev. Then came a sudden, chilling shock. Zinoviev remembered that the leader's face was ashen. 'Malinovsky', he shouted, 'has turned out to be a provocateur.'[42]

This time the blow was personal ('The swine,' fumed Lenin, 'shooting is too good for him'). As he read *Pravda*'s scathing commentary on Roman Malinovsky's dealings with the old secret police, the Bolshevik leader must have thought back to the allegations of 1914, the angry rumours that he had dismissed at that brief trial in Poronin. As *Pravda* distanced itself from the traitor, Lenin may also have remembered a letter he had sent to Malinovsky only weeks before, containing greetings from his wife and relating all their recent news from Switzerland.[43] Proof of the double-agent's treachery was now in front of him in black and white, along with the case against that pre-war editor of *Pravda*, Miron Chernomazov. Both, it turned out, had been working for the tsarist secret police for years. The story was not new by April, but (to judge by a piece by Eremeev in the issue for 29 March/11 April) *Pravda*'s editors were still having to pay for it. The situation was in fact far worse than Lenin could yet know. Spinning a web of innuendo, some writers had started alluding to a rumour that the Bolshevik Party and its newspaper were funded by 'German millions'.[44] Petrograd was full of jokes on the theme, and in some circles *Pravda* itself had been dubbed 'Provocateur'. It was not hard to imagine how Lenin's own adventure in the German lands was set to be portrayed.

It was already dark when Lenin's train slowed for the border at Beloostrov. Though Finland was a Russian province, it had kept some of its freedoms. The real Russia, with all its prisons, gendarmes and repressive laws, began at Beloostrov, a fact that called for yet another well-staffed guard post. According to Nikitin, it was here that patriotic passengers were urged to point out any suspicious-looking travellers to the local police.[45] Fresh from his reading of *Pravda*, Lenin braced himself for a long interrogation. Instead, his train was all but mobbed. Lev Kamenev had warned the comrades that 'Ilyich hates any kind of ceremony.'[46] As usual, his words had no effect at all.

It had been difficult to organize a fitting party. A telegram from Fürstenberg that should have warned the Bolsheviks about the time of Lenin's train had been held up, so the news arrived late, on Monday morning, when Lenin's sister Mariya informed the Central Committee about her brother's message from Tornio. With less than fifteen hours in hand,

Shlyapnikov worked on the welcome preparations at Petrograd's Finland Station, while a small detachment (including Kamenev and Fedor Raskolnikov) travelled the 25 miles to the border to meet the leader's train. They were joined by a group of enthusiastic workers from Petrograd, who squeezed on to the evening service for Beloostrov in the hope of a spectacle. By far the largest crowd on the platform, however, had come to the border station on foot from the provincial town of Sestroretsk. These people, veteran Bolsheviks from the local weapons factory, had walked nearly 10 miles to see their leader's train pull in.

The platform at the isolated halt was in darkness, and as they waited in the rain the men could barely make out their own neighbours' faces, let alone the banners they had made and brought along. 'At last,' Raskolnikov remembered, 'the three blinding lights of the locomotive rushed by us, and behind it the lighted windows of the carriages began to twinkle – more and more gently and slowly. The train stopped, and at once we perceived, over the crowd of workers, the figure of Comrade Lenin.'[47]

The conductor had told the Sestroretsk workers where to look for Lenin in the line of carriages. They rushed aboard before the train had even stopped and swept him out, carrying him shoulder high. Shocked, frightened and then overwhelmed, the leader was borne into the station hall. He was so relieved to be home that he kissed everyone in sight, including Raskolnikov (whom he had never met). As the young party worker remembered, 'the smile never left his face for a moment.' A few moments later, Kamenev joined the group, holding Zinoviev by the hand. Most of the Bolshevik exiles had crammed into the station hall by now, and Lenin climbed on to a chair to treat the room to an impromptu speech. He was still talking, smiling, blinking in the station lights when the bell rang for the train to leave for Petrograd.[48] The comrades all rushed to the same carriage at once, talking in chorus without drawing breath. At one point, Lenin turned to Kamenev and asked: 'What have you been writing in *Pravda*? We've seen a few copies and have called you all kinds of names.'[49] For the moment, in recognition of this gala night, there was no hint of menace in the question.

He could believe Kamenev now. There would be no police to arrest him at the Finland Station. What Lenin could not have imagined was the scale of the reception that his supporters had planned. On Easter Monday, and with very little time to prepare, the party had spurred all its local networks into action, even groups for whom the name of Lenin was an unfamiliar one. There were no newspapers over the public holiday, but Petrograd's poorer districts operated an informal bush telegraph, and soon thousands of people were talking about this new leader's return. Factory committees of Bolsheviks assembled and chose delegates to line the route. The banners were unfurled, resewn, and greeting placards painted. A military band assembled, though it had played the same music so often that rehearsal was unnecessary. After a scratch meeting at their base in Kronstadt, the sailors sent a detachment to Petrograd to act as a guard of honour.[50]

The Soviet Executive was also alerted to Lenin's approach. Unwilling to endorse the troublemaker from abroad, Tsereteli refused to go to the station to meet him. Instead, it fell to Chkheidze and Skobelev, neither of whom was glad to turn out late on Easter Monday night, to push their way through the enormous crowd and then sit like forlorn bridesmaids in the Finland Station's Imperial Waiting Room. The Ex Com had not opposed Lenin's return. It had not even objected to his accepting German help, though that had been a tougher call. But Chkheidze had already suffered many blows at the hands of the exiled leader, and he was not eager to invite another round. He also had a lot to lose, for the revolution had reached a delicate stage, relations with Lvov were improving, and there were hopes for peace-talks in Europe. The chairman of the Soviet, still deep in mourning for his son, sat dolefully rehearsing a welcoming speech while Skobelev cracked feeble jokes to pass the time.

Although he had not received a specific invitation, Sukhanov also joined them late that night. It took a while to get close to the station building, let alone to make his way inside. The crowds that blocked his route were vast, and there were soldiers, sailors, throbbing ranks of motor-cars. As he concluded, the Bolsheviks, who 'shone at organization', were clearly 'preparing for a really triumphal entry'.[51] There was more going on here than a reception for some travellers. The organizers were also trying to counteract the impression created by Lenin's decision to accept German help. If they had whispered about *Pravda*'s 'German millions' before, the bourgeois press now had a live traitor to shout about, a Russian who had just enjoyed the kaiser's hospitality. Making their leader look like a returning super-star was one way for the Bolsheviks to respond to a press campaign that even Sukhanov thought to be 'bristling with malice'.

Petrograd's Bolsheviks excelled themselves. Sukhanov found the station's main platform ablaze with red and gold. The route was hung with banners calling for peace and brotherhood, justice for the working class, freedom and revolution for the world. Triumphal arches spanned the track.

At the end, where the train was due to come to a halt, a band was waiting and there were women holding large (and expensive) bouquets. The organizers had even turned the lateness of the hour to their advantage. In two or three places, Sukhanov observed, 'the awe-inspiring outlines of armoured cars thrust up from the crowd. And from one of the side-streets there moved on to the square, startling the mob and cutting through it, a strange monster – a mounted searchlight, which abruptly projected on the bottomless void of the darkness tremendous strips of the living city, the roofs, many-storeyed houses, columns, wires, tramways, and human figures.'[52]

9. From the Finland Station

Stranglers of the revolution, by honeyed phrases –
Chkheidze, Tsereteli, Steklov – are dragging the
revolution back, away from the Soviets of Workers'
Deputies towards the undivided sway of the
bourgeoisie, towards the usual bourgeois
parliamentary republic.

V. I. Lenin

Lenin's train was late. Anticipation added to the drama as the crowd outside the station swelled with late-night passers-by. Though many chance onlookers barely knew who Lenin was, this was clearly shaping up to be a classic Vyborg night. It was already nearly midnight when someone picked out the lights of an approaching locomotive. Only one train was ever due at this hour. The band struck up the Marseillaise (a mistake: Lenin preferred the Internationale) and the sailors stood to attention. As Sukhanov had several times observed, the Bolsheviks could always be relied on for a spectacle.

The brakes went on, the rolling stopped, and Lenin stepped into a bitter cloud of fumes. Air that cold and that pungent was a shock after the train. A woman – was it Kollontai? – swam up and handed him a florist's bouquet of spring flowers, a pointless object in his view and one he did not want.[1] The blaze of colour was a fresh surprise: his eyes took in the scarlet banners, station lights, more flowers, and the flashing brass of cornets and trombones. Somewhere in this unexpected human sea, a guard of honour from the Second Baltic Fleet had just presented arms. In their blue uniforms and jaunty caps, the lads looked like hangovers from the old empire. Lenin was irritated by the show, which reeked of bourgeois pageantry and pride. Haloed by steam, he took the opportunity to tell the sailors and his loyal friends that they had made an error in their class analysis. The Provisional Government, he shouted, could only ever betray them. That done, the leader sprinted from the platform, making straight for the Imperial Waiting Room. Hurrying into the middle of that, wrote Sukhanov, 'he stopped still in front of Chkheidze as though he had run into a completely unexpected obstacle.'[2]

The 'obstacle' was speaking now. The Ex Com had committed itself to inclusive team-work, and Chkheidze was about to make an offer that came close to choking him. 'The principal task of the revolutionary democracy', he insisted, 'is now the defence of the revolution from any encroachments either from within or from without. We consider that what this goal requires is not disunion, but the closing of the democratic ranks.'[3] A sailor called out that he hoped that Lenin would become a member of the Provisional Government.[4] The leader of the Bolsheviks did not reply. Instead, after a short pause while he fiddled with those flowers, he turned to the rest of the assembled crowd (admittedly a small one, for he was still in the waiting room) and hailed a revolution that was set to sweep the entire globe. 'The piratical imperialist war is the beginning of civil war throughout Europe,' he announced. ' . . . Any day now the whole of

European capitalism may crash. The Russian revolution accomplished by you has prepared the way and opened a new epoch. Long live the worldwide socialist revolution!'[5]

The words were shocking and completely fresh, 'a bright, blinding exotic beacon', in Sukhanov's words, 'straight from the train . . . novel, harsh and somehow deafening'.[6] For a few moments, Sukhanov pictured himself as he had been in February, felt all the fire of his first hopes and even glimpsed how much of that momentum had been lost in the tactical manoeuvring of the past six weeks. But though his heart was telling him that, as he put it, 'Lenin was right a thousand times over,' he forced himself to disapprove. Like almost everyone else that night, he could not let himself be swayed by any heresy. When faced with such a challenge to the fragile compromises that the revolution had achieved, the correct response was to be scandalized.

Lenin was struggling, that was plain. He had not travelled back to join a coalition, nor did he expect pretty speeches and a military band. On the train from Beloostrov, he and his wife had been more worried about finding transport into the city. Ever practical, Krupskaya had pointed out that it was a public holiday as well as late (and no one in her group was sure what that meant for a city in the throes of revolution). Now mere impatience took the place of their concern about the trams. Lenin's group would never have got out of the station if Shlyapnikov, as master of ceremonies, had not cleared a path through the crowd. A few yards on, not one but many cars were waiting. Confused, excited, protesting, Lenin was lifted high by smiling strangers and passed above the mass of bodies to the gleaming bonnet of a car. He could not simply let this go, he had to seize the chance to speak.

Sukhanov, standing some way off within the crowd, could make out only isolated phrases: 'Shameful slaughter . . . lies and deceit . . .capitalist pirates . . .'[7]

The armoured car had been for show, but now its size and shape suggested a new kind of use. Through the confusion and the glaring lights, Sukhanov watched as Lenin was ushered up on to its turret. This part of the performance was entirely unrehearsed, but the leader took advantage of the platform instantly. Now raised above that mass of heads, he could project his words to all. He was still shouting at full voice, a wild messiah in round hat, tie and flapping coat, when the driver began to pull away from Station Square. The mounted searchlight followed, sweeping round the city as the procession made its way over the Sampson Bridge to the Petrograd Side. With Lenin and his entourage marched hundreds of admiring citizens, and though some must have been committed Bolsheviks, large numbers had been drawn along by the spectacle itself and (in snatches caught on the chill midnight breeze) by Lenin's astonishing words.

As far as anyone could guess, the man up on the armoured car was telling them that they had been betrayed; he seemed to promise longed-for peace but talked of class struggle and victory. No one made out each last detail, but his slogans felt like a sudden electric shock after six weeks of compromise and confusion: a call to life, a blinding glimpse of futures some had privately begun to doubt. At each crossroads along their route, the vehicles paused so that Lenin could roar at a fresh crowd, waving that hat and summoning the proletariat to fulfil its historic task. 'The triumph', Sukhanov conceded, 'had come off brilliantly.'[8]

The Bolsheviks' destination was to be their new headquarters in the capital. Where once that might have meant a dismal flat, the armoured car was heading for a mansion in a leafy district not far from the Peter-Paul Fortress. Built for the ballerina Mathilde Kshesinskaya, a former mistress of Nicholas II, it was an art deco palace with a substantial hall for private performances, an exotic winter garden for sub-tropical palms and a balcony on the first floor that opened on to a wide street. The whole estate, complete with a gazebo large enough for a rhinoceros, was more or less opposite the British embassy, whose own balcony faced it from the other side of the Neva.

The diplomats had seen the uproar when the Bolsheviks had commandeered the place. Kshesinskaya had been in residence at the time, though she took refuge elsewhere as the first profaning boots began to trample in. Before long, a red banner was billowing from the front windows, and in time the whole building was draped with them. It was a strange fate for the residence of a woman who had starred in the gala performance of *The Sleeping Beauty* for the allied del-egation not two months before.[9] Local people believed that Kshesinskaya had been targeted, in a city wracked by fuel-shortages, because she had a huge stockpile of boiler-coal, the gift of a well-connected grand duke.[10] Whatever the reason, the mansion, once so feminine, now served as prem-ises for the Bolshevik Central Committee. The antique furniture had been removed, the palms were dying and the silk-lined boudoir reeked of onions and cheap hand-rolled cigarettes.

On the night of Lenin's return, as the car-engines cooled in the courtyard below, the final touches were being added to a generous late-night buffet in a room on the first floor. Meanwhile, in Kshesinskaya's white recital room, where pride of place was still claimed by a grand piano from Berlin, old friends were embracing, laughing, all talking at once. A lesser man might have joined his colleagues beside the samovar, but Lenin did not linger in the midst of the mêlée. Instead, he found his way upstairs and out on to the balcony.

It was the only place in the main building that was visible to passers-by beyond the garden walls. Kshesinskaya's nearest neighbour, just a silhouette of dark on dark at this late hour, was the Petrograd mosque, and all around was open space with ghostly, leafless parkland trees. Leaning into the night, Lenin could sense the perfect opportunity to make a speech. 'Germany is in ferment,' he told the small crowd that still lingered in the shadows below. In Britain, he bellowed, the anti-war agitator John Maclean had been imprisoned. The names and details might have been a little alien to Russian ears, but the news was thrilling and the speaker's hoarse but raging tone entirely original. It was only when Lenin began to rail against the capitalist war that the atmosphere started to curdle. 'Ought to stick our bayonets into a fellow like that,' a soldier shouted. ' . . . Must be a German.'[11]

Although he went inside at last, it would be a while before the leader got to drink his tea. At about two o'clock in the morning, Lenin's Bolshevik hosts called everyone to order for the formal speeches of welcome. These had been carefully rehearsed and featured all the usual clichés about democracy and freedom and the progress that was being made. 'Lenin endured them like an impatient pedestrian waiting in a doorway for the rain to stop,' wrote Trotsky (though he was not there).[12] The charade was as stifling as the ruched white curtains at the ballerina's windows. The last hand-clapping had yet to die away when Lenin launched into an aggressive and even frightening reply. His performance was a tour de force by any standards, but for a man of middle age who had just spent eight days and nights on perilous slow-moving trains, it was miraculous.

He lectured his comrades for two whole hours. The only person who kept a record at the time was Sukhanov, who had been smuggled in by Kamenev. 'I will never forget that thunderlike speech,' he wrote. 'I am certain that no one had expected anything of the sort. It seemed as if all the elements had risen from their abodes, and the spirit of universal destruction, knowing neither barriers nor doubts, neither human difficulties nor human calculations, was hovering around Kshesinskaya's reception-room above the heads of the bewitched disciples.'[13] When Trotsky tried to picture the effect, he imagined a teacher's wet sponge being drawn across a blackboard, wiping clean the confused scribbles of a very dim pupil.[14]

The thunder rolled as Lenin accused his old friends. He attacked the Provisional Government (which they had been advising everyone to tolerate) and dismissed any collusion with it as 'the death of socialism'. More thunder crashed as he denounced revolutionary defencism ('a betrayal of socialism') and rejected the idea of coalition with any socialist party – the Mensheviks especially – because they had acquiesced in the continuation of the war. But his insistence that the first phase of the revolution was at an end was the mightiest bolt of all. 'The specific feature of the present situation', Lenin declared, was that society was 'passing from the first stage of the revolution . . . to its second stage, which must place power in the hands of the proletariat and the poorest sections of the peasantry'.[15] The idea was so mad that it reduced the room to silence.

The whole point was to understand the hidden politics of class. The bourgeoisie, Lenin explained, could never give up on the war, for their future was bound to it. It was a mistake to expect them to abandon their quest for plunder, too, and any concession they appeared to make would be a trap. By working with the bourgeoisie, the Mensheviks in the Ex Com had betrayed the whole future of the revolution, and any Bolshevik who advocated an alliance with such people was doing the same. '*Pravda* demands of the government that it should renounce annexations,' Lenin declared. 'To demand of a government of capitalists that it should renounce annexations is nonsense, a crying mockery.'[16] The meetings about forms of words, the little victories over war aims, the deals and phone calls in the night – all were dismissed as vanity and foolishness. It was time for the proletariat to look to a future in which it would take power itself. As Sukhanov remembered, the effect was to confirm 'Lenin's complete intellectual isolation, not only among Social-Democrats in general but also among his own disciples'.[17] By the small hours of the next day, even Krupskaya was heard saying to a friend: 'I am afraid it looks as if Lenin has gone crazy.'[18]

Almost no one could credit that Russia's people were ready for power. When they had coaxed the politicians of the Duma into forming a Provisional Government, the Mensheviks (including Sukhanov) had been relieved. They had all been convinced that the revolution would be doomed unless a few respectable figures stepped in to lead it, the kind that generals and bankers could be induced to accept, the kind that armies follow without question. This calculation had been based in part on the well-grounded fear of counter-revolutionary military force, but there were theoretical considerations, too. For almost every socialist who witnessed it, what was happening in February 1917 was a march towards democracy and liberal reform. The pace might be a little brisk by world standards, but Russia's task was to trace the route that Britain had blazed, that France had followed in its 'bourgeois' revolution of 1848, the route that led to parliaments and party politics and a free press. Socialism, which required the people to take control of everything from economic life to war and peace, was not thought to be possible in a land of boorish peasants. In private, moreover, a good many socialists in Petrograd had been more than a little terrified of responsibility in any form.

Although at first some Bolsheviks had disagreed, their leaders in the Russian capital had more or less kept to this line. Indeed, they had started to act and think more like a loyal opposition than a revolutionary force. Now Lenin told them that they had been making a mistake. The muddled feuds and complex arguments in *Pravda* were irrelevant. Though he accepted that the compromise of February had been everyone's error (a lapse arising from what he called 'the insufficient class-consciousness and organization of the proletariat'), there could be no excuses now. The Bolsheviks must prepare the workers and poor peasants for a transfer of state power. To most of his audience, this was not just bad Marxist theory; it was an invitation to political suicide.

The sole crumb of comfort was that Lenin did not call for instant revolutionary action. He recognized that his ideas were out of tune with current orthodoxy, and that it would be 'necessary with particular thoroughness, persistence and patience' to explain them to the revolutionary masses. The mention of patience (a word that did not feature much in Lenin's lexicon) suggested that there might be time to talk some sense into the ill-informed newcomer after he had slept a bit. But this was an extremely fragile straw, and almost no one in the audience opted to clutch at it. The only person who defended Lenin that night was Alexandra Kollontai, whose sympathetic comments brought down 'mockery, laughter, and hubbub'.[19] Lenin did not seem to mind the criticism or the snubs. He concluded his long speech with a threat that his party had heard before. 'You comrades have a trusting attitude to the government. If that is so, our paths diverge. I prefer to remain in a minority.'[20]

In the course of the next few days (beginning, after that late night, at noon the next day, 4/17 April 1917), Lenin defended his ideas at meetings of the Bolshevik Central Committee Bureau and at the local Petersburg Committee. On no occasion were his proposals accepted; the Petersburg Committee rejected them by thirteen votes to two.[21] The first discussion ended early because the Central Committee had already scheduled a coalition meeting with the Mensheviks for the afternoon. 'At this "unifying" conference,' Sukhanov would remember, 'Lenin was the living incarnation of schism.'[22] The leader appeared out of touch, the victim of his long exile. Yet Lenin did not abandon his explosive ideas. They were summarized, soon after the fateful speech in the ballerina's mansion, in the shortest treatise that he ever wrote. 'The April Theses', published in *Pravda* on 7 April, ran to just 579 words.

When they get to Lenin's impact, textbooks about the revolution often cite the short slogan: 'Bread, Peace and Land'. In fact, those words had been part of the Bolshevik

20. (*top*) Barrels awaiting transport through Haparanda-Tornio during the First World War. Though these were said to contain tar, similar ones were used to smuggle sanctions-busting contraband through Sweden.

21. (*bottom*) Sacks of international post at Tornio. The office here was vital to wartime communications between Europe, Russia and the Far East.

22. (*right*) Lenin on his way to Petrograd in the sealed train. A romantic view by Soviet artist P. V. Vasiliev (1899–1975). The real carriage was too small for such a large assembly, and the Russian section had no armed soldiers in it.

23. (*below*) The Customs House in Tornio during the First World War.

24. (*above*) Lenin's arrival at the Finland Station, April 1917, in a painting by M. G. Sokolov (1875–1953). With no regard for history (but a keen sense of self-preservation), the artist added Stalin to the scene.

25. (*below*) The Finland Station in the 1910s.

26. (*left*) Lenin speaking on the Balcony of Kshesinskaya's Mansion on the night of 3 (16)–(4) 17 April 1917. Painting by A. M. Lyubimov (1879–1955).

27. (*above*) Kshesinskaya's mansion and its balcony today.

28. (*below*) The prow-shaped drawing-room at the Elizarov Apartment Museum, St Petersburg.

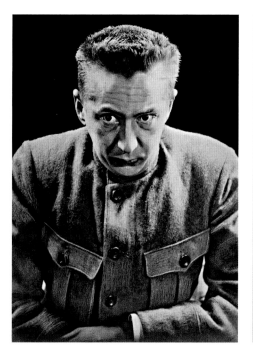

29. (*top left*) Alexander Fedorovic Kerensky at the height of his fame.

30. (*top right*) Death in the guise of an Englishman: cover of the German satirical magazine *Kladderadatsch* for 8 April 1917, the eve of Lenin's departure from Zurich.

31. (*bottom*) Soviet-era painting by Isaak Brodsky (1883–1939) showing Lenin addressing workers at Petrograd's Putilov factory in May 1917.

32. (*top*) Petrograd on 1 May 1917. Gathering on Palace Square. The banners call for a republic, land and liberty.

33. (*bottom*) Lenin's office at the headquarters of *Pravda*, April–July 1917. The room was re-created to match the painting on display at the far end.

34. (*above left*) Finnish Railways Steam Locomotive No. 293. The engine that pulled Lenin's train in April 1917 was not preserved, so this one, which helped him flee to Finland in July, enjoyed the honour in its place.

35. (*above right*) Fritz Platten's memoir of the sealed train was published in 1924, the year of Lenin's death.

36. (*below*) Memorial at Sassnitz. This is the Empress Carriage, built in 1912. Though not the 'sealed' car itself, the relic gave a focus to the town's small Lenin museum throughout the lifetime of the GDR.

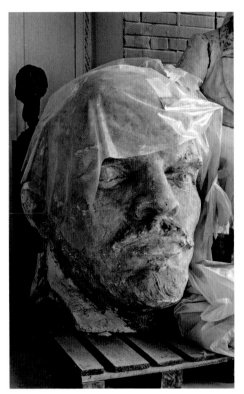

37. (*above left*) Lenin in the cupboard: discarded model plaster head from the Memorial Workshop of Sculptor M. K. Anikushin (1917–1997), St Petersburg.
38. (*above right*) Lenin in the nude: plaster model created to inspire and guide the work of sculptor M. K. Anikushin.
39. (*right*) Lenin in triumph: Sergei Evseev's 1926 statue of the leader at the Finland Station, St Petersburg.

mantra for weeks. What was new, deriving from Lenin's analysis of class, were the positions on the war and the revolution. Although the leader was tactful enough to avoid referring to a worldwide civil war, his first thesis was a direct attack on current socialist orthodoxy. The present war, he insisted, 'unquestionably remains on Russia's part a predatory imperialist war' and 'not the slightest concession to "revolutionary defencism" is permissible.' The way ahead lay in a revolution against capitalism, for 'without overthrowing capital, it is impossible to end the war by a truly democratic peace, a peace not imposed by violence.'[23] The second thesis repeated the class-based analysis of revolution that had shocked his comrades on the night of 3–4 April. 'We must ably, carefully, clear people's minds,' he wrote in a note to himself, 'and lead the proletariat and poor peasantry forward, away from "dual power" towards the full power of the Soviet of Workers' Deputies.'[24]

There was no sense, he urged, in waiting for the bourgeoisie to turn into a revolutionary force. It was already bent on the defence of property, profit and caste. 'No support for the Provisional Government,' Lenin wrote. 'The utter falsity of all its promises should be made clear, particularly of those relating to the renunciation of annexations.' In private notes in defence of this line, Lenin also dismissed the Menshevik leaders of the Soviet Ex Com – the self-appointed titans of the left – as 'stranglers of the revolution'. 'The "revolutionary defencism" of the Soviet of Workers' Deputies, i.e. of Chkheidze, Tsereteli and Steklov,' he scribbled, 'is a chauvinist trend a hundred times more harmful for being cloaked in honeyed phrases, an attempt to reconcile the masses with the Provisional Revolutionary Government.'[25]

The remaining theses dealt with the governance of any

future revolutionary state. With brief, almost manic strokes of his pen, Lenin sketched out a soviet system: 'not a parliamentary republic . . . but a Republic of Soviets of Workers', Agricultural Labourers' and Peasants' Deputies throughout the country, from top to bottom. Abolition of the police, the army and the bureaucracy.' Lenin also proposed that the banking system should be nationalized and that officials' salaries should be restricted so that even high-ranking advisers could earn no more than 'the average wage of a competent worker'. As for the land, the issue that concerned the largest number of future Soviet citizens, Lenin's plan did not envisage giving it to peasants. Instead, he called for it to be entrusted to the state. Like the limiting of official salaries and the abolition of police, this proposal would prove more difficult to implement than the proletarian dictatorship itself, but no one could have guessed that in the early spring. Most readers were too busy wondering how Lenin had managed to lose his mind.

His critics raised the issue of his journey home. The right-wing press was most forthright, openly attacking the Bolshevik leader for striking a deal with Germany's blood-stained tyranny. 'It is a great pity', sneered Miliukov's newspaper, *Rech*, 'that the conditions of the Bolshevik leader's arrival are such that even in the socialist camp they can provoke at best only a feeling of dismay . . . No citizen of Russia deems it possible to manifest his love of peace by rendering services to an enemy who is ravaging his country.'[26] The smear would prove indelible, but Lenin had prepared his own riposte. He placed an article in *Pravda* on exactly the same day, choosing to lash out at the British and French governments for refusing, in their own military interests, to grant safe passage to all returning Russian citizens. A debate about Lenin's relations with the enemy had already been tabled in the Soviet Ex Com. 'We shall make a report of our journey to the Executive Committee of the Soviet of Workers' and Soldiers' Deputies,' the leader continued. 'We hope that the latter will obtain . . . a permit for all emigrants, not only the social-patriots, to return to Russia.'[27]

Lenin received a mixed response in the Ex Com. Though no one went as far as to condemn him openly, Tsereteli managed to insinuate that the Germans might have used the exiled Bolshevik for their own ends.[28] The meeting's mood was not improved by Lenin's mulish attitude. Instead of meekly explaining 'How We Arrived', he soon returned to the terrain of the 'April Theses'. It was the line that he would always take. 'Lenin was a hopeless failure at the Soviet yesterday,' reported a gleeful Miliukov. 'He argued the pacifist cause so heatedly, and with such effrontery and lack of tact, that he was compelled to stop and leave the room amidst a storm of booing. He will never survive it.'[29] Though Miliukov was not impartial, it did appear that every socialist in sight was scandalized. One member of the audience called Lenin's speech 'the ravings of a madman', while Fedor Dan, another of Tsereteli's 'Siberian' Mensheviks, described it as 'the [Bolshevik] party's funeral'.[30] As Kerensky would later confide to a government colleague, Lenin seemed to be 'living in a completely isolated atmosphere, he knows nothing and sees everything through the lens of his own fantasies, and he has no one to help him get his bearings on what is going on.'[31]

His party was not reconciled, but only Kamenev ventured to challenge Lenin's views in print. The idea that the workers should seize power now, he wrote in *Pravda*, 'proceeds from the assumption that the bourgeois-democratic revolution is completed, and builds on the immediate transformation of this revolution into a socialist revolution'.[32] It was a criticism every Menshevik would have echoed, a view that called for patience, calm and good solid committee work. But Lenin was not demanding the immediate introduction of socialism, nor trying to create an earthly paradise at once. Repeatedly, he insisted that the point was not merely to build on any revolutionary gains, but to defend them from the class whose very nature was opposed to true democracy and peace. The Marxist talk of bourgeois-democratic revolution was now obsolete, he said. 'It is no good at all. It is dead. And it is no use trying to revive it.'[33]

If Lenin had not conquered his party, and if he had not also gained a following outside it in the next two months, the 'April Theses' might have disappeared into the mousy corner of an archive. One reason for his triumph was the force of his conviction. While others talked and traded exquisite concessions, picking their way along the path of revolution as if they were avoiding mines, Lenin knew where he wanted to go and he knew exactly why. His energy was prodigious, and he wrote and argued tirelessly, repeating the same themes until his opponents wearied of concocting new rebuttals. 'Lenin displayed such amazing force,' wrote Sukhanov, 'such superhuman power of attack that his colossal influence over the Socialists and revolutionaries was secure.'[34] The Bolshevik Party had been his creation in the first place, and he had a long record of triumphing over any rival in its ranks. As for the rest, his ideas sometimes did the trick, but it was that dynamic energy that held the loyalty of followers when all else failed.

There was a good deal more to Lenin's victory, however,

than sheer brute force. Above all else, he had struck upon a kind of truth that people would soon want to hear. The finer details of constitutional change were irrelevant to hungry workers or impatient garrison troops. Tsereteli might lead the Soviet Ex Com into protracted talks about war aims, but the people on the streets had made the revolution to secure peace, jobs and bread. As the euphoria of having toppled a hated regime began to dissipate, the problems that had driven them to risk their lives for freedom in the first place resurfaced, often with redoubled force.

The war had wrecked the European trade-system, and fighting it had emptied Russia's stocks of everything from food to medicines and fuel. Price inflation increased because of shortages. Factories closed for the same reason, leaving workers without pay. The transport crisis did not ease, supplies of flour and coal stayed scarce. Though Russia's problems were not unique (almost all European economies were facing comparable calamities), it was striking that the liberals of Petrograd could think of nothing more imaginative than giving pre-war rules another try. They wanted order, property and due legal process, they wanted educated voters to create a civilized new state, but the truth was that they were at war. Every bloodstained day of that helped to destroy the prospects for a new democracy. Whatever Miliukov might say, or even Tsereteli with his formula for compromise, it was not clear why anyone was fighting any more.

The problems were so evident that Lenin had not been the only one to notice them. There were elements in the lower ranks of the Bolshevik Party who were beginning to arrive at similar conclusions without his help. The Vyborg Committee had never been happy with the concept of dual power, the left was critical of Kamenev's *Pravda*, and there were radicals in Petrograd who could not stomach any truce with Menshevism. To that extent, the leader's words struck home because parts of his audience were well prepared. But a new tide of activists was also flooding in. From a relatively small movement (23,600 members) in February 1917, Bolshevik numbers had swelled to just under 80,000 by the end of April.[35] Unlike the older ranks of party stalwarts, whose lives had taught them how to play a longer game, the new wave were shop-floor radicals who wanted more than talk and promises.

Younger, more optimistic and often ready for a fight (Colonel Nikitin, the head of Petrograd counter-intelligence, described them as 'the dregs of the nation'),[36] the new recruits knew little about ideology or the niceties of Zimmerwald internationalism. They joined the Bolshevik Party because it was known to be the most extreme, the party of the dispossessed, the one whose members talked the toughest line. By April, some had started to resent the hesitations of the current leadership. In a process that almost every revolution comes to face, the joy of liberation was beginning to give way to envious, watchful impatience. 'Almost everywhere in the provinces,' Trotsky would write, 'there were Left Bolsheviks accused of maximalism, even anarchism. These worker revolutionaries only lacked the theoretical resources to defend their position. But they were ready to respond to the first call.'[37] It did not need a Lenin to ignite these people's zeal. In many ways, they were ahead of him.

So far ahead were some, indeed, that Lenin soon found himself issuing a call for calm. The atmosphere in Petrograd was growing tenser almost by the hour. 'We have received a number of reports,' Lenin declared to readers of *Pravda* on 15/28 April, 'written as well as oral, concerning threats of violence, bomb threats, etc. . . . We not only have not been guilty, directly or indirectly, of any threats of violence against individuals, but, on the contrary, we have always maintained that our task is to explain our views to all the people.'[38] Mere explanation, however, had started looking just a little feeble to some of Petrograd's hard-working poor. 'It was becoming harder and harder to live,' Trotsky explained. 'Prices had risen alarmingly; the workers were demanding a minimum wage; the bosses were resisting; the number of conflicts in the factories was continually growing; the food situation was getting worse; bread rations were being cut down; cereal cards had been introduced; dissatisfaction in the garrison had grown.'[39] Then came a pause. On 18 April/1 May, the city once more gathered on the streets.

The occasion was a public holiday, the festival of international labour, and it was also an opportunity (one of the last) to celebrate the dreams of February. Among the many witnesses was a French politician, Albert Thomas, who had arrived in Russia a fortnight before. His diary entry for that night reads like a requiem for innocence:

> The demonstrations . . . are like religious processions. The crowd is gentle, calm and orderly. The voices are pure. On Nevsky Prospect, a procession of prisoners [of war] distributes leaflets calling for a war to the finish against the Germans. On the square outside the Winter Palace, the crowd is enormous. A crowd of nuns, all in white, has gathered on the palace balconies. On the red bridge . . . an immense procession is going by: it is made up of the most

varied groups: revolutionary groups, groups from the villages round Petrograd, groups of professors and students from the Botanic Garden, with large palms and large crowns emblazoned with crosses made of red immortelles. Banners proclaim the accord between free Science and a free people. Groups of people from Turkestan, Muslims, with banners proclaiming freedom of conscience, freedom of religion, freedom to write in any language. From every side, the Marseillaise, in a slow tempo. The Square of Mars Field is littered everywhere with red flags . . .[40]

This was the day Miliukov chose to issue the diplomatic note that ended his career. He timed it cleverly, so it was only on 19 April/2 May, as the palms and red banners were being cleared away, that the press got hold of the wording. The whole of Petrograd had known that there was pressure from the Ex Com for the Provisional Government to clarify its new policy on war aims to its allies and the world. In time, the ministers agreed that their Declaration of 27 March, the one that had cost so much wrangling, should be reissued as a formal Diplomatic Note.[41] A binding document like this would certainly put paid to any plan for Russian expansion in the Black Sea region, and Miliukov remained deeply opposed to it. As Tsereteli recalled, the foreign minister 'received our proposals with obvious displeasure'.[42] But pressure from his own colleagues, and from Kerensky in particular, forced him to find a form of words.

A small group was convened to check the text. Because Guchkov, the minister of war, was confined to his bed (the strain of recent weeks had affected his heart), the cabinet agreed to hold the meeting in his apartment. 'I remember very clearly that the first reading of Miliukov's draft impressed

234

everyone, even Kerensky,' recalled the elder Vladimir Nabokov.[43] Kerensky himself would concede that the wording 'should have satisfied the most violent critic of Miliukov's "imperialism"'.[44]

That satisfaction turned to rage, however, when it leaked out that Miliukov had added a covering explanation of his own, disguising it as an informal statement of his views. The idea, Miliukov would later claim, was 'to eliminate the possibility of interpreting the Declaration to our detriment'. But his words suggested that he had his own priorities in mind. What Miliukov had done was to affirm the 'general aspiration of the whole Russian people to bring the war to a decisive victory'. His explanatory remarks also promised that Russia would 'fully observe' existing treaty obligations, which was as good as calling for the annexation of the Straits.[45] Though he passed the whole thing off as a mere gloss, Miliukov appeared to have committed Russia to the same old war, the war of annexations and imperialism, the war the Soviet had battled to renounce.

'This Note', thundered Lenin in a short piece for *Pravda* on 20 April/3 May, 'has had the effect of a bombshell.'[46] However hard the politicians might protest that they had approved every word of the main document, the news of dissent within the cabinet was marvellous for him. Better still was the prospect that all that smug deal-making by the Ex Com was about to blow up in its face. 'Lenin gloated like Mephistopheles,' recalled a socialist critic, 'he positively crowed with delight, realizing at once how well it boded for his own campaign. I saw him at the time, on the very afternoon when Petersburg turned into an arena for popular unrest . . . Oh, how he gloated.'[47]

The crowds were out in force well before dark. Their

banners read 'Down with the War', 'Down with Miliukov' and even 'Down with the Provisional Government'. The next day's demonstrations were larger still, and included a stream of stern-looking workers marching on the centre from the Vyborg district. A counter-demonstration blocked Nevsky Prospect, this time composed of supporters of Miliukov.[48] Firearms that had been missing since February now reappeared, and other protesters were armed with clubs. It was as well that all the ministers were once again round at Guchkov's, for the Mariinsky Palace was besieged. Then came the news that Kornilov, the right-wing military governor of Petrograd, was moving cannon into Palace Square. The crisis threatened to turn into full-scale civil war.

The leaders of the Soviet had foreseen this to some extent. As if anticipating an attempted coup, the Ex Com had issued orders to soldiers in the city to remain in their barracks unless they received a direct order from the Soviet itself. Having thus thwarted any plot by Kornilov, Tsereteli joined Nikolai Nekrasov, the transport minister, at Prince Lvov's house to work out a solution to the Miliukov crisis. Outside, the streets were in uproar, with chanting, shouting and the sound of breaking glass. Refusing to give in to an illegal show of force, Lvov decided that he ought to stand by his troublesome foreign minister. Meanwhile, however, the politicians had no option but to draft a fresh explanatory note in place of Miliukov's.

When it was issued, on 22 April/5 May, this further note was as desperate as it was limp. Its purpose, explained the text, was to clarify any 'misunderstandings' that might have arisen from the previous communication. Defence, it stipulated, meant no more than 'defence against the invader' (not conquest or the securing of borderlands), while 'guarantees and sanctions' had nothing to do with Constantinople but translated as 'limitation of armaments'. As they went through each line and comma of the wretched draft, the Ex Com members were surprised and then relieved, for what it meant was that they had again been spared the poisoned chalice of real power. Another concession, perhaps, and another round of horse-trading with kindly Prince Lvov, and then they could all turn their minds to workers' problems and the fight for jobs. When Fedorov, a Bolshevik, suggested that Miliukov's note should prompt the Soviet to seize the reins of government, he received such a hostile response that no left-winger in the room ventured to speak again.[49]

Whatever Prince Lvov might say, Miliukov had probably been planning to resign for some time, and he did so within a matter of days. He refused to abandon the view that Russia would never be secure until it controlled the sea-lane from the Black Sea to the Mediterranean. A liberal and old-school patriot, moreover, he could not bear to see his government hijacked by those he viewed as coarse-tongued demagogues. As he put it, when he listened to the shouts of 'Down with Miliukov' from angry crowds, 'I was not afraid for Miliukov, I was afraid for Russia.'[50]

His famous note, however, was a gift that Lenin seized upon at once. 'No class-conscious worker, no class-conscious soldier will support the policy of "confidence" in the Provisional Government any longer,' he wrote on 21 April/4 May. 'The policy of confidence is bankrupt . . . Not even we had expected events to move so fast . . . Workers and soldiers, you must now loudly declare that there must be only one power in the country – the Soviets of Workers' and Soldiers' Deputies.'[51]

There was still a long way to go. The violence that surfaced in those troubled days had not all worked to Lenin's benefit. Between nine and ten-thirty in the evening on 20 April, wrote Buchanan, 'I had to go out three times on the balcony of the embassy to receive orators and to address crowds who were demonstrating for the government and the Allies. During one of them a free fight took place between the supporters of the government and the Leninites.' It turned out that some Bolsheviks, acting without Lenin's personal sanction, had been calling for insurrection, demanding that the Soviet seize power at once. By the next evening, according to one of Buchanan's government contacts, the 'workmen' had become 'disgusted with Lenin, and the latter would, he hoped, be arrested at no distant date.'[52] War-wounded soldiers helped the cause by openly accusing the Bolsheviks of working for Germany.[53] On 25 April/8 May, the right-wing *Russkie Vedomosti* cheered all its readers up by calling the most recent soldiers' pro-war demonstrations 'a vote of confidence in the regime'.

Miliukov's resignation also paved the way for a new ministry, and Prince Lvov was bent on making it a coalition. As he put it to Buchanan, the Provisional Government had become 'an authority without power', while the 'Workingmen's Council [the Soviet]' was clearly 'a power without authority'. The two had to combine, there was no other way. After a few ritual protestations (in February, after all, the socialists of the Soviet had vowed to stay out of any bourgeois government) Victor Chernov was given the ministry of agriculture and Skobelev became minister for labour.

Kerensky replaced Guchkov as the minister of war. Tsereteli continued to claim that a ministerial portfolio would prevent him from carrying out his more important duties in the Soviet, but in the end, reluctantly, he accepted the ministry of post and telegraph.

Aside from any nagging scruples about ideology and class, the coalition might have seemed like a victory for common sense. As Kerensky told his guests, the British socialists Thorne and O'Grady, at a dinner in late April, 'the Communist doctrines preached by Lenin have made the Socialists lose ground.'[54] Not a day went by, observed Paléologue, without a demonstration of some sort, but most were protests against pacifism. The war-wounded, the blind, the amputees, all had been on the streets, many carrying banners with the slogan 'Down with Lenin!'[55] Another member of the British diplomatic corps, William Gerhardie, made a detour on his way home each evening to listen at the balcony of Kshesinskaya's mansion, for Lenin's tirades had become a nightly spectacle. 'I would linger a while, but not for long,' he remembered, 'for there was nothing in the man's speech or looks to give an inkling of his future career.'[56]

Still, all that talk and persuasion were slowly bearing fruit. The turning-point came at the Bolsheviks' spring conference, which opened on 24 April/7 May. Lenin's theses still encountered opposition, but one by one, over the coming days, the leader hammered his proposals home.[57] The party rejected collaboration with bourgeois democracy, effectively accepting the idea that power should pass to the soviets. A resolution condemning the imperialist war (and, with it, the revolutionary defencism that Kamenev and Stalin had been advocating in *Pravda*) was passed unanimously. On the grounds that 'unity with defencists' was impossible, the conference also ruled out any coalition with the Mensheviks and Socialist Revolutionaries.[58]

No one had even mentioned insurrection. But Lenin had achieved two triumphs. First, through sheer hard work as well as charisma, he had resumed the undisputed leadership of his party (at the April conference he topped the poll in a ballot for its new Central Committee). Next, and far more crucially, he had defined the Bolsheviks as the only clear alternative to dual power. When the mass of the Russian people finally wearied of the well-intentioned chatter that drifted between the Tauride and Mariinsky Palaces, when hardship and exhaustion began to breed a sense of outraged betrayal, only one party could claim that it had not colluded with big business and foreign capital, landowners, generals or the flag-waving proponents of war.

Lenin had also managed to muster something of the patience he had advocated in his first great speech. He had insisted that the workers should be well informed and organized and he had set about arranging that, spending his nights and days in a small room in *Pravda*'s offices and bashing out thousands of words. The newspaper was everywhere; it seemed to speak directly to the dispossessed. Meanwhile, a sister paper, *Soldatskaya Pravda*, was launched for distribution to the army. 'Most of the soldiers come from the peasantry,' he wrote on its first ever page. 'All the landed estates must be taken over by the people. All the land in the country must become the property of the whole people . . . and to dispose of it properly, while preserving order and guarding against any damage to property, the peasants must be supported by the soldiers . . . No one can stop the majority, if it is well organized, if it is class-conscious, if it is armed.'[59]

The tone and wording were exactly right. The paper was a

huge success. What no one knew was where the funding for it could be coming from. On 8/21 April 1917, however, the day after the publication of Lenin's 'April Theses', Foreign Ministry Liaison Officer Grunau at the imperial German court had forwarded a note to his colleagues. It came from the political section of the General Staff in Stockholm, which meant the people who controlled the spies, and its message was triumphant: 'Lenin's entry into Russia successful. He is working exactly as we would wish.'[60]

10. Gold

It is not the business of socialists to help the younger
and stronger robber (Germany) to plunder the older
and engorged robbers. Socialists must take
advantage of the struggle between the robbers to
overthrow all of them.

V. I. Lenin

The rumours were already rife as Lenin stepped down from his train. 'What Lenin brought to Russia', alleged Colonel Nikitin, 'was class hatred, German money and elaborate works on the application of Marxism in Russia.'[1] The views of the police chief were extreme, but he was not alone in suspecting a plot. 'If Lenin had not had the support of all the material and technical power of the German propaganda apparatus and the espionage system,' Kerensky was later to write, 'he would never have succeeded in destroying Russia . . . Not only did Lenin come to Russia with the knowledge and consent and at the desire of the German government, but even in Russia he worked with the mighty financial backing of the enemies of his country.'[2] Here was the bleak Greenmantle of the north, the prophet with his baleful sack of German gold.

The only awkward detail was that no one had a shred of proof. Lenin's views were not in doubt; what was uncertain was the true extent of Germany's financial backing for him.

Throughout that tense summer in Petrograd, his reputation would turn largely on this point, for where a pacifist might call for an immediate cease-fire out of some deep conviction of his own, Lenin's words were said to have been paid for by the enemy himself. 'Each day of war enriches the financial and industrial bourgeoisie and impoverishes and saps the strength of the proletariat and the peasantry of all the belligerents, as well as of the neutral countries,' Lenin announced in one of the resolutions that he prepared for his party's April conference. 'In Russia, moreover, prolongation of the war involves a grave danger to the revolution's gains and its further development.'[3] This would have been inflammatory stuff at any time, but what the pro-war camp in Russia ached to prove was that it was premeditated treason.

By late April, the hunt was on in earnest. The first scent of possible evidence came from the French. In early May, Albert Thomas, the politician who had recently arrived from Paris, informed War Minister Kerensky and the new foreign minister, Mikhail Tereshchenko, that his country's intelligence service was on the trail of documents that ought to clinch the case for good. A captain in the French intelligence mission in Petrograd, Pierre Laurent, would keep the Russian government informed of any developments. Pavel Pereverzev, the Russian minister of justice, was also told of the suspicions, as was Nikitin. They related to a series of intercepted telegrams between Lenin's headquarters in Petrograd and a cast of characters in Stockholm that the Swedish police had been watching for several months.[4]

In secret, two inquiries were begun at once, one headed by Lvov and Tereshchenko, the second (more unscrupulous) by Colonel Nikitin. Lvov and his colleagues soon decided to drop the case, not least because they thought that Lenin's influence, after April's brief blaze of publicity, was insignificant and dwindling. But Nikitin continued to assemble piles of intercepts, aided by French intelligence and an assortment of Petrograd's literary unemployed. The justice ministry assigned his team new premises on the lower two floors of a large building on the Voskresensky (now Robespierre) Embankment that had formerly housed the Imperial Body-guard. On arriving at his new headquarters, however, the colonel discovered that the upper floor had been occupied by a group that called itself the combat section of the Liteinyi District Bolshevik Party. 'The place was already full of their banners, posters, pamphlets and weapons,' Nikitin complained. 'Fixed bayonets were also in evidence. We could scarcely be expected to permit the very people whose seditious activities we were investigating to sit down cheek by jowl with us, as it meant exposing the comings and goings of all our outside agents to the enemy's observation.'[5]

The Bolsheviks never moved out, nor did Nikitin's masters offer him a new address. The truth was that most people had more pressing issues on their minds. Kerensky had approved a fresh offensive in Galicia, the campaign that the allies needed to relieve the pressure in the west. It was a bold, not to say a reckless move, for it was far from clear how Russia's army would respond to the demands of an offensive operation. Kerensky, however, had boundless faith in his powers of persuasion. He swapped his dark suit for an officer's tunic (the outfit that eventually became a sort of uniform for the Bolshevik officials who succeeded him) and set off for the front in a lather of posturing and rhetoric. Even Sukhanov remarked on his dashing style. 'Everywhere he was carried shoulder-high and pelted with flowers,' the Soviet left-winger recalled. 'The whole bourgeoisie had leapt to its feet: the agreeable smell of blood was in its nostrils again, and once again almost abandoned imperialist illusions had revived.'[6]

Buchanan's office had been longing for some good news to report. With a mixture of apprehension and relief, Sir George relayed the story that Kerensky's 'speeches all along the front have had an enthusiastic reception'. London would be delighted: Kerensky was 'daily being recognized as the real leader of the revolutionary movement'.[7] The strutting politician seemed to revel in the limelight. 'Not a single drop of blood will be shed for the wrong cause,' he promised Russian servicemen. 'It is not for the sake of conquest and violence but for the sake of saving free Russia that you will go forward where your commanders and the government lead you. On the points of your bayonets you will bring peace, right, truth and justice.'[8] The words were thrilling, but the men themselves remained confused. 'Kerensky toured the front,' commented a world-weary Trotsky, 'adjured and threatened the troops, kneeled, kissed the earth – in a word, clowned it in every possible way, while he failed to answer any of the questions tormenting the soldiers.'[9]

As an observer of the Russian military, Alfred Knox had also harboured doubts about the offensive. 'The Russian peasant soldier formerly fought because he was afraid of his officers and of punishment,' he ruminated as the campaign was prepared. 'Now he has lost all respect for his officers and he knows he cannot be punished. He has no patriotism or any possible motive force for enthusiasm.'[10] Knox's gloom only deepened as the army started to dissolve. 'Yesterday disorders took place in Kiev when agitators induced a large party of deserters . . . to attempt to disarm the militia and officers,' he wired London on 30 May. 'Every day reports are received from the interior of Russia of deserters in the form of murder, pillage and forcible taking of land.'[11] Some units remained sound (even to the exacting eyes of Knox), but a battle had surely begun for the hearts and muscle of Russia's remaining troops, and Lenin's anti-war ideas were altering the odds. 'The Russian and Austrian soldiers play cards together and visit each other freely,' Knox added. His contact, an old friend in the army, still thought 'the men may attack but it is all a question of propaganda.'[12]

The June offensive turned into a July rout. No strutting and no rhetoric could rebuild Russia's army at this stage. As Trotsky (himself to be a brutal leader of Red troops) explained, 'The ministers thought of the masses of soldiers, stirred to their very depths by the revolution, as so much soft clay to be moulded as they pleased.'[13] It turned out that the men had ideas of their own. News of their panic and retreat provoked hysteria in Petrograd. The tension had been building in the city for some weeks, but it exploded now, as crowds poured through the streets with red flags, black flags, rifles and knives. Armed sailors from the Kronstadt naval base played a key role. So many massive guns appeared that the British embassy, in the sights of artillery outside the Peter-Paul Fortress on the embankment opposite, prepared for an evacuation. For two days in a row the Buchanans went without their breakfast, preferring to get ready to flee as servants started up their car. The armed police protecting them were backed up, in some places, by extremist thugs from the right-wing Black Hundreds. In three days of confused street fighting, more than 700 demonstrators were killed. The July Days came to an end without a working-class seizure of power, but they had brought the country to the brink of an abyss.

The Bolsheviks had not created the protests, but the tenor of their rhetoric, and especially their call for a transfer of power to the soviets, made them obvious scapegoats. Kerensky felt betrayed, humiliated. He was also vulnerable, for though the government of Prince Lvov collapsed, allowing him to step into the premiership, the way had also been opened for a potential coup, perhaps by monarchists within the army. On 4 July, at the height of the crisis, Justice Minister Pereverzev complicated everything by taking a personal initiative. Without official sanction, he released a portion of the material that, he hoped, would prompt a public trial, a shift of blame and Lenin's swift imprisonment. By the next day, the press was full of it. The story went that Lenin was a spy. He had a contract with the kaiser. The Germans had paid him, and his task was to commit a string of murders and spread panic in the sacred Russian land.[14]

The charges were corroborated by the testimony of a certain Ensign Ermolenko, a wretched former prisoner of war, who had given himself up in April and confessed to taking German money to commit criminal acts. He told his Russian interrogators that the details of his mission had been settled at a meeting in Berlin in 1916 at which he had also seen Lenin. A Captain Stenning of the German General Staff was alleged to have written Lenin's contract soon after their talks. Ermolenko claimed to have signed a similar agreement, and while it mentioned blowing up some key munitions factories, his version promised a reward of 200,000 rubles if he could assassinate Sir George Buchanan. Lenin, his critics hoped and prayed, would turn out to have put his name to deeds at least as dark.[15]

Even Nikitin balked a little at fairy-stories like this. Ermolenko was gabbling from sheer terror, and fled to Siberia as soon as the police had done with him (this did not stop the Bolsheviks from arranging for his grisly end, much later, in the dungeons of the Kremlin).[16] But Nikitin had some real documents by now, a pile of intercepted telegrams, and these were just the sort of proof that could be used in court. A cursory reading pointed to links between the Bolsheviks, the German foreign ministry and a Swedish commercial bank. The details might be blurry, but here was the spy thriller that everyone from Kerensky to Buchanan and the allied intelligence services had been longing to read. As head of the reconfigured Provisional Government (and armed with a range of emergency powers), Kerensky initiated an inquiry of his own in mid-July. In its short lifetime – a few months – the inquiry collected more than twenty volumes of evidence.

Trotsky had a word for most of it. 'Never before did people lie as much as they did during the "great war for liberty",' he wrote. 'If lies could explode, our planet would have been blown to dust long before the Treaty of Versailles.'[17] Ermolenko had lied from desperation. There was no likelihood at all that Lenin had signed a contract to deliver a dead Buchanan to General Ludendorff, but once launched on that wild goose chase, the inquiry could go on looking for rumours almost indefinitely. Esmé Howard, for instance, had contributed a useful piece to the jigsaw when he wired London shortly after Lenin had crossed Sweden in April. According to a third-hand story, the Stockholm-based ambassador reported, 'Lenin and his party of Russian extremists had received safe conduct from German government some time before the [February] revolution broke out in Russia. It is clear therefore Germans were ready with a plan . . . if Protopopoff failed.'[18] The source for this particular fable was alleged to have been Nikolai Chkheidze.

Not to be shown up by the Scandinavians, Europe's other secret agents set off in pursuit of news. In August, an American called Frank Chester turned up in Zurich. He claimed to have been recruited in April, under pressure, by German agents in Bern, and one of his tasks was to have been liaison with Lenin. His handler, a German called Franken, had given him precise orders: 'You are to say to Mr Lenin that the contract No. 55 is in order: you must also assist Mr Lenin as much as possible.' This same Franken, Chester believed, had provided Lenin with four million rubles in the spring of 1917. The money, he supposed, went through a line of go-betweens, one of whom was a woman in Stockholm whose name he thought was Sumenson.[19]

Chester's ramblings ended there, but it was clear that the cocktail of wartime treachery and spy-thriller was going to a lot of people's heads. Alexandra Kollontai, according to one British source, 'is Lenin's speech-maker, Lenin being a rather uneducated man, and relying on her for all his speeches'. Another story (also British) held that 'Lenin's sister went to Salonika as a spy, and that . . . a sum of 300,000 rubles has been received from Germany, probably for the purpose of paying Lenin's agents'. In June, the story briefly circulated that 'Nikolai Lenine has been murdered by his followers.' Refusing to be left behind, the newspapers piled in with speculation of a different kind, including a substantial dash of trademark anti-semitism. 'Lenin's real name is Zeder-bluhm,' announced the *Morning Post*, 'but for many years he passed under the name of Uljanoff.' 'It is said', a fascinated *Daily Telegraph* chipped in, 'that Lenin's real name is Mytenbladm.'[20]

Treason, spying and murder – these were crimes that everyone could picture by this time, especially if the accused were obvious outsiders like refugee dissidents and Jews. The machinery of wartime propaganda, already running at white heat, seemed set for its most dazzling hour, and everyone wanted to share the thrill. 'Our success', Kerensky later claimed of the campaign, 'was simply annihilating for Lenin. His connection with Germany was established unquestionably.'[21] One of Pereverzev's final acts as justice minister was to sanction a raid on the *Pravda* press and offices. The printshop was closed, the papers scattered. Soon afterwards, Trotsky was imprisoned, along with the now famous Sumenson and a lawyer and businessman called Kozlovsky. Lenin himself, meanwhile, had fled, quitting Petrograd at night on 10 July with the faithful Zinoviev at his side and taking refuge on some farmland near the armaments works at Sestroretsk.[22] Beardless and heavily disguised beneath a ginger wig, he eventually made his way into hiding in Finland, a disappearing act that only confirmed what everyone was longing to believe. This man just had to be a traitor. The sailors who had formed his guard of honour at the Finland Station all claimed to have been sickened by the thought.

The Bolsheviks' detractors had an open field for several weeks. The indefatigable *Daily Telegraph* announced that Lenin had been arrested in Finland, though as it turned out he was nowhere to be found. The secret services of Britain, France and Russia approved a Europe-wide search. Some thought that Lenin was in Switzerland, others traced him to Copenhagen, but the darkest fear was that he might have gone to Berlin for fresh orders and another pile of German cash. Like strands of dried grass from the haystack in which Lenin genuinely did hide on his flight from Petrograd, the slanders clung tenaciously. Three months later, Lenin still needed to use thick disguise as he slipped back into

Petrograd to organize his party's bid for power. A good deal had changed for Russia by then, but Lenin's enemies had not forgotten him.

Throughout the crisis years to come, the search for traces of the rumoured German gold remained a veritable industry. In February 1918, four months after the Bolsheviks had come to power, an organization called the American Committee on Public Information sent a new agent to Petrograd. His name was Edgar Sisson, and he had formerly worked as an editor of *Cosmopolitan* magazine. He arrived in a city rent by anger, fear and cold. As a man with no experience of local intrigue and plenty of dollars to spend, he soon became a magnet for stories. He was also in the market for any documents that he might use, and in a matter of weeks he had managed to procure – often for large cash sums – a batch of papers linking Lenin and Trotsky with the German High Command. Some were copies of leaked intercepts from Pereverzev's inquiry, but the most controversial ones appeared to show how Germany was still dictating its peace terms to members of the Bolshevik elite. Trotsky came out of it as badly as Lenin, for both were said to be in line for fabulous sums – in personal reward – once they had signed away Ukraine. Sisson believed every word. The Committee on Public Information published the so-called Sisson Papers as a pamphlet in October 1918, and it was only the euphoria at the war's end that stopped the affair from creating a world-wide scandal.[23]

No one reviewed the Sisson Papers for a generation after that (it did not help that the entire trove was lost inside a White House safe for more than three decades). It was only after Stalin's death that the former diplomat and Russian expert George F. Kennan found the time to work on them.

In an article of 1956, he argued that the whole lot had to have been forgeries, but this did not completely close the case. Instead, the scandal had an unexpected afterlife beyond the English-speaking world. In the early 1990s, in the maelstrom that followed the Soviet Union's collapse, a team of Russian historians was permitted to work in the archive of the Soviet secret police. The papers that they found there – copies of the very ones in Sisson's wartime file – were irresistible. The Russians did not know George Kennan's work, so they had no doubt that the dirt here must be weapons-grade. The stuff was classified after all, which surely meant that it was good.

The man who always got to read the secret papers first in those days was Colonel-General Dmitry Volkogonov, and it was he who broke the story to the world. As he explained, he had come to believe that Lenin was a criminal and that his crimes went back to the Great War. He now revealed to Russian readers (and to the credulous western scholars who continue to cite him)[24] that the Bolsheviks had organized a cover-up as soon as they came to power. At a time of national emergency, two trusty comrades had been spared from other duties in order to weed the Provisional Government's paperwork and destroy anything that might prove dangerous. The pair, Volkogonov continued, were found to have informed Trotsky on 16 November 1917 that they had removed at least one file: German Imperial Bank Order No. 7433, dated 2 March 1917. This, like some other bank details that they had checked, related to the payment of money for peace propaganda in Russia and named 'Comrades Lenin, Zinovieff, Kameneff, Trotsky, Sumenson, Kozlovsky and others'.[25]

Volkogonov was certain he had found his smoking gun. Had he been able to read English, however, he might have asked some tougher questions. Three decades earlier, George

Kennan had been very thorough. He had checked the hand-writing on Sisson's papers, he had identified the typewriters, he had tracked watermarks and rubber stamps to find the offices from which the things were sent. He concluded that the author of the most explosive forgeries was an anti-German journalist called Anton Ossendowski, a character also associated with the Provisional Government's earlier inquiry. Several motives were imputed, but Ossendowski's need for cash was probably the overriding one. To the most damning of the documents, the German Imperial Bank Order cited by Volkogonov, Kennan had applied his own experience as a former diplomat: 'It is unusual', he pointed out, 'for governments to record unnecessarily in written documents . . . data that can be used against them.' If the Soviet leadership's ambition was to suppress this sort of evidence, 'the last thing it would have wanted would have been to have it spread out in another official document.'[26]

The actors at the centre of the story had indeed been careful. Even people on the German side were not always completely certain who was helping whom. In March 1918, when his country's envoys were poised to sign their long-awaited treaty with Soviet Russia at Brest-Litovsk, a German diplomat considered the peace process that so fascinated Sisson. 'What do we want in the East?' State Secretary Hintze allowed himself to muse. 'The military paralysis of Russia. The Bolsheviks are taking care of this better than any other Russian party, without our contributing a single man or a single penny. We cannot demand that they . . . should love us for squeezing their country like an orange . . . We are not co-operating with the Bolsheviks, we are exploiting them. That is what politics is about.'[27]

*

The intercepted telegrams dated April to June 1917, however, were genuine. Nikitin had placed an agent in the Tauride as soon as he learned that a Bolshevik official in the Soviet was using telegraph apparatus there to transmit messages for Lenin's group.[28] The colonel read each intercept, he read them fast and he drew the only conclusion that his imagination allowed. The French were also on the case, and so was British Military Intelligence, whose agents spent the month of August 1917 poring over a report on 'documents which clearly prove that Lenin was implicated in a German plot to undermine the prestige of the Russian government. Money was sent from Berlin through a certain Svedson, connected with the German Embassy at Stockholm to Madame Sumensohn, and Kozlovsky through whom it was transferred to Lenin and other German agitators.'[29]

The wires converged in Stockholm, which meant that Fürstenberg must be involved. The dapper crook was still the local manager of the Handels Og-Eksport Kompagniet, but he remained one of Lenin's closest aides as well, and certainly the most active Bolshevik in Sweden. It was also suspicious that the import–export company for which he worked was owned and run by Parvus and Sklarz, both known to be German agents. The problem was that the cables themselves turned out to be boring and mundane. 'Madame Sumensohn', otherwise known as Evgeniya Sumenson, was the Petrograd agent of a Polish export firm that handled some of Fürstenberg's business in north-western Russia. At other times, as her telegraphic output affirmed, she also dealt with food imports on behalf of the Swiss Nestlé firm. Kozlovsky, a lawyer very close to Lenin, was the chief representative of Parvus' company in Russia, and most of his telegrams confined themselves to business news.

The full collection of sixty-six telegrams was never published by Kerensky's legal team, and after Lenin's coup in 1917 the Soviet state locked them away. In 1991, however, the file became available to researchers. Reading them now, they seem repetitive, curt and transparent. Sumenson cables for fresh stock, Kozlovsky with details of payments and consignment times. Finding nothing more suspicious, as they thumbed through all this for themselves, Kerensky's agents decided that certain words must be in code. 'Sold two hundred fifty pencils thirty seven boxes,' reported a telegram from Moscow.[30] In the old days of the Russian underground, codes had been used for everything, so why not now, when so much more depended on such words? 'The investigation', fumed Trotsky, 'was in the hands of practitioners of justice seasoned under the regime of the Tsar. They were unaccustomed to treating facts or arguments honestly.'[31]

In August 1917, the Russian public prosecutor declared himself satisfied. Reuter's news agency carried the story on behalf of the world's press. The Bolshevik leaders, starting (in absentia) with Lenin and Zinoviev, were all found guilty. 'The Public Prosecutor adds', readers of English newspapers would learn, 'that an investigation has shown the existence of a vast German spying organisation at work throughout Russia, and that certain facts pointed irresistibly to the conclusion that M. Lenin was a German agent, whose part it was to return to Russia and there work for the success of the German cause.' According to this bulletin, Lenin's local network included Parvus, Kozlovsky, Sumenson and Fürstenberg. A new name, Paschal, also featured on the list.

The trouble was that there was still no proof. No one had tracked real German money to the Bolsheviks' accounts; no one could even show a direct link between Lenin and Parvus (who was certainly flush with German gold). Fürstenberg protested that his involvement with Parvus' firm was purely commercial and that he took no interest in pro-German politics. Radek, who still shared Fürstenberg's handsome villa, was busy writing pieces for the German left-socialist (and anti-military) press. As for the mysterious Paschal, a note addressed directly to the British Prime Minister David Lloyd George (and fishy enough in itself) pleaded that he was in fact Frank Paswell, a former advertiser of American soap in Petrograd, 'pushing, go ahead disposition, plausible talker', who had accepted German money on his own account to place disruptive pieces in the Russian press.[32]

Instead of proof, then, there were only probabilities and lies. The Bolsheviks certainly had plenty to explain. Their modest accounts for 1917 showed that their income, which came in part from membership fees, was growing steadily, but there was a large gap between their declared wealth and the operations that they were able to fund. In April 1917, their income was about 11,500 rubles and their outgoings, according to their accounts, no more than 5,500. In May, thanks to an increased membership and rising paper sales, their income was 18,000 rubles; in June, it had reached nearly 30,000.[33] They did not pay rent for their premises, they had seized a functioning printing press, and Lenin set a standard for austerity in private life, but with a daily print-run of 85,000 in the first instance, *Pravda* alone was an expensive undertaking, and the printing and distribution of other papers and pamphlets, the design and production of posters and the costs of running a growing party in a vast and war-torn country represented serious money. In his 'Proposal for Propaganda in Russia', a report delivered in July 1917, an enterprising British general's suggested budget for countering the Bolsheviks' pacifist publicity was a staggering £2 million for three initial months and £500,000 a month thereafter.[34]

There can be no doubt that Germany was pouring money into Russia. In just one instance, on 3 April 1917, the German foreign ministry approved a grant of five million marks for propaganda purposes, much of which probably passed to Parvus (who always refused to sign receipts).[35] While Lenin's cheap seat on the sealed train had been a gamble on the part of a small group in Germany's civilian government, other departments and agencies had budgets of their own. The military might have been counting on its submarines to throttle and defeat the enemy, but it still ran a lavish propaganda campaign on the eastern front throughout 1917. As the British War Cabinet noted in April, 'German agitators and German money would seem to be having much to do with the unrest in Russia.'[36] The idea of a 'vast spying organisation' was fanciful, but with large piles of foreign notes in circulation, many of them forged, it was a challenge to work out who was bankrolling whom.

In Bern, the Germans used an agent called Karl Moor. A German citizen, he had settled in Switzerland in the 1870s. His career had encompassed journalism and the law, but later he began to finance the twilight world of émigré socialist politics. In March 1917 he also agreed to work for Germany (and Austria). His new code-name was Bayer, and his main job was to pass information about the socialist community to his handler in Bern, Dr Walter Nasse. In the summer of 1917, he travelled to Stockholm several times, though he had no dealings with Parvus' group. The extent of his activities remained obscure until the end of the Second World War, but some writers now describe him as the Bolsheviks' 'Quartermaster No. 2' (after Parvus).[37] Declassified papers from Russia suggest that he passed at least 230,000 German marks to the Bolsheviks in August 1917. To the frustration of those who believed that they had found their evidence at last, however, it turned out that the money had gone no further than Stockholm. As far as anyone can tell, it never got beyond Radek, who used it to finance a project for an international left-socialist peace conference.[38]

Illicit finance was also a game that anyone could play. A game, that is, but one where cash alone could never guarantee results. In Bern, Walter Nasse was appalled by what he saw as a tide of 'English gold'. 'The Entente', he reported, 'was spending enormous sums on the support of the war-effort and on bribing influential people.'[39] When it came to agents on the ground, even the cricket-playing British turned out to have the worthy Captain Bromhead and his film-screenings. The French had a propaganda bureau in Petrograd headed by the Comte de Chevilly, another enthusiastic promoter of cinema who was also a representative of the Lyon Private Bank.[40] These people's efforts, and the pamphlets, gifts and speaking tours, all came at a substantial price, though 'English gold' was putting it a bit strongly. In May, in fact, Buchanan appealed to London on the grounds that 'army workmen and peasantry are so utterly ignorant that they know nothing about the origin of the war or the aims for which we are fighting while they believe implicitly all lies told them by countless agitators who are poisoning their minds against the Allies and advocating peace on any terms.' He received a grudging (and inadequate) £10,000.[41]

The British had good reason to keep hold of the purse-strings. In Whitehall, as officials totted up the monies spent on Russian propaganda, what struck them most was the egregious failure rate. Plenty of chaps had gone to Petrograd, but somehow never quite the right ones for the job. It was not gold they needed, maybe, but a change of tack. The British must have guessed by May that Plekhanov had failed to make a whit of difference to the Russian war effort. Their other approach (which hinted at a craving for a bedtime story to console) involved sending writers into the breach, which accounted for Arthur Ransome and some of his unshaven friends. In July 1917, the Wilson government in the United States joined in when it agreed to send Somerset Maugham to Petrograd by way of Tokyo.[42]

Once in the Russian capital, Maugham would quarrel, as many did, with the head of the British propaganda effort, the novelist Hugh Walpole. Both collected a good deal of material for later books in the process, but neither made much headway with the Russian public. As Alfred Knox put it in a private letter of October 1917, 'Walpole the man who has been running the [propaganda] work lately is NOT the man for the job at present because he does not know Russia and is only a novelist and a man with balls is required.'[43] No one ever said that of Lenin. Whatever backing he may have had, the fact was that his message really had hit home. Anyone who toured the front lines could see the difference that he and his followers were making by the end of May, and all the English gold in Russia was worthless against them.

The Germans had not been particularly discerning. Their agents had been willing to finance anyone from Finnish and Estonian separatists to Turkmen preachers of jihad. When they compared Lenin with some of these wilder characters, however, officials in the foreign ministry could pride themselves on the risk they had taken. The Bolshevik did not quite have the sort of pedigree they liked, nor did he promise loyal cossacks for the western front, but his writing had given voice to the soldiers' weariness and his party was a focal point for dreams and discontent. When all they needed was for Russia to be neutralized, Lenin's German sponsors did not even have to think about his future, let alone the viability of his regime. Cartoon insurgents carried knives between their yellow teeth, but this one did a grand job merely with his pen.

Still, sending Lenin back had been a gamble and the costs (especially if the Parvus account were included) had not been trivial. Inevitably, the small group that accepted the responsibility found that they sometimes had to justify themselves. State Secretary Kuhlmann ventured to boast a little when he wrote to the foreign ministry liaison officer at General Headquarters on 3 December 1917, less than a month after the Bolsheviks' successful coup. His main aim this time was to secure further support for Lenin's group while they arranged the details of a separate peace. He did not think the Bolsheviks would be in power for long, so he was anxious to create the best conditions for a treaty before Russia changed course yet again.

Kuhlmann made a good job of his case. 'The disruption of the Entente and the subsequent creation of political combinations agreeable to us constitute the most important war aim of our diplomacy,' he wrote.

> Russia appeared to be the weakest link in the enemy chain. The task therefore was gradually to loosen it, and, when possible, to remove it. This was the purpose of the subversive activity we caused to be carried out in Russia behind the front – in the first place promotion of separatist tendencies and support of the Bolsheviks. It was not until the

Bolsheviks had received from us a steady flow of funds through various channels and under different labels that they were in a position to build up their main organ, *Pravda*, to conduct energetic propaganda and appreciably to extend the originally narrow base of their party.[44]

Exactly how that cash flowed east remains a matter for speculation. It is entirely reasonable to suppose that some of Parvus' German millions reached Lenin's fighting fund. It is possible that the big man used his research group in Denmark to channel money to the Bolsheviks, a course he could have sorted out with Radek at their secret meeting in April. Some researchers have named the likely handler as a confidential agent called Vladislav Shatsenstein.[45] The other route for moving cash may have been through Stockholm. The most convenient intermediary would have been the firm that Fürstenberg managed for Parvus and his German friend Georg Sklarz, which ploughed some of its profits back into trading but may have used the rest for political operations in Russia.[46] The file is open, although many of the documents have disappeared. What is beyond doubt is that Lenin accepted 2,000 rubles from Fürstenberg in April 1917 when he was planning his journey to Russia, and he took 800 more for Zinoviev.[47] He did not balk at that variety of German gold. For those who still refuse to credit that the greatest socialist on earth could ever lie about a wad of German notes, the alternative is to concede that he subsidized himself with profits from the war's black-market trade in lead pencils and condoms (with teat end).

It was not obvious that Lenin had to lie for ever. He was afraid at first, of course; he could not know how his plans would turn out, and though free Russia had abjured the gallows, he had cause enough to be wary of a treason trial in the summer of 1917. He also thought himself to be a target for assassination; he kept armed bodyguards around him everywhere he went.[48] A man with more faith in the people, however, might yet have thought that he could win the final argument, for the thrust of the 'April Theses' was that bourgeois rules and bourgeois justice were about to fall. A braver leader might eventually have boasted of that German cash, for he would soon be using it to help the German proletariat defeat the kaiser. Germany's home front had been fragile for some time; people were hungry, and Lenin's brand of revolution was already threatening the peace of Berlin's streets. The situation was even more critical in Austria.[49] Lenin's appeal for worldwide revolution was addressed to the armed forces of Germany as well as his own side, and as he repeatedly insisted, 'We consider the German capitalists to be as predatory as the Russian.'[50] Even the fraternization that he advocated was a two-way process. If Lenin was a 'bacillus', as Churchill once alleged, then like a real pathogen he might infect more than one victim at a time.

He could have turned the tables and attacked his accusers head on. If taking German money was one kind of crime, after all, then trampling on the people's dreams, making them fight against their will and even starving them were surely worse. A man who genuinely trusted the Russian people's sense of justice might have pointed to the poetry of taking money from the robbers of the poor, whatever country they were from. From Miliukov's ill-judged devotion to the Straits to Kerensky's ill-fated offensive at the front, from lock-outs and long working hours to the rationing of bread, the Russian bourgeoisie seemed set on a course of renewed oppression. There were also contributions from its cousins overseas; few outside influences were as damaging to the fragile democratic Russian state as the pressure from London and Paris. In the teeth of advice from their own agents, the war leaders of Britain and France continued to hold Russia to the letter of its Entente treaty obligations.

It was a policy that disgusted Arthur Ransome. In July, after the defeat of Russia's armies, he wrote to his mother that the British attitude to Russia resembled 'that of a man towards a tool that has worn itself out'. The upshot was a self-defeating callousness. 'For some reason or other the war does not hurt every man woman and child in England permanently continuously as it does those of the continental nations, and Russia most of all,' he told her. 'You do not see the bones sticking through the skin of the horses in the street. You do not have your porter's wife beg for a share in your bread allowance because she cannot get enough to feed her children . . . It is because things are like that here that German agents and extremists who promise an immediate millennium do succeed in carrying away the absolutely simple-minded Russian soldier . . . The time may come when England will be the best-hated country in Russia.'[51]

In proclaiming that he had taken a share of the kaiser's gold, Lenin might have made more of British perfidy like this. The Germans had been bad enough; the British were voracious. 'With great respect,' O'Grady and Thorne reported to London on their return from the Russian capital, 'we urge that Russia is an empire of great area, with a population of 180 millions, and with enormous possibilities of not only being a great market, but of developing into the greatest economic power in the world. Its mineral, oil, and food processing resources are practically untapped. When war is over, the struggle in exploiting those resources will, if no effort is now put forward by Great Britain, remain a matter of conquest between America and Germany, with advantages in favour of the latter.'[52]

Even more overt was the cupidity of an itinerant British businessman called William Henry Beable. To him, the end of tsarism had created an enormous market. As long as Germany could be excluded, the British stood to make a killing from the Russian middle class, a virgin clientele that did not yet suspect its need for bicycles and cameras and Sanatogen tonic wine. In a report published in the darkest hour of 1918, as news of starving children started coming in from the wastelands of Russia's civil war, Beable listed the most profitable market openings, including pharmaceuticals, scientific instruments and optical supplies, photographic material and, 'since shaving is becoming fashionable', razors and patent soap. 'The piano trade', Beable proposed, 'is one in which Russia offers splendid opportunities.'[53]

In theory, then, if he had cited anything of this, Lenin's case about the imperialist and capitalist nature of the war should have been clear to everyone. He could also have made more of the British refusal to allow other Russian exiles to go home, another policy that showed the bourgeoisie in its true light. As he might further have remarked, he was the one who had taken the risk, who had come home against all odds. He could not say how long it might take to bring socialism to the world, but he was certain that the project would succeed, and then all debts would disappear and all corruption wither. The fact that his train-ride suited the Germans, he might have added, was regrettable but irrelevant. As Trotsky later put the case: 'On Ludendorff's part this was an adventure dictated by the grave military situation in Germany. Lenin took advantage of Ludendorff's plans to further thereby his own.'[54]

Perhaps the problem was that in the end (as later history would show), most Russians were likely to prefer one of Mr Beable's bicycles – or even a drop of his tonic wine – to the joys of Lenin's version of class war. Lenin, of course, suspected that; false consciousness was the term that some Marxists used for people's fondness for mere ease. He also knew that real peasants wanted only justice and a piece of land. To force his revolution through against such odds, the leader had to steel himself to play the part of Robespierre. If people could not see where their true freedom lay, he would impose a revolutionary dictatorship until they were prepared to understand. Meanwhile, he had to put himself above the ordinary ruck, becoming the ideal instrument of History with a big H, a new man, incorruptible and without sin. As Paléologue put it in April 1917, Lenin appeared to be 'a compound of Savonarola and Marat'.[55] In real life, he mixed those unattainable ideals with a schoolmaster's hard-working probity and the controlling passions of a man who kept his pencils in neat rows, whose lampshades had hand-beaded trim.

Illicit finance is a dirty little crime, but lying is corrosive in the longer term. Instead of trusting the masses with the truth about his German funds, Lenin opted to lecture them. Instead of confiding in them, he lied. It was the price he paid in the short term, on their behalf, to save them from their own weakness. He then went on to make 150 million people free (or so he claimed) by subjecting them to a merciless political elite.

In years to come, Bolshevik Party members were obsessed by the idea of foreign spies and traitors in their midst. Their activists had to appear perfect. It was an impossible burden with which to begin rebuilding any empire, let alone the first ever proletarian one, and the conditions at the end of 1917 could hardly have been worse. 'One wondered', mused Trotsky as he looked back on those dreadful months, 'if a country so despairing, so economically exhausted, so devastated, had enough sap left in it to support a new regime and preserve its independence.'[56] The darkest secret of all was that the men in charge had private doubts. Though they preached dogma to the world, they did not quite believe it for themselves.

11. Fellow Travellers

The Jacobins of the Twentieth Century would not
guillotine the capitalists – to follow a good example
does not mean copying it.

V. I. Lenin

St Petersburg has many revolutionary shrines. Among the
oddest, accessible only to pre-booked groups, is a small flat
on an upper floor. Opened as a museum in 1938 (the blackest
year of Stalin's political terror), it is based on the apartment
where the Alliluevs, the family of Stalin's second wife, had
their home in the first two decades of the twentieth century.
Though Stalin visited more often, Lenin himself sought refuge here in July 1917, and that fact made the place a holy site
in the years of Soviet power. The museum has gone through
many transformations since, but a striking painting has survived and still hangs in the tiny exhibition space. The work
of a Soviet artist called Mikhail G. Sokolov (1875–1953), its
subject is Lenin's arrival at the Finland Station on 3 April
1917. In three rooms, small and stuffed with chintz, it is by
far the brightest object on display.

An art historian would know the picture as a work of
socialist realism, a style that was near universal in the Soviet
Union by the 1930s. Like many compositions of its kind – all
muscles, square jaws and sunshine – it is stronger on the
socialism than the reality, but the figure of Lenin in the main

spotlight is clear enough. Wearing a dark suit and tie and brandishing his trademark hat, the Bolshevik leader is stepping from a wagon that is clearly marked 'III class'. His general expression is a little wooden, but that may be the artist's way of giving him the same look as the icon-painters gave to saints. In every other way, this is a work of the secular age. As members of a brass band struggle with their music-sheets (it is hard to see how the trombonist in the foreground will ever move his elbows), everyone else has gathered at the dark-green door of the train, some waving caps and others holding banners high above their heads. The faces shine, the colours blaze, and everyone is having a good time.

Apart from Lenin himself, only one character has been allowed to look out of the picture in full face. His gaze bores out of the dark train, his black moustache is unmistakable (as is that crooked eyebrow line). With no regard for awkward facts, Sokolov has placed Stalin among the illustrious passengers. Indeed, although the man was never in Lenin's carriage at all, Sokolov has put Stalin one step above the late leader, suggesting that he could be a mentor or chaperone. Such lies were not unusual by the 1930s. In April 1937, for instance, as the Soviet Union celebrated the twentieth anniversary of Lenin's triumph at the Finland Station, *Pravda* felt obliged to pretend that Stalin had been the real impresario in Petrograd.[1] Sokolov went even further, creating a visual fairy-tale, a foretaste of communist joys to come. A mere glance at the picture is enough to show that one day the bouquets and glinting steel will be for Stalin, rightfully. The succession is direct and utterly secure. Lenin might have founded the unbreakable Union of Soviet Socialist Republics, but Stalin, his heir and truest disciple, will be the man who builds it into the greatest, freest and happiest land the world has ever seen.

The antidote to that idea lurks in a dull glass case at waist height in another corner of the room. Suppressed during the years of Stalin's tyranny, it is a typed list, in Cyrillic, of the passengers who completed the journey on the famous sealed train.[2] Stalin does not feature anywhere this time. Many of the other names seem unfamiliar, especially where people's pseudonyms were later changed, and those of Fritz Platten and Karl Radek are missing because they could not enter Russia when the others did. The exhibition offers no commentary, but the document should not be treated casually, for it would once have been a rare and secret thing. Most of the names on it were censored out of Soviet history books, and by the time of Stalin's death the lives of those who bore them had largely been forgotten. They knew too much, that was the problem; they knew that Lenin had not thought of Stalin as his heir, they knew what the alternatives had been. They even had a few ideas about the sort of state that they had hoped to build in the far-off days before each fascinating dream dissolved.

It is a hundred years now since the sealed train crossed Europe under German guard, and yet the story still has important, even disturbing, resonances. In Russia, where moments of hope, of mass engagement in national life, have been so lamentably rare, they have a special poignancy. The mere idea of taking power appalled the politicians who were thrust into office in the early spring of 1917. Instead of addressing the grievances that had placed them in government, moreover, they mainly used them to manipulate the crowds. Nationalist newspapers co-opted hungry and disfigured veterans to blackmail an exhausted public into accepting another year of war. The right blamed Jews and socialists, the left set every-one against the types they chose to call the bourgeoisie, and in the end democracy could only skulk around the fringes of the revolution like a dog with mange. By contrast, Lenin's answers may have looked seductive for a while, but people are not set free by dictatorships, and violence is not the way to bring them peace.

The drama had intriguing roles for foreigners as well. A story that began as high adventure for the likes of Hoare and Knox soon turned into a tragedy for everyone involved. In the same way, there have been many hopeful springs in recent times, not only in the Slavic world, and all have witnessed chanting crowds with flowers, flags and candles for the sacred dead. As modern tyrannies are swept away (and every honest heart delights), the quick-thinking servants of the world's great powers still proffer plans to intervene, to jostle, scheme and sponsor factions that they barely understand. In 1917, their predecessors in western Europe had a clear set of objectives where Russia was concerned. They wanted military edge to win the war, they wanted all their global influence to last. They also wanted to be winners in the peace, to buy up Russia's minerals and sell their branded shaving soap to merchants in its thriving towns. The order of priorities may well have changed since then, but not the character of government advisers or their basic aims. In 1917, the plans of all the foreign actors in the Russian tragedy backfired. In the process, the European powers succeeded, between them, in destroying the first and last chance for a free and democratic Russian polity that any could have hoped to see.

The most unwelcome lesson for the European actors in the story was the eventual price-tag. The German foreign ministry might once have balked at Parvus' unabashed demands, but in the aftermath of Lenin's coup the big man's expenses would come to look like pocket money. By May 1918, with Russia now a battleground for every shade of Red and White, the secret agents of the warring European powers were all running up massive bills. Writing from Moscow, which had become the capital of the new Soviet state, the German minister, Count von Mirbach, requested guidance from Berlin. 'I am still trying to counter efforts of the Entente and support the Bolsheviks,' he explained. 'However, I would be grateful for instructions as to whether overall situation justified use of larger sums in our interests if necessary.' The reply was unequivocal. 'Please use larger sums,' read his instruction. 'If further money required, please telegraph how much.' Mirbach believed that he would need a monthly income of three million German marks. Two weeks later, a secret German memorandum increased the estimate to forty million marks or more. Among the reasons was competing pressure from Britain and France.[3]

Expense alone was not the worst of it, however. Another unpleasant discovery was that Lenin and his followers had plans that even German officers could not control. Less than two months after the Bolsheviks' accession to power, Radek's centre in Stockholm was agitating inside Germany, calling on German troops to lay down their arms, inciting revolution and (according to a memorandum of January 1918) attacking loyal servants of the kaiser. 'We are portrayed as slave-drivers and oppressors of the workers,' complained an outraged deputy state secretary in Berlin. 'It is claimed that we put the workers' leaders into concentration camps and that we appease the hunger of women and old men with lead and gunpowder.'[4] As German civilians' suffering deepened in the final winter of the war, such propaganda (presented in Radek's fluent German prose) was bound to find a ready audience.

The hardest truth of all was that no subterfuge on Russian soil could ever be enough to save the German state. The foreign ministry had planned to exploit Lenin only till the Russian army failed; as soon as he had served his purpose they could leave him to the wolves. Duplicity like that was justified to win the war, and no one was supposed to mourn collateral damage. 'In the hands of the Bolsheviks,' wrote Mirbach in April 1918, 'Moscow, the sacred city . . . represents what is perhaps the most glaring destruction of taste and style that has resulted from the Russian revolution.' 'That is not our concern,' commented Kaiser Wilhelm II, 'the war lacks style as well.' Two weeks later, reading Mirbach's gloomy report of a meeting in the Kremlin, Wilhelm concluded that 'He [Lenin] is finished.'[5] In fact, within six months, the one who turned out to be finished was Wilhelm himself.

Defeat brought catastrophe to the German government and misery to the majority of German people, but everyone had suffered as the pressure grew. 'If I do ever get home,' Arthur Ransome told his mother in the summer of 1917, 'I shall drink too much beer, and shun the acquaintance of all people who know the difference between a liberal and a conservative . . . I shan't read a newspaper EVER.'[6] Sir George Buchanan's health collapsed at several points, but so did that of almost every foreign official in Petrograd. When Harold Williams looked back on Russia's revolutionary year, his first thoughts ran to excitement and happiness. 'There were great emotions,' he wrote. 'There was a deep and singing joy, and a bitter despair, and anger and contempt and reverence, and, besides and apart from all that, the sheer and constant fun of it all.' But even Williams became a disappointed man. 'Sometimes one had the feeling that too many illusions had been torn away,' he concluded, 'that one had seen things that it was not good to see in this life.'[7]

Buchanan could not stay in Russia once the Bolsheviks had taken power. He left in January 1918, exhaustion close to breaking him. Not one of London's goals had been fulfilled. The Entente as a whole now fell apart. There was an Anglo-Soviet trade agreement in 1921, but relations were always hostile and the wartime dream of booming trade never materialized. Despite their conspicuous ideological differences, the Germans were the Soviets' main partners in the inter-war decades, not least because the victors in the First World War had managed to exclude them both from the European mainstream. Moscow was still involved in a tactical alliance with Berlin on the summer night in 1941 when the Luftwaffe flew unchallenged through its airspace and destroyed 1,200 of Stalin's military aeroplanes in one long-planned surprise attack.

Sir Samuel Hoare left Russia without seeing the revolution. In that respect, he did not have the opportunity to learn from the mistakes that everyone else was beginning to make as tsarism dissolved. On a posting to Italy later that year, however, he continued to play the spying game. The strain of war was testing all of Britain's continental allies, including Italy, and morale was further dented by the activities of left-wing pacifists who drew their inspiration from the Petrograd Soviet. In an attempt to neutralize these local peace protesters, Hoare authorized the covert payment of £100 a month to a promising Italian journalist. At thirty-four, Benito Mussolini was already starting to emerge as a persuasive and red-blooded type. He and Hoare would meet again some years later. As Britain's foreign secretary, Hoare was the architect of the Hoare–Laval Pact of 1935, a scandalous deal, never implemented, intended to give Mussolini a free hand with his tanks and poison gas in parts of Abyssinia.[8]

The reckoning for the defeated German empire came in 1919. As they filed into the mirrored hall of the Palace of Versailles, its diplomats could count on few old friends. The leader of the German delegation was Parvus' sponsor from wartime Copenhagen, Ulrich von Brockdorff-Rantzau. Like Parvus, he had seen his happiest and most creative days. Lenin did not honour any debt incurred to patrons from his past, and most would understand what was about to happen only when it was too late.

Now a German national at last, Parvus was horrified by the news from Versailles. 'If you destroy Germany,' he warned the victors from his new base near Berlin, 'you will make the German nation the organizer of the next world war.'[9] The big man had come to believe that the only future – for himself, for Europe and for mankind – lay in a strong Germany and a united western Europe. He harboured no illusions about Lenin's Russia; he considered the place to have assumed the grisly proportions of a reincarnated tsarism. It did not help that Lenin had not ventured to reward him, nor that the Soviet state had branded him a traitor, shutting him out of a drama that he once dreamed of orchestrating. Closer to home, the Swiss police had orders to arrest him for his wartime economic crimes.[10] Thwarted but still in fighting mood, he used a portion of his wealth to build himself a mansion at Schwanenwerder just outside Berlin. The Wannsee had its own romantic shore, but it was a far cry from the Baur au Lac. 'This is terrible,' he wrote to a young friend. 'I need change and life, and all I see is decay, slime, dislocation ... I want intellectual creativeness, the joy of hope, the triumph of spiritual achievements, the joy of new discoveries – I would like to feel again the heartbeat of civilization.'[11]

That joy eluded him for ever. Parvus died in 1924, aged fifty-five. 'The younger generation knows his name as the name of a betrayer of the working class, a social-patriot,' wrote Karl Radek. 'He combined in one person the spirit of a German social-democrat and of a speculator.'[12] Coming from his erstwhile friend, the words were cruel enough, but worse was to come. Stalin quickly added Parvus' name to the list of enemies and former men. The millionaire socialist was never mentioned in Moscow again; there were no plaques or statues and no footnotes in Soviet books. As if anticipating that darkness, Parvus had destroyed most of his papers in the last months of his life. His fortune also disappeared – burned, buried, squandered – and with it vanished the last trace of his remarkable career.

Parvus had underestimated Lenin's ruthlessness, and the Germans had failed to realize in time that they were sponsoring a man whose personal sense of mission appeared – to him – to warrant any violence. The greatest sufferer of all, however, was Lenin's own society. The hatreds from the old days had not had the chance to heal, while new ones, stoked by the language of class, swept through the masses like a blaze. 'A leader who is not in some degree a tyrant is impossible,' wrote Maxim Gorky in the sycophantic mood of his old age. 'More people, probably, were killed under Lenin than under Thomas Müntzer; but without this, resistance to the revolution of which Lenin was the leader would have been more widely and powerfully organized.'[13]

Though he had witnessed not a single battle at first hand, Lenin came to power in a world distorted by the shock of mechanized slaughter. On the pretext of ending that, he used the new technologies of war himself, while in the course of three years of internal conflict his people also tore at human flesh with pitchforks, mattocks, knives and teeth. There was no refuge for compassion or remorse. A struggle for survival, the bloodbath was justified (on all sides) with slogans, lies and ideology. 'Explode / Chop apart / The old world!' a poem of the time enjoined. 'Be / Merciless / Strangle / The bony body of destiny!'[14]

As trusted and experienced comrades, Lenin's companions of the sealed train were bound to be swept up in revolutionary storms. Grigory Usievich was the first to die, killed in an early battle of the civil war. As the new banking commissar, however, an economist called Grigory Sokolnikov had other ways of repaying the cost of his cheap seat to Petrograd. In 1918, when Lenin's government was desperate for usable hard cash, he presided over the long-promised expropriation of Russia's robber-capitalists, which meant opening tens of thousands of private safe-deposit boxes and stealing ('revising') the contents. By the end of its first year, this wholesale raid had yielded 500 million tsarist rubles (or roughly $250 million).[15] At the same time, the loyal Fürstenberg was also put to work in his specialized area of trading and supply. He spent months buying boots in bulk before he was promoted to the directorship of the Soviet national bank, a role in which he could exploit financial contacts in Stockholm.

It was not as easy for everyone. After years of tireless underground work, Shlyapnikov made the mistake (in political terms) of retaining a direct association with the factory workers of Petrograd. He felt he could do nothing else, for they were his comrades in arms, and as a skilled lathe-operator he identified with their concerns. Like them, therefore, he could only watch in horror as Lenin's government became as dictatorial and as merciless as any industrial baron of the past. Shlyapnikov's group began to clash with Lenin on questions of workers' control and the rights of trade unions from 1920, but it was the introduction of a mixed economy, the so-called 'New Economic Policy', with its concessions to capitalist practices, that drove his Workers' Opposition to full-scale revolt. In 1921, Lenin described the new faction as 'the greatest danger to our continued existence'.[16] None of poor Shlyapnikov's pre-revolutionary loyalty counted for anything as loaded guns dispersed his following and its ideas. Thereafter, factional activity of any kind was banned for ever. In the space of only four years, the Bolshevik Party had turned its back on the very source of dynamism that had propelled Lenin to power.

The Soviet dictatorship, a government that promised freedom for all working people, had created a tyranny. But the dream remained powerful, and when Lenin died, in 1924, the country genuinely mourned. Stalin was another matter. 'Your socialism', Raskolnikov, the former Petrograd activist, informed the people's leader in an open letter of 1939, 'can find room for those who built it only behind prison bars . . . Your personal dictatorship is without anything in common with the dictatorship of the proletariat.'[17] Soon after he had written that, and though he had escaped to France, Raskolnikov was dead, quite possibly from poisoning. No one ever found a culprit, however, and very few would ever look. The problem was that communists in general were wary of assigning blame. No individual, their ideology had taught, could ever question the collective cause. Stalin's future victims clung hard to Lenin's Marxist rhetoric in an attempt to justify themselves, eschewing the notion of individual wickedness by reference to social forces and class struggle.

None ever challenged the desirability of revolution as a goal. Instead, they thought of all the reasons why, on this or that occasion, Russia might have failed to measure up. When they had finished blaming the peasants (this remained Russia's national sport), they reverted to a damaging self-scrutiny. History, after all, could not be wrong, so the people whom it had called to serve must somehow have failed it. For decades, communists of every kind picked at the fraying edges of their ideology, defining and denouncing each other's mistakes. The debates echoed something of the Soviet of 1917, for they were abstract, well-intentioned, literate and doomed. 'Having grown up under the conditions of revolutionary struggle against the old regime,' wrote one contemporary, 'we had all been trained in the psychology of oppositionists, of irreconcilable non-conformists ... In short, we were all critics, destructionists – not builders.'[18]

By the end of 1927, just ten years after Lenin's own triumphant coup, Stalin was more or less omnipotent in the Kremlin. When the French communist Victor Serge visited Radek in his Kremlin suite in December that year, he found the disgraced politician packing up to leave. Instead of riches, all he had to show for his career was a vast pile of books. 'We've been absolute idiots!' Radek fumed. 'We haven't a halfpenny, when we could have kept back some pretty spoils of war for ourselves! Today we are being killed off through lack of money. We, with our celebrated revolutionary honesty, we've just been over-scrupulous sods of intellectuals.'[19]

The 'over-scrupulous sods' had lost. Trotsky was exiled to Central Asia. Zinoviev and Kamenev were expelled from the party and hounded by Stalin's policemen. Radek was packed off to the Siberian town of Tobolsk. Even Krupskaya, who had shared their opposition to the Stalin line, was targeted in an obscene whispering campaign. 'Within the ranks of the apparatus,' wrote Trotsky, 'they systematically compromised her, blackened her, degraded her.' The rumour spread that it was Inessa Armand who had been the leader's real love, that Krupskaya had been a deadweight, dowdy and absurd. At one point, Stalin even muttered that he could 'make someone else Lenin's widow'.[20] Blackmail and bullying behind the scenes ensured the ailing woman's silence after 1926. In years to come (she died in 1939), this tireless underground conspirator and lifelong socialist was gagged, her rich experience of Lenin now too dangerous to share. She could not even get her memoirs into print until they had been purged of Trotsky's name.

Zinoviev was shot with Kamenev in 1936. His son Stefan – who as a little boy in Switzerland had enchanted Lenin so much that the leader once attempted to adopt him – was shot in 1937. Zinoviev's second wife and travelling companion of 1917, who was exiled to one of the most northern labour colonies, was shot in 1938. His first wife, Olga Ravich, the woman who had irritated Lenin with her piercing laugh, was arrested for her part in the alleged opposition and spent two decades in the Arctic camps. Neither age nor gender was a defence, and nor was infirmity. Shlyapnikov's torment was particularly cruel. In 1933, he wrote to Stalin personally, pleading that he had gone almost completely deaf and that he wanted to retire into his silent world. The following year, by way of answer, Stalin had him tried and exiled to the Kola peninsula, one of the coldest places on the planet. He was recalled several months later, humiliated and frightened, before being freed, arrested and then tried again. Nothing that he had witnessed at the hands of the tsarist police had been remotely as sadistic or gratuitous. In September 1937, and still protesting his innocence, he was shot for his supposed involvement in Zinoviev's so-called conspiracy.[21]

If the deaf and enfeebled Shlyapnikov was marked for death, then Sukhanov, a Menshevik and author of the best eye-witness chronicle of Petrograd's brief revolutionary spring, was bound to end up in the Kremlin's sights. Acerbic though he always was, he had remained in Russia to take part in the future he had glimpsed with so much rapture from the steps of the Tauride. Ambition proved to be a trap. 'How can one describe the condition of people who sensed with all their being the approach of a terrible disaster,' asked Soviet writer Boris Yefimov, 'and did not know how to escape it, how to save themselves, and remained bound and helpless in a nightmare?'[22] Sukhanov was arrested in an early cull of 1931. Arriving in the labour camp at Verkhne-Uralsk, he attempted to evade his fate by reminding his captors that he had co-operated willingly in the weeks before his trial. He had betrayed a lot of friends, he had a right to his reward. The secret police spirited him from the convicts' crowded dormitory and no one in the outside world would ever hear from him again.[23]

Karl Radek's tactics were broadly the same. His exile in Tobolsk was unbearable, so he wrote to Stalin in the spring of 1929, accepting the new party line, denouncing Trotsky as a terrorist and pleading to come back and serve in Moscow. The tyrant was amused enough to grant his wish, and for a few years Radek acted as Stalin's fawning spokesman. But he had already been warned about his promiscuous wit. Muscovites quipped that Radek was the origin of every anti-Stalin joke in Russia. 'Most men's heads control their tongues,' Stalin remarked. 'Radek's tongue controls his head.'[24] Radek was arrested in October 1936 on treason charges, and stood trial the following January. Among his fellow defendants was Grigory Sokolnikov, the banker and economist, another veteran of Lenin's train. Unusually, neither man received a death sentence: Radek had bought his paltry reprieve by implicating former comrades in a new (and imaginary) terrorist network. The betrayal spared him a bullet but it did not save his life for long. Though their murders were made to look like the result of accidental brawls, Radek and Sokolnikov were beaten to death in their respective labour camps within a few days of each other.[25]

As a Pole and a businessman, efficient and still sporting a crisp suit, Fürstenberg had no idea that his cards had also been marked. It was true that he had not kept his original job in the financial world. With the absurdity that was characteristic of the times, he had been moved to the State Administration of Music and Entertainment and then, in yet another reshuffle, he had taken over the management of Moscow's circuses and public concerts. His danse macabre would end in July 1937. As the police went through his flat, he tried to scribble a note to Stalin, clutching his pencil so tightly that it kept breaking. 'A nightmarish tragic accident has occurred,' he scrawled. 'They have arrested me tonight! They are already calling me an enemy! What's going on? How could such a ghastly mistake be made?'[26]

There never were mistakes, of course. The police confiscated a pile of 'compromising' books from the Fürstenbergs' flat, including works by many of the comrades that the businessman had helped: Radek and Trotsky, Zinoviev, Kamenev and Shlyapnikov. The arresting officers may well have pocketed a souvenir or two before they wrote it, but their report insisted that Russia's former banker possessed no other valuables worth mentioning beyond two US dollars and a collection of antique revolvers. The next steps were the usual ones: a short but polite questioning, a beating, tearful pleading and humiliation in a bloodstained room. His torturers were more fastidious than usual (the party did not want to draw attention to those past transfers of German cash), but Fürstenberg was shot, as were his wife and son, after a fifteen-minute trial.[27] His daughter spent years in the camps, still believing her mother and brother to be alive. As for Fritz Platten, the Swiss socialist and on-train go-between, he had crossed the border into Russia many times after his failed attempt in 1917. Having spent nearly two decades in the service of the Soviet state, he was arrested in 1939 and sentenced to exile in the Archangel region, where he died in 1942.[28]

Lenin's real opponents often had a better time. In the brief interval when flight was possible (that route through Finland was busy again), a number of former members of the Provisional Government and Soviet Executive escaped to France (Germany, after all, was not an option). By the 1920s, there was a lively, disputatious Russian colony in Paris. Chkheidze and Tsereteli both lived there, and they shared their exile with an array of their former adversaries, including Prince Georgy Lvov, Mikhail Tereshchenko and Paul Miliukov. While never loath to argue as they smoked their long, fragrant cigars, these gentlemen tended to use the leisure that they now enjoyed to justify themselves in print. Many would contribute to

Russian-language newspapers, new titles in the émigré tradition of the ones that had flourished in France before the war. The most determined, however, wrote memoirs. Miliukov remained obsessed with the issues of foreign policy and liberal reform that had inspired his brief political career, while Tsereteli (who wrote his memoirs later, in New York) laboured to reconstruct the agonizing compromises of that fatal spring.

Neither enjoyed the same celebrity as Kerensky. Drama had followed him until the last. Most members of his final cabinet were arrested in October 1917 (they had repaired to the White Dining Room inside the Winter Palace), but he made his escape in an American embassy car.[29] He had a plan to organize an uprising against the Leninists, but it did not come off. Months later, Robert Bruce Lockhart (by now the head of the British mission) helped him to emigrate on a false visa. Kerensky, once adored and fêted, often showered with bouquets, was to live modestly at first, joining the Russian community in France and continuing to rail against the Bolsheviks. He escaped for a second time as Hitler's troops approached in 1940. His future lay in the United States.

Lenin remained his nemesis. Where others skimmed over the drama of the sealed train, Kerensky wallowed in it, always regretting the fact that he had not (as he put it) had time enough to prove the case about Lenin's connection with the German government. Blaming Lenin, then, became a way of letting himself off the hook; it also allowed him to claim that Russia might not have been doomed, in battle and on the home front, despite the mounting pile of evidence suggesting otherwise. While he deplored those tragedies, however, Kerensky quickly reconciled himself to the new world and his old age was an agreeable combination of scholarship and minor celebrity. He published several versions of his own memoirs and helped to edit a classic multi-volume selection of primary documents from 1917.[30] 'Although Kerensky could be standoffish at times,' a fellow professor at Stanford remembered, 'he developed a great circle of academic friends, loved a good party and mixed well, especially with the ladies.'[31]

By 1937, according to a Russian observer, the Soviet public was 'utterly sick of politics' and wanted 'nothing but to be left in peace and to be able to live in peace'.[32] It was a cry that everyone had heard before, and the mature Soviet regime certainly needed something more than violence to get people to slave for it. As Trotsky had said, in a different context, 'masses of men cannot be led to death unless the army command has the death penalty in its arsenal . . . Yet armies are not built on fear.'[33] The propaganda of the 1930s set the standard for its genre. Combining all the fun of mass events with stirring messages of hope, it offered citizens a shining dream in place of private comfort and traditional community. The dream was false: the party's leaders were a charmless and malicious clique, but Lenin was always with them (that was the slogan, anyway), and he was not the type to let them down.

The cult of Lenin was a flagrant lie. Simplifying anything that it did not fake, it reduced its hero to an unconvincing plaster saint, a sort of cartoon Uncle Vlad. Lenin was both more and less than this; no statue, song or festival could capture the ambition of his dream, and none could blot the bloodstains from its execution. This uncle had sent tens of thousands to their deaths; the system he created was a stifling, cruel, sterile one, a workshop for decades of tyranny.

And yet his cult was all that stood between the people and their fear of chaos and another civil war. The idea of turning his body into a permanent exhibit developed slowly over several years, but by the 1930s his mausoleum and the corpse within it were on Red Square to stay.

That mausoleum was an insult to the countless bodies Lenin had destroyed, and there was no excuse for keeping the remains inside except to demonstrate beyond all doubt that one monster really was dead. Though Stalin was more than capable of formulating those ideas in private, however, outwardly he exploited the body like a holy relic. The high hopes of 1917 were fading by the time he came to power; Lenin's death-cult boosted them again by invoking the ghosts of ideas that had set the wartime world alight. Immortal Lenin put all doubt to shame; his shrine reminded everyone that Russians were the pioneers of mankind's progress towards socialism. In life, the greatest Bolshevik on earth had led his people in their sacred, world-historic struggle; in faith, and with his help, announced the propaganda in its boldest print, they would fight on, and die if need be, for the sake of a collective human destiny. To avoid distraction and weakness, meanwhile, even Soviet people needed leadership, and that happened to be Stalin's forte.

The cult survived for sixty years because it kept a bankrupt polity intact. Lenin stayed dead; yet he was always near at hand, convenient and dependable. For as long as the Soviet empire lasted, the Lenin statues could be mocked but they were not torn down. The anti-Lenin jokes were funny precisely because Lenin was there, as dowdy, reassuring and immovable as a black-lead kitchen range. 'The jubilee year!' read *Pravda* on 16 April 1967, the fiftieth anniversary of Lenin's return to the Finland Station. 'Let's start it well!' The words were meaningless, and the newspaper would end up in pieces on the paper-nail in some earth privy within hours, but Lenin held the universe aloft, and the alternative (as the leaders occasionally ventured to hint) was almost guaranteed catastrophe. By sleight of hand, one of the most epic revolutions in history was made to double as a sermon on the value of a strong, vigilant state.

The most dangerous time was the late 1980s, when Mikhail Gorbachev announced his policy of glasnost. Over the next few years, historians stripped Soviet mythology of each lie in succession, beginning with the Gulag but soon turning to October 1917. In the process almost every Soviet hero was exposed as a blackguard or a thief, but though he took a few half-hearted blows, Lenin came off better than the rest. His relationship with Inessa distracted many readers from genuine stories of his cruelty. For a few years in the early 1990s, the government withdrew its funding from the team that maintained the dead leader's corpse, but the approach of the millennium brought better times and ever fatter envelopes of cash. 'Even the hireling scribblers did not manage to blacken his name,' a latter-day communist wrote in *Pravda* in April 1997.[34] This was another false statement, for researchers had found abundant evidence of Lenin as mass-murderer, but it was true that his cult – like his mummified remains – had made it safely into the post-Soviet age.

Vladimir Putin became president in 2000, and for a while after that Russia's leaders chose to focus on an undisputed victory – the triumph that they called the Great Patriotic War – rather than reflecting too much on the controversial revolutionary stuff. The public celebration of Lenin's coup (marked annually on 7 November) was replaced in 2005 by something called 'National Unity Day' (celebrated on 4 November), an allusion to events that took place in a long-forgotten century (the seventeenth) and whose heroes did not look at all like anyone around today. But as the centenary of Russia's year of revolutions approached, it was clear that Lenin's role would have to be commemorated. The state needed to take the lead, to seize control lest others might. Bishops were called to the Kremlin. Historians, slack-jowled from years of euphemism, assembled at their reserved seats. Microphones were positioned, and warm sparkling wine awaited as the speeches, as they always do, ran well past their allotted time.[35] The budget for Russia's centenary events in 2017 was stupendous. In general, the message (though the transcripts use more words than this) was that a lot of people suffered and the Russians of the present day will not forget.

The technique was to keep things bland. Long speeches in assorted overheated rooms were excellent for this, while cartoon strips could tell the public stories that already bored them in a pleasantly nostalgic way.[36] At all costs, the image of Petrograd as it had been in a far-off spring, with angry crowds and troops abandoning their posts, had to stay firmly in the past, for recent re-runs, springs for people close to home, had been disastrous to Russia's interests in the Baltic, Georgia and Ukraine. 'We will commemorate the four-hundredth anniversary of the Romanovs,' observed *Novaya Gazeta*'s Kirill Martynov in 2015, 'and immediately after it the centenary of the October Revolution. We will mark the day of the Chekist [Lenin's secret police] and then, without delay, the day of remembrance for the victims of political repression . . . Putin, Stalin, Lenin and Nicholas II, holding each other by the hand, are leading Russia from victory to victory.'[37] Like concrete smothering precocious shoots, the festival would flatten any awkward curiosity before it could be vocalized. As Culture Minister Vladimir Medinsky put it, a series of centenary commemorations in 2017 would encourage people to 'understand the importance for Russia of strong state power, supported by all layers of the population'.[38]

If Lenin's corpse survives all this, it will not be by accident. It takes a lot of skill to keep him fresh. Each year, not long after the Christmas break, vigilant Muscovites watch for an ambulance bumping across Red Square. Inside it, Lenin is being taken for maintenance. In 2015, as the leader's 145th birthday loomed, someone with influence decided that he also deserved a new suit. Experts in a special lab removed the existing trousers and jacket, the old shirt, tie and woollen socks. Beneath them, the corpse was clothed, as always, in a double-layered bodysuit of clear rubber whose purpose is to trap a film of embalming fluid over what is left of the skin. The removal of this demands a delicate touch, but there are practised fingers to command, for the embalming coat – a gruesome sort of bodystocking – has needed changing regularly for more than ninety years. While it is off, the naked corpse, with waxy patches here and there, must be revived in a series of chemical baths, each one infused with a more sinister preservative cocktail. A brand-new rubber film is then eased on, sealing the fluid underneath. That done, the tailors may come in to measure up.[39]

Dead though he is, this Lenin is an awkward presence in the Russia of Vladimir Putin, which is itself an artefact whose oily coat conceals unfathomable depths of rot. The current regime takes its cue from Russia's old-time tsars. The president has borrowed a good deal from the Romanovs' faux-Byzantine style (that gold, those uniforms, the whole imperial parade), and like them he makes ample use of Russia's ultra-nationalist church. In January 2016, perhaps to test the public appetite for getting rid of the expensive body in Red Square, Putin ventured to accuse Lenin of undermining Russia's unity – and, more importantly, its tight hold on Ukraine – by encouraging movements for national autonomy in the old tsarist empire. Ideas like that, Putin informed a scientific conference, 'planted an atomic bomb under the house that we call Russia, and it eventually collapsed.'[40] An outcry led to recantation, with Putin's press secretary hastily claiming that the president's words were just a 'personal view'.[41] He may be noxious and he may cost millions to keep in shape, but Lenin has a charisma that still holds many Russians in its grip.

'We are grateful to Lenin,' the curator of the *Pravda* museum explained. 'It is because of Lenin that we still have all of this, that we survived.' We were in a fine building on the Moika, and she had been showing me the floor where *Pravda* had been written and produced from February to July 1917. Thanks to state money over many years, a good deal of the old clutter has been preserved, including Lenin's small office (large leather-topped desk with green-shaded lamps, papers, Bakelite telephone) and the staff room next door (bentwood chairs, round table, scattering of antique newspapers, more books). Next comes the print room, airy and flooded with light. Few of the presses are original – the ones that produced *Pravda* have been lost – and the room, whose tiled floor keeps it always cool, was used to store meat carcasses for many years, but the curators have restored it as an exhibition of printing history and it is beautiful.

The problem, and it afflicts every Lenin site, is that visitor numbers have declined since 1991. The collapse of the Soviet state was bad news for the revolution industry in general, and latterly few Russians have much time to spare from shopping and computer screens. The *Pravda* museum no longer features on prescribed school tours in Russia, and negative political publicity in the foreign press has caused a drop in tourist visits by outsiders in the past few years. To save their jobs, to say nothing of their heritage, museum staff have been forced to adapt. My guide took up the story as we walked. 'These rooms', she said, 'are now called the museum of tolerance.' Since I was visiting during a sanctions war, I found the idea startling, and Lenin might have bridled too, for 'tolerance' was never his strong point. On Russia's new curriculum for schools, however, the relevant module is compulsory. 'The exhibit shows us what Russia owes to Europe,' the guide explained (as we spoke, European cheese was being bulldozed into landfill somewhere near the Russo-Belarusian border). 'The piano is English, for instance, and the typewriter was made in Germany before 1914.'

Museum staff are not to blame. Inventive, energetic, committed, they do their best to keep the interest alive. But as long as Russia's electorate continues to evade responsibility for what its government chooses to do, investing in a set of fantasies as wild as many of the Lenin years, no light can be allowed to shine on the hard questions of the past. Too much reality is disturbing, especially when Putin's media strategy is based so heavily on his ability to soothe. Keep Lenin dead, that's the idea. If people cannot live without his relics, then store the lot like nuclear waste: contain the fall-out, make sure everyone stays calm. A rubber skin across the top will trap both lifeblood and corruption out of sight. The history of Lenin's train must be preserved and yet it must not be allowed to move. Everything is sacred, but nothing must ever signify.

I remember my first apartment-museum, the one where Lenin lived with his sisters. The prize exhibit there was one of Lenin's wheelchairs (ironically English-made) that someone had rescued when a museum near Moscow closed in the difficult 1990s. It was incongruous in St Petersburg, especially in an apartment that the leader himself did not revisit in the years of his infirmity. The curator was glad to have the object, however, and prouder still to wheel it out and let me touch. But then she talked about the clock. 'We cannot have it repaired,' she told me as I raised an eyebrow at the lifeless pendulum. 'It was here when Lenin was, so it is too precious to send out to a repair shop. But we cannot afford to have an expert come to us. All we can do is keep it here. We must look after it.' The clock has stopped in every sense, and the effect is suffocating.

There was another Lenin once, and he was neither bland nor dead. This man belongs to the springtime of hope, and it was revolution that defined his life. The only lively Lenin monument is also one of the very first, the work of someone who had known the man for real. The statue stands outside the Finland Station in St Petersburg and it was erected in 1926, two years after the leader's death. Despite its monstrous size and weight, this Lenin has all the energy of the original. He stands high on an armoured car, his feet in shop-bought Swedish shoes, and while his left hand has been tucked into the armpit of his bronze waistcoat, the right is thrusting forwards: emphatic, strong, forever in command.

Notes

Abbreviations

LCW   Lenin: *Collected Works* (English-language edition, 47 vols, Moscow, 1960–80)

PSS   Lenin: *Polnoe sobranie sochinenii* (55 vols, Moscow 1958–65)

TNA   The National Archives, London

VoVIL   G. N. Golikov et al. (eds), *Vospominaniia o Vladimire Il'iche Lenine v piati tomakh* (5 vols, Moscow, 1979)

Introduction

1 For this story, and pictures of the train, see http://www.historiskt.nu/normalsp/staten/sb_bd_haparanda/haparanda_station_07.html (accessed January 2016)

2 In principle, anyway. In the autumn of 2015, when Finnish nationalists began a general panic about the numbers of new migrants that might flood through from Haparanda, sporadic border controls resumed.

3 John Buchan, *Greenmantle* (London, 1916), Chapter 3

4 F. W. Heath (ed.), *Great Destiny: Sixty Years of the Memorable Events in the Life of the Man of the Century Recounted in his own Incomparable Words* (New York, 1965), pp. 388–9

5 The worst culprit is Martin Gilbert, *Russian History Atlas* (London, 1972), whose map (p. 87) indicates a route around the Baltic from Stockholm via Hangö to Petrograd, thereby

cutting more than a thousand miles off Lenin's real route. The same map was reproduced in subsequent versions of the book (*The Routledge Atlas of Russian History*, London, 2002 and 2007). Following Michael Pearson (*The Sealed Train*, Newton Abbot, 1975), most other historians send Lenin up the Swedish coast along a track that was not even laid until the 1920s.

6 Edmund Wilson, *To the Finland Station: A Study in the Writing and Acting of History* (New York, 1940)

7 Alan Moorehead, *The Russian Revolution* (London, 1958)

8 Pearson, *Sealed Train*

9 Marcel Liebman, *Leninism under Lenin* (London, 1975), p. 22

10 Cited in Maksim Gorky, *Days with Lenin* (London, 1932), p. 52

Chapter 1: Dark Forces

1 For more on Hoare's recruitment and this first mission, see J. A. Cross, *Sir Samuel Hoare: A Political Biography* (London, 1977), pp. 39–40

2 Keith Jeffery, *MI6: The History of the Secret Intelligence Service, 1909–1949* (London, 2010), pp. 30 and 103; Samuel Hoare, *The Fourth Seal* (London, 1930), p. 31

3 Hoare, *Fourth Seal*, p. 184

4 Jeffery, *MI6*, p. 96

5 Keith Neilson, *Strategy and Supply: The Anglo-Russian Alliance, 1914–17* (London, 1984), p. 312; Michael Smith, *Six: The Real James Bonds, 1909–1939* (London, 2011), p. 187.

6 Hoare, *Fourth Seal*, p. 30; see also Michael Hughes, *Inside the Enigma: British Diplomats in Russia, 1900–1939* (London, 1997), pp. 55–7

7 Hoare, *Fourth Seal*, p. 34

8 Ingvar Andersson, *A History of Sweden* (London, 1956), pp. 426–7; A. Nekludoff, *Diplomatic Reminiscences* (London, 1920), pp. 332–4

9 Hugh Brogan (ed.), *Signalling from Mars: The Letters of Arthur Ransome* (London, 1998), p. 18

10 Hoare, *Fourth Seal*, p. 40

11 Ibid., pp. 277–81

12 Arthur Ransome, *The Autobiography of Arthur Ransome* (London, 1976), p. 172

13 Paul Miliukov, *Political Memoirs, 1905–17*, edited by Arthur P. Mendel (Ann Arbor, 1967), p. 342

14 Hoare, *Fourth Seal*, p. 41

15 Ransome, *Autobiography*, p. 145

16 Hoare, *Fourth Seal*, p. 43

17 Nekludoff, *Reminiscences*, p. 386 (he made the same journey in 1916)

18 For figures, see T. Hasegawa, *The February Revolution: Petrograd, 1917* (Seattle and London, 1981), pp. 66–70

19 Robert B. McKean, *St Petersburg between the Revolutions: Workers and Revolutionaries, June 1907–February 1917* (New Haven and London, 1990), p. 40

20 Meriel Buchanan, *The Dissolution of an Empire* (London, 1932), p. 5

21 Anthony Cross, 'A Corner of a Foreign Field: The British Embassy in St Petersburg, 1863–1918', in Simon Dixon (ed.), *Personality and Place in Russian Culture: Essays in Memory of Lindsey Hughes* (London, 2010), pp. 345 and 353

22 Hoare, *Fourth Seal*, p. 237

23 Robert Bruce Lockhart, *Memoirs of a British Agent* (London, 1974), p. 117

24 W. Somerset Maugham, *Ashenden, or, The British Agent* (London, 1928), p. 209; Mayhew, cited in Hughes, *Enigma*, p. 20

25 Hoare, *Fourth Seal*, p. 243

26 Alan Moorehead, *The Russian Revolution* (London, 1958), p. 183

27 Lockhart, *Memoirs*, p. 116

28 Hoare, *Fourth Seal*, p. 48

29 Ibid., pp. 50–52

30 Cited in Jeffery, *MI6*, p. 102

31 Smith, *Six*, pp. 187–96

32 William Gerhardie, *Memoirs of a Polyglot* (London, 1990), p. 115

33 Hughes, *Enigma*, p. 55; Jeffery, *MI6*, p. 99

34 Smith, *Six*, p. 196

35 Ransome, *Autobiography*, p. 167

36 Hoare, *Fourth Seal*, pp. 58, 82

37 M. Paléologue, *An Ambassador's Memoirs* (London, 1923–5), vol. 3, p. 44

38 Meriel Buchanan, *Petrograd: The City of Trouble, 1914–1918* (London, 1918), p. 77

39 Miliukov, *Memoirs*, p. 362

40 Hoare, *Fourth Seal*, p. 242; Ransome, *Autobiography*, p. 167

41 Miliukov, *Memoirs*, p. 362

42 Hoare, *Fourth Seal*, p. 105

43 Charlotte Alston, *Russia's Greatest Enemy?: Harold Williams and the Russian Revolution* (London, 2007), p. 112

44 Miliukov, *Memoirs*, p. 334

45 Hoare, *Fourth Seal*, p. 105

46 William G. Rosenberg, *Liberals in the Russian Revolution: The Constitutional Democratic Party, 1917–1921* (Princeton, 1974), pp. 20–21

47 On Kadet demands, see Melissa Kirschke Stockdale, *Paul Miliukov and the Quest for a Liberal Russia* (Ithaca, NY, 1996), pp. 224–5

48 Miliukov, *Memoirs*, p. 317

49 For the stories, see Paléologue, *Memoirs*, vol. 3, p. 63

50 Stinton Jones, *Russia in Revolution: By an Eye-Witness* (London, 1917), p. 60

51 Sir George William Buchanan, *My Mission to Russia and Other Diplomatic Memories* (2 vols, London, 1923), vol. 2, p. 56, citing his report of 18 February 1917

52 Nekludoff, *Reminiscences*, p. 447; Paléologue, *Memoirs*, vol. 3, p. 46; Stockdale, *Miliukov*, p. 232

53 Paléologue, *Memoirs*, vol. 3, p. 111

54 Ibid., p. 49

55 The National Archives (TNA) FO 371/2995 (reports by Buchanan and John F. Douglas, November and December 1916)

56 Hoare, *Fourth Seal*, p. 109

57 Buchanan, *Mission*, vol. 2, p. 41. See also M. V. Rodzianko, *Krushenie imperii: gosudarstvennaia duma i fevral'skaia 1917 goda revoliutsiia* (Moscow, 1986), p. 210

58 For the speech itself, see V. D. Karpovich (ed.), *Gosudarstvennaia duma, 1906–1917: stenograficheskie otchety* (4 vols, Moscow, 1995), vol. 4, pp. 43–8

59 Cited in Stockdale, *Miliukov*, p. 236

60 Alexander Rabinowitch, *Prelude to Revolution: The Petrograd Bolsheviks and the July 1917 Uprising* (Bloomington, Ind. 1968), p. 20; Paléologue, *Memoirs*, vol. 3, p. 74; Sir Alfred Knox, *With the Russian Army, 1914–1917* (2 vols, London, 1921), vol. 2, p. 515

61 Hoare, *Fourth Seal*, pp. 117–18 (italics in original)

62 Cited in Jeffery, *MI6*, pp. 106–7

63 Paléologue, *Memoirs*, vol. 3, p. 135

64 Hoare, *Fourth Seal*, p. 147

65 Smith, *Six*, pp. 199–200

66 Lockhart, *Memoirs*, p. 100

67 Buchanan, *Mission*, vol. 2, p. 44; Knox, *Russian Army*, vol. 2, p. 515

68 On the Milner mission, see Elizabeth Greenhalgh, *The French Army and the First World War* (Cambridge, 2014), p. 181; Hoare, *Fourth Seal*, p. 201

69 Lockhart, *Memoirs*, p. 162

70 Meriel Buchanan, *Petrograd*, pp. 89–90; Hoare, *Fourth Seal*, pp. 204–5

71 Lockhart, *Memoirs*, p. 107

72 Jeffery, *MI6*, p. 104. The eighteen men that Jeffery notes included Hoare himself.

73 Neilson, *Strategy*, p. 243

74 Lockhart, *Memoirs*, p. 163

75 Meriel Buchanan, *Petrograd*, p. 90

76 Alexander Kerensky, *The Kerensky Memoirs: Russia and History's Turning-Point* (London, 1966), p. 182

77 TNA FO 371/2995, 14 February 1917

78 TNA CAB 24/3/42, David Davies, Notes on the Political Situation, 10 March 1917

Chapter 2: Black Markets

1 A. Scherer and J. Grunewald (eds), *L'Allemagne et les problèmes de la paix pendant la première guerre mondiale: documents extraits des archives de l'Office allemand des Affaires étrangères* (3 vols, Paris, 1962–76), vol. 1, p. 37 (Bethmann-Hollweg to Ballin, 25 December 1914)

2 For examples, see ibid., p. 68 (Bethmann-Hollweg to Copenhagen with information for Scavenius to transmit to the tsar, 6 March 1915); p. 70 (Brockdorff-Rantzau to Bethmann-Hollweg on Scavenius' information, 10 March 1915); p. 416 (Jagow to Brockdorff-Rantzau, 26 July 1915)

3 Ibid., p. 45 (Brockdorff-Rantzau to Bethmann-Hollweg, 8 January 1915)

4 On Brockdorff-Rantzau, see Z. A. B. Zeman and W. B. Scharlau, *The Merchant of Revolution: The Life of Alexander Israel Helphand (Parvus), 1867–1924* (London and New York, 1965), p. 166

5 Scherer and Grunewald, *Documents*, vol. 1, pp. 166 and 150–51

6 Rosenberg, *Liberals*, p. 11

7 George Katkov assisted by Michael Futrell, 'German Political Intervention in Russia during the First World War', in Richard Pipes (ed.), *Revolutionary Russia* (Cambridge, Mass., 1968), pp. 63–96

8 Ibid., p. 71

9 Michael Futrell, *Northern Underground: Episodes of Russian Revolutionary Transport and Communications through Scandinavia and Finland, 1863–1917* (London, 1963), p. 112

10 Alfred Erich Senn, *The Russian Revolution in Switzerland, 1914–1917* (Madison, 1971), pp. 63–4

11 Wayne C. Thompson, *In the Eye of the Storm: Kurt Riezler and the Crises of Modern Germany* (Iowa City, 1980), p. 97

12 On Ireland, see Reinhard R. Doerries, *Prelude to the Easter Rising: Sir Roger Casement in Imperial Germany* (London, 2000). On the east, see A. Will: *Kein Griff nach der Weltmacht: Geheime Dienste und Propaganda im deutsch-österreichisch-turkischen Bundnis 1914–18* (Cologne, 2012)

13 The treaty of 23 December 1914 obliging them to do this was never ratified by the Irish republican leadership. See Doerries, *Prelude*, p. 10

14 For evidence, see TNA CAB 24/143/2 (Eastern Report, 4 February 1917)

15 The team that worked on Ukraine, for instance, was headed by one Dr Zimmer. See Z. A. B. Zeman (ed.), *Germany and the Revolution in Russia, 1915–1918: Documents from the Archives of the German Foreign Ministry* (London, 1958), p. 1 (Document of 9 January 1915)

16 Anthony Curtis, *Somerset Maugham* (London, 1977), pp. 94–5; Jeffery, *MI6*, p. 90

17 Leon Trotsky, *My Life: An Attempt at an Autobiography* (Harmondsworth, 1984), p. 245

18 On Maugham's mission, see the commentary in Curtis, *Maugham*, pp. 94–5, and the fictionalized account in his own *Ashenden*

19 Senn, *Switzerland*, p. 14

20 Alexander Shlyapnikov, *On the Eve of 1917: Reminiscences from the Revolutionary Underground* (London and New York, 1982), pp. 47 and 120

21 Nekludoff, *Memoirs*, p. 383

22 Moorehead, *Revolution*, p. 129

23 Boris I. Nikolaevsky, *Tainye stranitsy istorii* (Moscow, 1995), pp. 271–2

24 See Lockhart, *Memoirs*, pp. 144–5; Keith Neilson, 'Joy Rides? British Intelligence and Propaganda in Russia, 1914–1917', *Historical Journal*, 24:4 (1981), p. 894

25 Senn, *Switzerland*, pp. 60–61 and 73

26 Fritz Platten, 'Revoliutsionery vostoka', in G. N. Golikov et al. (eds), *Vospominaniia o Vladimire Il'iche Lenine* (5 vols, Moscow, 1979; hereafter VoVIL), vol. 5, p. 90; Trotsky, *My Life*, pp. 257–8

27 For Zivin/Weis, see Zeman, *Documents*, pp. 18–23 (Minister in Bern to Chancellor, 24 August 1916)

28 Nikolaevsky, *Tainye*, pp. 269–81

29 Zeman, *Documents*, p. 1 (Berlin, 9 January 1915)

30 Zeman and Scharlau, *Merchant*, pp. 20 and 29

31 Trotsky, *My Life*, p. 172

32 Zeman and Scharlau, *Merchant*, pp. 55–8

33 Trotsky, *My Life*, p. 172

34 Zeman and Scharlau, *Merchant*, pp. 98–9

35 Ibid., p. 128

36 Dmitry Volkogonov, *Lenin: Life and Legacy* (trans. Harold Shukman, London, 1994), p. 112

37 There is a hint to that effect in Wangenheim's report of 9 January 1915 (Zeman, *Documents*, pp. 1–2). For more on Parvus' financial dealings in wartime Turkey, see M. Asim Karaömerlioglu, 'Helphand-Parvus and his Impact on Turkish Intellectual Life', *Middle Eastern Studies* 40:6 (November 2004), p. 158

38 Zeman, *Documents*, p. 2

39 Ibid., pp. 140–52; the document was undated, but appeared in the register for 9 March 1917. For further commentary, see Moorehead, *Revolution*, p. 132; Zeman and Scharlau, *Merchant*, p. 149

40 Zeman, *Documents*, p. 3 (Fröhlich to Diego von Bergen, Berlin 26 March 1915 and notes)

41 Ibid., p. 4 (Rantzau, 14 August 1915); for the money in July, see ibid., pp. 3–4 (Jagow to the State Secretary of the Treasury, 6 July 1915)

42 Curt von Westernhagen, *Wagner: A Biography* (Cambridge, 1981), p. 222

43 Zeman and Scharlau, *Merchant*, p. 156

44 Zeman, *Documents*, pp. 140ff (memorandum by Dr Helphand)

45 Zeman and Scharlau, *Merchant*, pp. 157–9

46 Volkogonov, *Lenin*, p. 113

47 V. I. Lenin, *Collected Works* (47 vols, Moscow, 1960–80; hereafter LCW), vol. 21 (London, 1964), pp. 421–2 (*Sotsial-Demokrat*, No. 48, 20 November 1915)

48 Zeman and Scharlau, *Merchant*, p. 164

49 Ibid., p. 199

50 On his unattractiveness, see Futrell, *Northern Underground*, p. 193; for the flower, Pearson, *Sealed Train*, p. 101

51 W. H. Beable, *Commercial Russia* (London, 1918), p. 215

52 Futrell, *Northern Underground*, pp. 192–4

53 Ibid., p. 181

54 He joined in April 1916. See Semion Lyandres, 'The Bolsheviks' "German Gold" Revisited: An Inquiry into the 1917 Accusations', *Carl Beck Papers in Russian and East European Studies*, No. 1106 (February 1995), p. 22

55 Futrell, *Northern Underground*, p. 191

56 Cited in Volkogonov, *Lenin*, p. 114

57 Ibid.

58 For the address, see Zeman and Scharlau, *Merchant*, p. 198

59 Thompson, *Riezler*, pp. 132–3

60 Futrell, *Northern Underground*, p. 145

61 Nekludoff, *Memoirs*, pp. 490–92

62 Futrell, *Northern Underground*, p. 145. Futrell's story was based on an interview with the aged Kesküla years later, but a different version appears in Moorehead, *Revolution*, p. 136

63 Shlyapnikov, *On the Eve*, pp. 51–2

64 Zeman, *Documents*, p. 7 (Romberg to the Chancellor, 30 September 1915)

65 The go-between was to have been Alexander Kesküla. For the document, see ibid., pp. 6–7 (Romberg to the Chancellor, 30 September 1915); Futrell, *Northern Underground*, p. 100

66 Zeman, *Documents*, pp. 11–12 (Steinwachs to Diego von Bergen, enclosing letter from 'Stein' [Kesküla] of 9 January 1916)

67 Ibid., pp. 17–18 (Steinwachs to Diego von Bergen on budget for agents, 8 May 1916); Futrell, *Northern Underground*, p. 148

68 Futrell, *Northern Underground*, pp. 17–18

Chapter 3: Red Lake

1 Carter Elwood, 'Lenin on Holiday', *Revolutionary Russia*, 21:2 (December 2008), p. 122

2 Nadezhda Krupskaya, *Memories of Lenin* (London, 1970), p. 284

3 Ivan Babushkin, cited in Helen Rappaport, *Conspirator: Lenin in Exile* (London, 2009), p. 8

4 LCW, vol. 22, pp. 184–304

5 Senn, *Switzerland*, p. 151

6 Rapport, *Conspirator*, pp. 255 and 201

7 Cited in Volkogonov, *Lenin*, p. 83

8 See Neil Harding, *Lenin's Political Thought* (Basingstoke, 1986), vol. 1, p. 194

9 Gorky, *Days with Lenin*, p. 12; VoVIL, vol. 5, p. 69 (Feliks Kon)

10 Valeriu Marcu, 'Lenin in Zurich, a Memoir', *Foreign Affairs* 21:1 (1943), p. 550

11 Ibid.

12 M. I. Vasil'ev-Iuzhin, in VoVIL, vol. 2, p. 185, referring to a meeting in 1905

13 Cited in Richard Pipes, *The Russian Revolution, 1899–1919* (London, 1990), p. 348

14 N. L. Meshcheriakov, cited in VoVIL, vol. 2, p. 91; Gorky, *Days with Lenin*, pp. 5 and 23

15 VoVIL, vol. 2, p. 185 (M. I. Vasil'ev-Iuzhin on Lenin in 1905)

16 Cited in Volkogonov, *Lenin*, p. xxxvi

17 Kharitonova, in VoVIL, vol. 2, pp. 362–3; Krupskaya, *Memories*, p. 272; Rappaport, *Conspirator*, p. 252

18 Nikolai Sukhanov, *The Russian Revolution, 1917: A Personal Record* (edited, abridged and translated by Joel Carmichael, London, 1955), p. 281

19 Marcu, 'Lenin', pp. 554–5

20 LCW, vol. 23, p. 81 (Military Programme of the Proletarian Revolution, September 1916)

21 Marcu, 'Lenin', p. 556

22 LCW, vol. 21, pp. 30–34 (The War and Russian Social-Democracy, September 1914)

23 Marcu, 'Lenin', p. 556

24 Cited in Futrell, *Northern Underground*, p. 65

25 Trotsky, *My Life*, p. 167

26 Cited in ibid., p. 157

27 Krupskaya, *Memories*, p. 239

28 Ibid., p. 241

29 Senn, *Switzerland*, p. 33

30 Ibid., p. 22

31 LCW, vol. 21, pp. 15–16; on the Bolsheviks' caution about publishing in Switzerland, see Krupskaya, *Memories*, p. 250

32 Volkogonov, *Lenin*, p. 79

33 Warren Lerner, *Karl Radek: The Last Internationalist* (Stanford, Calif., 1970), p. 31

34 Cited in Krupskaya, *Memories*, p. 252

35 Ibid., p. 67

36 Rhiannon Vickers, *The Labour Party and the World*, vol. 1: *The Evolution of Labour's Foreign Policy, 1900–1951* (Manchester, 2004), pp. 56–8

37 Merle Fainsod, *International Socialism and the World War* (Cambridge, Mass., 1935), p. 42

38 Senn, *Switzerland*, p. 21

39 Miliukov, *Memoirs*, p. 305

40 Brogan, *Signalling from Mars*, p. 15

41 Fainsod, *International Socialism*, p. 42

42 Lerner, *Radek*, p. 33

43 Fainsod, *International Socialism*, p. 50

44 LCW, vol. 21, p. 163

45 Ibid., p. 192

46 Ibid., p. 299

47 Ibid., p. 382 ('The Defeat of Russia in the Revolutionary Crisis')

48 Ibid., pp. 196–8 (*Sotsial-demokrat*, No. 42, 21 May 1915)

49 Trotsky, *My Life*, p. 257

50 Senn, *Switzerland*, p. 91; Rappaport, *Conspirator*, p. 247

51 Senn, *Switzerland*, p. 91

52 Fritz Platten, cited in VoVIL, vol. 5, p. 90

53 Senn, *Switzerland*, p. 94

54 Lerner, *Radek*, p. 13

55 For Radek's biography, see ibid., and the excellent Jean-François Fayet, *Karl Radek: biographie politique* (Bern, 2004); on the

rumours about Parvus and the Institute, see Volkogonov, *Lenin*, p. 114

56 R. C. Elwood, *Inessa Armand: Revolutionary and Feminist* (Cambridge, 1992), pp. 167–9

57 Robert Service, *Lenin: A Political Life*, vol. 2: *Worlds in Collision* (Basingstoke, 1991), pp. 134–6

58 VoVIL, vol. 5, p. 66, memoir by Feliks Kon

59 Marcu, 'Lenin', p. 559

60 LCW, vol. 23, p. 132 (*Sotsial-demokrat*, No. 56, 6 November 1916)

61 Ibid., p. 79 (Military Programme of the Proletarian Revolution)

62 Service, *Lenin*, vol. 2, p. 129

63 Marcu, 'Lenin', p. 558

64 Sukhanov, *Revolution*, p. 44

65 Victoria E. Bonnell, *Roots of Rebellion: Workers' Politics and Organizations in St Petersburg and Moscow, 1900–1914* (Berkeley and London, 1983), pp. 436–7

66 A. G. Shliapnikov, *Kanun semnadtsatogo goda: semnadtsatyi god*, vol. 1 (Moscow, 1992), p. 274

67 M. A. Tsiavlovskii, *Dokumenty po istorii bol'shevizma s 1903 po 1916 god byvshego Moskovskago Okhrannago otdeleniia* (Moscow, 1918), p. ix

68 Simon Sebag Montefiore, *Young Stalin* (London, 2007), p. 229

69 Service, *Lenin*, vol. 2, p. 122

70 McKean, *St Petersburg*, p. 145; on *Pravda*, see R. C. Elwood, 'Lenin and Pravda, 1912–1914', *Slavic Review*, 31:2 (June 1972), pp. 355–80

71 Kerensky, *Memoirs*, pp. 134–5

72 Futrell, *Northern Underground*, p. 112; see also Shlyapnikov, *On the Eve*, pp. 19, 92 and 106

73 Shliapnikov, *Kanun*, vol. 1, p. 308

74 Ibid., vol. 2 (Moscow, 1992), p. 22

75 Service, *Lenin*, vol. 2, p. 123

76 Shlyapnikov, *On the Eve*, p. 62

77 For the size of organizations, see Hasegawa, *February*, p. 117

78 A. Kondrat'ev, cited in ibid., p. 108

79 Paléologue, *Memoirs*, vol. 3, p. 118

80 Shliapnikov, *Kanun*, vol. 1, pp. 274–6

81 Kerensky, *Memoirs*, p. 184

82 McKean, *St Petersburg*, p. 108

83 Cited in Elwood, 'Lenin and Pravda', p. 364

Chapter 4: Scarlet Ribbons

1 A. I. Savenko, cited in Hasegawa, *February*, p. 182

2 M. V. Rodzianko, *Krushenie imperii i Gosudarstvennaia Duma i fevral'skaia 1917 goda revoliutsiia* (Moscow, 1986), p. 222

3 Sukhanov, *Revolution*, p. 5

4 Okhrana report, cited in Hasegawa, *February*, p. 201

5 Ibid., pp. 217 and 201

6 Ibid., p. 199

7 Rabinowitch, *Prelude*, p. 24; Paléologue, *Memoirs*, vol. 3, p. 65; Jones, *Russia in Revolution*, pp. 119–20

8 TNA CAB 24/143/5 (Eastern Report, 28 February 1917)

9 Shliapnikov, *Kanun*, vol. 2, p. 42; McKean, *St Petersburg*, p. 409

10 Paléologue, *Memoirs*, vol. 3, p. 213

11 Kerensky, *Memoirs*, p. 170; Buchanan, *Mission*, vol. 2, p. 51; Paléologue, *Memoirs*, vol. 3, p. 215

12 Hasegawa, *February*, p. 161

13 Ibid., p. 160

14 See Shliapnikov, *Kanun*, vol. 2, p. 140

15 Knox, *Russian Army*, vol. 2, p. 516; Paléologue, *Memoirs*, vol. 3, p. 80

16 Shliapnikov, *Kanun*, vol. 2, p. 60

17 Ibid., vol. 1, p. 308; see also Hasegawa, *February*, pp. 215–16

18 Hasegawa, *February*, pp. 217–19

19 Cited in D. A. Longley, 'The Mezhraionka, the Bolsheviks and International Women's Day: In Response to Michael Melancon', *Soviet Studies*, 41:4 (October 1989), p. 632

20 Shliapnikov, *Kanun*, vol. 2, p. 70

21 Knox, *Russian Army*, vol. 2, p. 527

22 Shliapnikov, *Kanun*, vol. 2, p. 78

23 See I. Iurenev, 'Mezhraionka, 1911–1917gg', *Proletarskaia revoliutsiia*, 1924, No. 2, p. 139

24 Hasegawa, *February*, pp. 238 and 248

25 Shliapnikov, *Kanun*, vol. 2, p. 103

26 Hasegawa, *February*, pp. 253–4

27 Knox, *Russian Army*, vol. 2, p. 528

28 Sukhanov, *Revolution*, p. 24

29 V. Iu. Cherniaev, 'Vosstanie Pavlovskogo polka 26 fevralia 1917', in O. N. Znamenskii (ed.), *Rabochii klass Rossii: ego soiuzniki i politicheskie protivniki v 1917 godu* (Leningrad, 1989), p. 156

30 F. F. Raskolnikov, *Kronstadt and Petrograd in 1917* (New York, 1982), pp. 4–7

31 Cherniaev, 'Vosstanie', pp. 157–8

32 Shliapnikov, *Kanun*, vol. 2, p. 110; Hasegawa, *February*, p. 220

33 Sukhanov, *Revolution*, p. 28

34 Cherniaev, 'Vosstanie', pp. 157–8

35 Sukhanov, *Revolution*, p. 36; Hasegawa, *February*, p. 282

36 Jones, *Russia in Revolution*, pp. 119–20

37 Knox, *Russian Army*, vol. 2, pp. 353–4

38 Jones, *Russia in Revolution*, p. 127

39 Ibid., p. 120

40 D. A. Longley, 'The Divisions in the Bolshevik Party in March 1917', *Soviet Studies*, 24:1 (July 1972), p. 64

41 Sukhanov, *Revolution*, p. 46

42 Miliukov, *Memoirs*, p. 391

43 Hasegawa, *February*, p. 357

44 Miliukov, *Memoirs*, p. 393

45 Hasegawa, *February*, p. 355

46 Raskolnikov, *Kronstadt*, p. 11

47 Sukhanov, *Revolution*, p. 41

48 Ibid., pp. 38–9

49 Kerensky, *Memoirs*, p. 232

50 Lockhart, *Memoirs*, p. 176

51 Sukhanov, *Revolution*, p. 31

52 Shliapnikov, *Kanun*, vol. 2, p. 167

53 Sukhanov, *Revolution*, p. 52

54 Kerensky, *Memoirs*, p. 232

55 Shliapnikov, *Kanun*, vol. 2, p. 135

56 Sukhanov, *Revolution*, p. 74

57 Ibid., p. 98

58 Hasegawa, *February*, p. 374

59 Sukhanov, *Revolution*, pp. 103–4

60 Cited in Liebman, *Leninism*, p. 121

61 Sukhanov, *Revolution*, p. 171

62 Ibid., pp. 104–5

63 Miliukov, *Memoirs*, p. 402

64 Sukhanov, *Revolution*, p. 145

65 Miliukov, *Memoirs*, p. 406

66 Sukhanov, *Revolution*, p. 141

67 Ibid., p. 143

68 Trotsky, *My Life*, p. 300; Knox, *Russian Army*, vol. 2, p. 671

69 Buchanan, *Mission*, vol. 2, p. 70

70 Paléologue, *Memoirs*, vol. 3, p. 239

71 On the powers of the Provisional Government, see the discussion in the final chapters of F. A. Gaida, *Liberal'naia oppozitsiia na putiakh k vlasti: 1914–vesna 1917g.* (Moscow, 2003)

72 Sukhanov, *Revolution*, p. 148

Chapter 5: Maps and Plans

1 Meriel Buchanan, *Petrograd*, pp. 95–8

2 TNA FO 371/2995

3 Hughes, *Enigma*, p. 88

4 TNA FO 371/2995 (cipher telegram to Buchanan, 16 March 1917)

5 Ibid.

6 TNA FO 371/2996 (letter from Frank Lindley to Mr George Clark, 20 March 1917)

7 Cited in Vickers, *Labour Party*, vol. 1, p. 64

8 Alston, *Harold Williams*, p. 115

9 Raymond Pearson, writing in Edward Acton, Vladimir Iu. Cherniaev and William G. Rosenberg (eds), *Critical Companion to the Russian Revolution, 1914–1921* (Bloomington, Ind., 1997), p. 170

10 Miliukov, *Memoirs*, pp. 396–7

11 Hoare, *Fourth Seal*, p. 256

12 TNA CAB 24/143/8 (Eastern Report, 22 March 1917)

13 Buchanan, *Mission*, vol. 2, p. 108

14 Miliukov, *Memoirs*, p. 436

15 Paléologue, *Memoirs*, vol. 3, pp. 263–5

16 Ibid., p. 269; Buchanan, *Mission*, vol. 2, p. 109

17 Paléologue, *Memoirs*, vol. 3, p. 270

18 Knox, *Russian Army*, vol. 2, p. 577; see also TNA CAB 24/143/8 (Eastern Report of 22 March 1917)

19 Knox, *Russian Army*, vol. 2, pp. 576–8

20 Kerensky, *Memoirs*, p. 220

21 Allan K. Wildman, *The End of the Russian Imperial Army* (Princeton, 1980), p. 260

22 TNA FO 371/2996 (telegrams from Sir George Buchanan (cipher), 9 April (27 March) 1917)

23 Kerensky, *Memoirs*, p. 243

24 Cited in Robert P. Browder and Alexander Kerensky (eds), *The Russian Provisional Government, 1917: Documents* (3 vols, Stanford, Calif., 1961), vol. 1, p. 157

25 Miliukov, *Memoirs*, p. 433

26 Kerensky, *Memoirs*, p. 199

27 Sukhanov, *Revolution*, p. 222

28 Ibid., p. 221; see also the clear summary in Rex A. Wade, *The Russian Search for Peace, February–October 1917* (Stanford, Calif., 1969), p. 15

29 Sukhanov, *Revolution*, p. 218

30 Cited in Miliukov, *Memoirs*, p. 434

31 *Izvestiia*, 15 March 1917 (K narodam vsego mira)

32 Paléologue, *Memoirs*, vol. 3, p. 275

33 *Izvestiia*, 16 March 1917

34 Cited from Siefeldt's 1924 memoir in Futrell, *Northern Underground*, p. 154

35 Volkogonov, *Lenin*, pp. 106–7; V. V. Anikeev, *Deiatel'nost' TsK RSDRP(b) v 1917 godu: khronika sobytii* (Moscow, 1969), vol. 1, p. 15

36 N. K. Krupskaia, 'Iz emigratsii v Piter', in F. Platten, *Lenin iz emigratsii v Rossiiu: Sbornik* (Sostavitel' A. E. Ivanov, Moscow, 1990), p. 117

37 V. I. Lenin, *Polnoe sobranie sochinenii* (hereafter PSS), vol. 49 (Moscow, 1962), p. 346

38 See Elwood, *Inessa Armand*, p. 200

39 Senn, *Switzerland*, pp. 222–3

40 Ibid., pp. 5 and 12

41 The Provisional Government's manifesto, telegraphed to London by Reuters, is reproduced in English in TNA CAB 24/143/8. On Kerensky and the early reforms, see S. V. Tiutiutkin, *Aleksandr Kerenskii: stranitsy politicheskoi biografii (1905–1917)* (Moscow, 2012)

42 Browder and Kerensky, *Documents*, vol. 2, p. 842

43 Volkogonov, *Lenin*, p. 107

44 LCW, vol. 23, pp. 297–308 (First Letter from Afar, written on 7/20 March 1917)

45 Ibid., p. 292

46 Ibid., p. 325 (Third Letter from Afar, 11/24 March 1917)

47 Pavel Moskovskii, *Lenin v Shvetsii* (Moscow, 1972), p. 86

48 V. I. Lenin, *Neizvestnye dokumenty, 1891–1922* (Moscow, 1999), p. 209

49 Moskovskii, *Lenin v Shvetsii*, p. 87; Anikeev, *Deiatel'nost' TsK*, vol. 1, p. 19

50 Krupskaya, *Memories*, p. 288

51 Fayet, *Radek*, p. 205

52 Pearson, *Sealed Train*, p. 62

53 Jeffery, *MI6*, p. 115

54 Alexander Watson, *Ring of Steel: Germany and Austria-Hungary at War, 1914–1918* (London, 2014), p. 341

55 Lieutenant A. Bauermeister ('Agricola'), *Spies Break Through: Memoirs of a German Secret Service Officer* (London, 1934), p. 123

56 Scherer and Grunewald, *Documents*, vol. 2, p. 46 (note from Lucius to Foreign Ministry, 9/22 March 1917)

57 Knox, *Russian Army*, vol. 2, pp. 600–601; see also the report from Lucius in Iu. G. Fel'shtinskii (ed.), *B. I. Nikolaevskii: tainye stranitsy istorii* (Moscow, 1995), p. 285

58 See Zeman, *Documents*, p. 25 (Minister in Copenhagen to Foreign Ministry, 21 March 1917); Volkogonov, *Lenin*, p. 120

59 Zeman, *Documents*, pp. 25–6 (State Secretary to Foreign Ministry Liaison Officer at General Headquarters, Berlin, 23 March 1917)

60 Volkogonov, *Lenin*, p. 119

61 Futrell, *Northern Underground*, p. 157

62 VoVIL, vol. 5, p. 380

63 Zeman, *Documents*, p. 34 (Minister in Bern to Foreign Ministry, 3 April 1917)

64 Volkogonov, *Lenin*, p 120

65 For Romberg's correspondence, see Scherer and Grunewald, *Documents*, vol. 2, pp. 72 and 78

66 The list of terms was sent for approval on 5 April 1917 (Minister in Bern to the Chancellor, 5 April 1917) and is reproduced in Zeman, *Documents*, pp. 38–9. See also Fürstenberg's account, VoVIL, vol. 5, pp. 380–81

67 Zeman, *Documents*, p. 31 (Minister in Copenhagen to Foreign Ministry, 2 April 1917)

68 Anthony D'Agostino, *The Rise of Global Powers: International Politics in the Era of the World Wars* (Cambridge, 2012), p. 93

69 Senn, *Switzerland*, p. 227

70 Zeman, *Documents*, p. 41 (Minister in Bern to the Foreign Ministry, 8 April 1917; dispatched 9 April)

71 N. Krutikova, *Na krutom povorote* (Moscow, 1965), pp. 53–61; Zeman, *Documents*, pp. 39–41 (documents relating to the final plans, 6–8 April 1917)

72 A. V. Maskuliia, *Mikhail Grigorevich Tskhakaia* (Moscow, 1968), p. 124

73 Lenin, *Neizvestnye dokumenty*, p. 211; see also Carter Elwood, *The Non-Geometric Lenin: Essays on the Development of the Bolshevik Party, 1910–1914* (London and New York, 2011), p. 116

74 LCW, vol. 23, pp. 371–3 (Farewell Letter to the Swiss Workers, read on 26 March/8 April 1917)

75 Kharitonova's account is in VoVIL, vol. 2, p. 368

76 A copy of the declaration is printed in Platten, *Lenin iz emigratsii*, p. 148

77 Platten, *Lenin iz emigratsii*, p. 58

78 Rappaport, *Conspirator*, p. 270

Chapter 6: The Sealed Train

1 Pearson, *Sealed Train*, pp. 81–2

2 Karl Radek, 'V plombirovannom vagone', in Platten, *Lenin iz emigratsii*, p. 129

3 Fritz Platten, 'K istorii vozvrashcheniia v Rossiiu v 1917 godu russkikh emigrantov, zhivshikh v Shveitsarii', in Platten, *Lenin iz emigratsii*, p. 56

4 Radek, 'V plombirovannom vagone', pp. 129–30

5 Ibid., p. 130

6 Sokolnikov, cited in Pearson, *Sealed Train*, p. 94

7 E. Usievich, 'Iz vospominanii o V. I. Lenine', in Platten, *Lenin iz emigratsii*, p. 149

8 Platten, 'K istorii', p. 57; Radek, 'V plombirovannom vagone', pp. 130–31. On Radek's pre-war record, see Lerner, *Radek*, pp. 13–21

9 On the deserters, see Wildman, *Imperial Army*, p. 235

10 TNA CAB 24/11/77, p. 2 (Knox to Director of Military Intelligence, 15 April 1917); Sukhanov, *Revolution*, pp. 170–71

11 I. G. Tsereteli, *Vospominaniia o fevral'skoi revoliutsii*, vol. 1 (Paris, 1963), p. 15

12 Ibid., p. 24

13 This was also the official instruction, issued by Rodzianko on 28 February/13 March, though in Irkutsk Tsereteli may not yet have heard of it. On the 'Bublikov telegram' on rail transport, see Wildman, *Imperial Army*, p. 207

14 Tsereteli, *Vospominaniia*, vol. 1, p. 24

15 Ibid., p. 23

16 Ibid., p. 30; see also *Izvestiia*, 16/29 March 1917

17 Tsereteli, *Vospominaniia*, vol. 1, p. 31; *Izvestiia*, 17/30 March 1917

18 Usievich, 'Iz vospominanii', p. 150

19 For a discussion, see Service, *Lenin*, vol. 2, p. 152

20 Pearson, *Sealed Train*, p. 102

21 Platten, 'K istorii', p. 58; Radek, 'V plombirovannom vagone', p. 131. Radek's instinct was not wrong. See Zeman, *Documents*, p. 44 (memorandum by Ow-Wachendorf, Berlin, 11 April 1917)

22 The allegation appears in Pearson, *Sealed Train*, p. 103

23 Zeman, *Documents*, p. 45 (memorandum by Ow-Wachendorf, 11 April 1917)

24 Jeffery, *MI6*, p. 108. See also TNA KV 2/585 (reports of 13 and 21 April 1917)

25 Maugham, *Ashenden*, p. 120

26 Trotsky, *My Life*, pp. 290–91

27 Jeffery, *MI6*, p. 108

28 Kesküla's conversation with Howard is reported in a note from Stockholm, TNA KV 2/585 (19 May 1917)

29 Zeman, *Documents*, p. 45 (memorandum by Ow-Wachendorf, Berlin, 12 April 1917)

30 Platten, 'K istorii', p. 59

31 Radek, 'V plombirovannom vagone', p. 131; Maskuliia, *Tskhakaya*, p. 124

32 Otto Grimlund, 'Na perevale', in VoVIL, vol. 5, p. 93; *Izvestiia*, 13 September 1963

33 For the background, see Ingvar Andersson, *A History of Sweden* (London, 1956), pp. 417–19

34 Zeman, *Documents*, p. 62 (Minister in Stockholm to State Secretary, 15 June 1917)

35 Grimlund, 'Na perevale', VoVIL, vol. 5, p. 94

Chapter 7: Leaderless

1 *Pravda*, No. 16, 23 March 1917

2 TNA FO 317/2996 (Lindley's report for 1–16 April 1917)

3 Cited in Harvey Pitcher, *Witnesses of the Russian Revolution* (London, 2001), p. 70

4 Sukhanov, *Revolution*, p. 246; Leon Trotsky, *The History of the Russian Revolution* (London, 1934), p. 345

5 TNA FO 317/2996 (report of 16 April 1917); diary cited in Pitcher, *Witnesses*, p. 71

6 Meriel Buchanan, *Petrograd*, p. 113

7 TNA FO 317/2996 (report of 16 April 1917)

8 Buchanan, *Mission*, vol. 2, p. 107; Paléologue, *Memoirs*, vol. 3, p. 285

9 Tsereteli, *Vospominaniia*, vol. 1, p. 59

10 Knox, *Russian Army*, vol. 2, p. 575

11 Wade, *Search for Peace*, pp. 22–4

12 Browder and Kerensky, *Documents*, vol. 2, p. 1043 (Miliukov's interview of 23 March 1917)

13 TNA FO 371/2996 (Buchanan's report to the Foreign Office, 8 April 1917)

14 Tsereteli, *Vospominaniia*, vol. 1, p. 60

15 TNA FO 371/2996 (Buchanan's report to the Foreign Office, 8 April 1917)

16 TNA FO 371/2996 (Buchanan telegram of 9 April 1917)

17 W. H. Roobol, *Tsereteli: A Democrat in the Russian Revolution* (The Hague, 1976), pp. 96–7

18 This was Sukhanov's own account. Sukhanov, *Revolution*, p. 240; see also Tsereteli, *Vospominaniia*, vol. 1, p. 45

19 Sukhanov, *Revolution*, pp. 247–8

20 Miliukov, *Memoirs*, p. 442

21 Text in Browder and Kerensky, *Documents*, vol. 2, p. 1045; see also Tsereteli, vol. 1, p. 69; Kerensky, *Catastrophe*, p. 245

22 Tsereteli, *Vospominaniia*, vol. 1, p. 72; Sukhanov, *Revolution*, p. 251

23 Sukhanov, *Revolution*, p. 253

24 V. B. Stankevich, cited in Roobol, *Tsereteli*, pp. 94–5

25 Knox, *Russian Army*, vol. 2, p. 569

26 Cited in Neilson, *Strategy*, p. 269

27 Cited in Liebman, *Leninism*, p. 125

28 TNA FO 371/2996 (telegram *en clair* praising the Petrograd Garrison for its pro-war resolution of 10 April 1917)

29 Browder and Kerensky, *Documents*, vol. 2, p. 860; see also Wildman, *Imperial Army*, p. 254

30 See Alexeyev's letter and reports from the front cited in N. E. Kakurin, *Razlozhenie armii v 1917 godu* (Moscow and Leningrad, 1925), pp. 25–33

31 TNA CAB 24/10/89

32 TNA CAB 24/12/35

33 TNA FO 371/2996; TNA CAB 24/11/77

34 Bernard Pares, *My Russian Memoirs* (London, 1931), p. 442

35 Knox, *Russian Army*, vol. 2, p. 582

36 Kakurin, *Razlozhenie*, p. 33; see also Wildman, *Imperial Army*, p. 333

37 TNA CAB 24/11/77; see also Wildman, *Imperial Army*, p. 309

38 Wildman, *Imperial Army*, pp. 235, 347 and 365–6; TNA CAB 24/15/1 (report from Northern Front, 18 April/1 May 1917)

39 Watson, *Ring of Steel*, p. 462

40 TNA CAB 24/11/29 (report by Knox, 10/23 April 1917)

41 Browder and Kerensky, *Documents*, vol. 2, pp. 526–7

42 Kakurin, *Razlozhenie*, p. 49

43 On the mood in the countryside, see Orlando Figes, *A People's Tragedy: The Russian Revolution, 1891–1924* (London, 1996), pp. 363–5

44 Raskolnikov, *Kronstadt*, pp. 22–3

45 Trotsky, *My Life*, p. 181

46 Raskolnikov, *Kronstadt*, p. 26

47 *Pravda*, No. 1, 5 March 1917, p. 1

48 Sukhanov, *Revolution*, p. 224

49 Longley, 'Divisions', p. 63

50 Ibid., pp. 68–9

51 Ibid., p. 68

52 Sukhanov, *Revolution*, p. 226

53 *Pravda*, No. 9, 15 March 1917, pp. 2–3. Also cited in Browder and Kerensky, *Documents*, vol. 2, p. 868, where the author is given as Stalin

54 Shliapnikov, *Kanun*, vol. 2, pp. 448–52

55 Ibid., p. 443

56 Paléologue, *Memoirs*, vol. 3, p. 297

57 TNA CAB 24/143/9 (report of note from Balfour to Buchanan)

58 Sukhanov, *Revolution*, p. 259

59 Ibid., p. 261

60 Lockhart, *Memoirs*, p. 120

61 Buchanan, *Mission*, vol. 2, p. 116

62 Ibid., p. 132; Harold Williams, cited in Pitcher, *Witnesses*, pp. 82–3

63 Sukhanov, *Revolution*, p. 263

64 Paléologue, *Memoirs*, vol. 3, p. 299

65 Rowland Smith, cited in Jennifer Siegel, *For Peace and Money: International Finance and the Making and Unmaking of the Triple Entente* (Oxford, 2014), p. 165

Chapter 8: Lenin in Lapland

1 The secret police report is dated 16 April 1917. National Archives, Stockholm, State Police Bureau for the Supervision of Foreigners in the Realm, vol. E3:2, VPM 1916–1917. I am grateful to Professor Lars Ericson Wolke for providing me with a copy of this report

2 *Bradshaw's Continental Railway Guide and General Handbook* (London, 1913), p. 1042

3 Ström, VoVIL, vol. 5, p. 100

4 Futrell, *Northern Underground*, p. 155, citing the Swedish daily *Politiken*

5 Ström's memoir used that phrase, though whether Lenin did in April 1917 remains unclear

6 Ström, VoVIL, vol. 5, p. 102

7 Grimlund, in VoVIL, vol. 5, p. 94

8 On Parvus' request for access to Lenin, see Zeman, *Documents*, p. 42 (Minister in Copenhagen to German Foreign Ministry, 9 April 1917)

9 Zeman and Scharlau, *Merchant*, p. 217

10 See below, pp. 254–7

11 I am grateful to Christina Engström, of the Swedish National Railway Museum in Gävle, for providing me with copies of the archive railway timetables for the week of Lenin's journey in 1917. The timings not only coincide with comments in participants' memoirs, but demonstrate the only possible route and trains that Lenin and his party could have taken

12 Anikeev, *Deiatel'nost' TsK*, vol. 1, p. 97

13 Hugo Sillen's account in VoVIL, vol. 5, p. 97

14 Pavel Moskovskii, *Lenin v Shvetsii* (Moscow, 1972), p. 131

15 The protocols of the meeting on the train are still in the Communist Party's main archive in Moscow. This account is cited from Moskovskii, *Shvetsii*, p. 133. On Borbjerg, see Brockdorff-Rantzau's telegram to Berlin, 13 April 1917, in Zeman, *Documents*, pp. 45–6. The Dane eventually reached Russia, though his mission was unsuccessful

16 Boris Nikitin, *The Fatal Years: Fresh Revelations on a Chapter of Underground History* (London, 1938), p. 27

17 Platten, *Lenin iz emigratsii*, p. 153 (account by Usievich)

18 The Swedes and Germans also counted on that fact. See Zeman, *Documents*, p. 70 (State Secretary Kuhlmann to

Foreign Ministry Liaison Officer at General Headquarters, 29 September 1917)

19 Information from the Torne city museum

20 For a photograph (also showing the Alatornio church), see http://commons.wikimedia.org/wiki/File:Tornio-Haparanda -ilmarata.JPG

21 A fact confirmed by Boris Nikitin. See Nikitin, *Fatal Years*, p. 113

22 Zinoviev, writing in Platten, *Lenin iz emigratsii*, p. 124

23 TNA FO 371/2996 (Lindley's report, forwarded by Buchanan on 1 April 1917)

24 Ibid.

25 On the War Cabinet and Russian support during the Nivelle Offensive, see TNA CAB 23/2/40; Buchanan, *Mission*, vol. 2, p. 109

26 TNA CAB 23/2/40 (on the artillery). On the war loan, see Browder and Kerensky, *Documents*, vol. 2, p. 1053 (Lansing to Ambassador Francis, 8/21 April 1917)

27 TNA FO 371/2996

28 Ibid.

29 For early impressions, see Rappaport, *Conspirator*, p. 61

30 TNA CAB 24/146/12

31 TNA FO 371/2995

32 German Minister in Bern to Foreign Ministry, 16 April 1917, cited in Zeman, *Documents*, p. 49

33 This, at least, is the version in A. M. Sovokin, 'Mif o "nemet-skikh millionakh"', *Voprosy istorii KPSS*, No. 4, April 1991, p. 70

34 Report cited in TNA KV 2/265 (18 June 1917)

35 Platten, *Lenin iz emigratsii*, p. 60

36 *New York Times*, 4 December 1919, p. 7

37 Nikitin, *Fatal Years*, p. 54; on Alley's responsibilities, see TNA CAB 24/3/37

38 Gerhardie, *Memoirs*, p. 130; see also Rappaport, *Conspirator*, pp. 275–6

39 https://www.thegazette.co.uk/London/issue/31843/supplement/ 3999

40 Rabinowitch, *Prelude*, p. 36; see also Elwood, *The Non-Geometric Lenin*, p. 55

41 See above, p. 134

42 Platten, *Lenin iz emigratsii*, p. 124

43 Lenin, *Neizvestnye dokumenty*, p. 190 (Lenin and Krupskaya to Malinovsky, August 1916)

44 *Pravda*, No. 20, 29 March 1917

45 Nikitin, *Fatal Years*, p. 28

46 Raskolnikov, *Kronstadt*, p. 68

47 Ibid., p. 71

48 A. M. Afanas'ev, 'Vstrecha na stantsii Beloostrov', in VoVIL, vol. 2, p. 388; Raskolnikov, *Kronstadt*, p. 70

49 Raskolnikov, *Kronstadt*, p. 71

50 Anikeev, *Deiatel'nost' TsK*, vol. 1, p. 57

51 Sukhanov, *Revolution*, p. 270

52 Ibid., p. 269

Chapter 9: From the Finland Station

1 E. D. Stasova, in VoVIL, vol. 2, p. 409

2 Sukhanov, *Revolution*, p. 272

3 Ibid., p. 273

4 Trotsky, *Revolution*, p. 311

5 Sukhanov, *Revolution*, p. 273

6 Ibid., p. 274

7 Ibid.

8 Ibid., p. 275

9 Pares, *My Russian Memoirs*, p. 235

10 Sukhanov, *Revolution*, p. 210; on the coal, see Paléologue, *Memoirs*, vol. 3, pp. 229–30

11 Woytinsky, cited in Rabinowitch, *Prelude*, p. 38; Sukhanov, *Revolution*, p. 276; Raskolnikov, *Kronstadt*, p. 74 (who notes that Lenin did get that tea in the end)

12 Trotsky, *Revolution*, p. 312; see also Raskolnikov, *Kronstadt*, p. 76

13 Sukhanov, *Revolution*, p. 280

14 Trotsky, *Revolution*, p. 319

15 Translation courtesy of Liebman, *Leninism*, pp. 129–30

16 Sukhanov, *Revolution*, p. 281; Lenin cited in Liebman, *Leninism*, p. 130

17 Sukhanov, *Revolution*, p. 288

18 Cited in Liebman, *Leninism*, p. 129

19 Sukhanov, *Revolution*, p. 288

20 Liebman, *Leninism*, pp. 130–31

21 For details of the meetings, see Anikeev, *Deiatel'nost' TsK*, vol. 1, pp. 57–60; Liebman, *Leninism*, pp. 131–2

22 Rabinowitch, *Prelude*, p. 40; Sukhanov, *Revolution*, pp. 286–7

23 All citations from the text in LCW, vol. 24, pp. 21–6

24 Ibid., pp. 32–3 (Notes in defence of the April Theses)

25 Ibid.

26 *Rech'*, 5/18 April 1917; cited in Browder and Kerensky, *Documents*, vol. 2, p. 1093

27 *Pravda*, No. 24, 5/18 April 1917

28 Browder and Kerensky, *Documents*, vol. 2, pp. 1094–5

29 Paléologue, *Memoirs*, vol. 3, p. 302

30 Sukhanov, *Revolution*, pp. 286–7; Service, *Lenin*, vol. 2, p. 166

31 Volkogonov, *Lenin*, p. 129

32 *Pravda*, No. 27, April 1917, cited in LCW, vol. 24, p. 50

33 LCW, vol. 24, pp. 50–51 (reply to Comrade Kamenev)

34 Sukhanov, *Revolution*, p. 290

35 Liebman, *Leninism*, p. 158

36 Nikitin, *Fatal Years*, p. 25

37 Trotsky, *Revolution*, p. 339

38 *Pravda*, No. 33, 15 April 1917, 'Against the Riot-Mongers', cited in LCW, vol. 24, p. 127

39 Trotsky, *Revolution*, p. 347

40 I. Sinanoglou (ed.), 'Journal de Russie d'Albert Thomas, 22 avril–19 juin 1917', *Cahiers du Monde Russe et Soviétique*, 14:1–2 (1973), p. 123

41 On the discussion, see Wade, *Search for Peace*, pp. 34–5; Rosenberg, *Liberals*, p. 105

42 Tsereteli, *Vospominaniia*, vol. 1, p. 85

43 V. D. Medlin and S. L. Parsons (eds), *V. D. Nabokov and the Russian Provisional Government, 1917* (New Haven, 1976), p. 122

44 Stockdale, *Miliukov*, p. 254

45 Browder and Kerensky, *Documents*, vol. 2, p. 1098; Wade, *Search for Peace*, p. 38; Miliukov, *Memoirs*, p. 446; Tsereteli, *Vospominaniia*, vol. 1, p. 86

46 LCW, vol. 24, p. 183, 'Bankruptcy?', published in *Pravda*, No. 36, 20 April/3 May 1917

47 G. A. Solomon, *Vblizi vozhdia: Svet i teni. Lenin i ego sem'ia* (Paris 1931: reissued Moscow, 1993), p. 45

48 See Miliukov, *Memoirs*, p. 448

49 Tsereteli, *Vospominaniia*, vol. 1, p. 97

50 Miliukov, *Memoirs*, p. 448

51 LCW, vol. 24, pp. 190–91, 'The Provisional Government's Note', published in *Pravda*, No. 37, 21 April/4 May 1917

52 Buchanan, *Mission*, vol. 2, pp. 124–5

53 Rosenberg, *Liberals*, p. 107

54 Buchanan, *Mission*, vol. 2, p. 117

55 Paléologue, *Memoirs*, vol. 3, p. 321

56 Gerhardie, *Memoirs*, p. 130

57 Service, *Lenin*, vol. 2, p. 171

58 Liebman, *Leninism*, pp. 132–4; Service, *Lenin*, vol. 2, pp. 171–7

59 LCW, vol. 24, pp. 137–8 (The Soldiers and the Land, *Soldatskaia pravda*, No. 1, 15 April 1917)

60 Zeman, *Documents*, p. 51 (Foreign Ministry Liaison Officer at the Imperial Court to the Foreign Ministry, 21 April 1917)

Chapter 10: Gold

1 Nikitin, *Fatal Years*, p. 273

2 Kerensky, *Catastrophe*, p. 127

3 LCW, vol. 24, p. 270 (Resolution on the War)

4 For a summary, see Lyandres, 'Inquiry', pp. 1–10

5 Nikitin, *Fatal Years*, p. 33

6 Sukhanov, *Revolution*, pp. 362–3

7 TNA CAB 24/15/36

8 Kerensky's address to the army and navy, 12 May 1917, Browder and Kerensky, *Documents*, vol. 1, p. 936

9 Trotsky, *My Life*, p. 323

10 Knox, *Russian Army*, vol. 2, p. 606

11 TNA CAB 24/15/20; see also the report from the returning labour delegation, TNA CAB 24/3/56, June 1917

12 TNA CAB 24/15/20

13 Trotsky, *My Life*, p. 323

14 Lyandres, 'Inquiry', p. 11

15 TNA KV 2/585 ('Lenin Nikola'), and see also Trotsky, *My Life*, p. 314

16 Nikitin, *Fatal Years*, pp. 109–10; see also Katkov assisted by Futrell, 'German Political Intervention in Russia', p. 74

17 Trotsky, *My Life*, p. 295

18 TNA KV 2/585 (telegram from Sir E. Howard to London, 16 April 1917)

19 Report filed in TNA KV 2/585

20 These extracts are all preserved in TNA KV 2/585

21 Cited by Trotsky, *My Life*, p. 315

22 Devotees of Lenin's exact movements from Petrograd to Razliv and on to Helsingfors may like to consult T. P. Bondarevskaia and others (compilers), *Lenin v Peterburge-Petrograde: Mesta zhizni i deiatel'nosti v gorode i okrestnostiakh 1890–1920* (Leningrad, 1977), pp. 279–89 and 359

23 For the papers and their history, see George F. Kennan, 'The Sisson Documents', *Journal of Modern History*, 28:2 (June 1956), pp. 130–54

24 Volkogonov's 'proof' gets a new airing, for instance, in Sean McMeekin's otherwise so careful *History's Greatest Heist: The Looting of Russia by the Bolsheviks* (New Haven, 2009), p. 102

25 Volkogonov, *Lenin*, p. 121

26 Kennan, 'Sisson', p. 138

27 Zeman and Scharlau, *Merchant*, p. 254

28 Nikitin, *Fatal Years*, p. 55

29 Report from Petrograd intelligence, 20 August 1917, TNA KV 2/585

30 Telegram 17, cited in Lyandres, 'Inquiry', p. 41

31 Trotsky, *My Life*, p. 312

32 TNA KV 2/585

33 Figures from Anikeev (*Deiatel'nost' TsK*, vol. 1), cited in Sovokin, 'Mif o "nemetskikh millionakh"', p. 75

34 Keith Neilson, 'Joy Rides? British Intelligence and Propaganda in Russia, 1914–1917', *Historical Journal* 24:4 (1981), p. 895

35 Zeman and Scharlau, *Merchant*, p. 219

36 TNA CAB 24/11/29 (23 April 1917)

37 A. G. Latyshev, 'Nemetskoe zoloto dlia Lenina', in his *Rassekrechennyi Lenin* (Moscow, 1996), p. 97; see also H. Schurer, 'Karl Moor – German Agent and Friend of Lenin', *Journal of Contemporary History* 5:2 (1970), pp. 131–52

38 Lyandres, 'Inquiry', p. 104; see also Iu. G. Fel'shtinskii, *Germaniia i revoliutsiia v Rossii, 1915–1918: sbornik dokumentov* (Moscow, 2013), p. 304

39 Memorandum by the Military Attaché of the Legation in Bern, 9 May 1917, cited in Zeman, *Documents*, p. 55

40 Sinanoglou, 'Journal de Russie', p. 94

41 TNA FO 295/105

42 Curtis, *Maugham*, pp. 109–12

43 Cited in Neilson, 'Joy Rides?', p. 902

44 Zeman, *Documents*, p. 94 (State Secretary Kuhlmann to the Foreign Ministry Liaison Officer, 3 December 1917)

45 Lyandres, 'Inquiry', p. 103

46 See Zeman and Scharlau, *Merchant*, p. 220, and also, for example, Helena M. Stone, 'Another Look at the Sisson Forgeries and their Background', *Soviet Studies*, 37:1 (January 1985), p. 92

47 Lyandres, 'Inquiry', pp. 66–7 (telegram of April 1917)

48 A point made in Michael Pearson, *Sealed Train*, p. 148

49 For British responses to the 1917 Berlin bread strike, see TNA CAB 24/146/12. On the general picture, see Watson, *Ring of Steel*, pp. 341–5, 477–9

50 LCW, vol. 24, p. 270 (Resolution on the War)

51 Arthur Ransome to his mother, 23 July 1917, cited in Brogan, *Signalling from Mars*, p. 49

52 TNA CAB 24/3/56 (report of labour delegation, June 1917)

53 W. H. Beable, *Commercial Russia* (London, 1918), pp. 162–5

54 Trotsky, *My Life*, p. 322

55 Paléologue, *Memoirs*, vol. 3, p. 304

56 Trotsky, *My Life*, p. 411

Chapter 11: Fellow Travellers

1 *Pravda*, No. 105, 16 April 1937

2 There are numerous lists in existence. This is a Soviet one, listing thirty-four names, but the Provisional Government had another (giving the names and dates of birth of only twenty-nine adults), and the Swiss and Swedes each had their own. For the Provisional Government's list, and a discussion of its later use, see V. A. Posse, *Vospominaniia, 1905–1917gg.* (Petrograd, 1923), p. 124. I am grateful to Dr Robert Henderson for this additional reference

3 Zeman, *Documents*, pp. 128–33 (Minister in Moscow to Foreign Ministry, 16 May 1918; State Secretary to Minister in Moscow, 18 May 1918; Minister in Moscow to Foreign Ministry, 3 June 1918; State Secretary of the Foreign Ministry to State Secretary of the Treasury, enclosure of 5 June 1918)

4 Zeman, *Documents*, pp. 112–13 (Deputy State Secretary to Minister in Stockholm, 4 January 1918)

5 Zeman, *Documents*, pp. 120–21 and 126–7 (Minister in Moscow to the Chancellor, 30 April 1918; Minister in Moscow to the Chancellor, 16 May 1918)

6 Cited in Pitcher, *Witnesses*, p. 118

7 Harold Williams, 'The Furnace of Democracy', cited in Alston, *Williams*, p. 131

8 http://www.theguardian.com/world/2009/oct/13/benito-mussolini-recruited-mi5-italy (accessed 25 July 2015)

9 Zeman and Scharlau, *Merchant*, p. 271

10 Ibid., p. 266

11 Cited in ibid., p. 267

12 Karl Radek, *Portrety* (Letchworth, 1979), p. 127

13 Gorky, *Days with Lenin*, p. 34. Thomas Müntzer (c.1489–1525) was a German preacher and critic of Martin Luther whose incitement to rebellion led to the deaths of tens of thousands of peasants before his execution in 1525

14 V. Aleksandrovich, 'Sev', cited in Mark D. Steinberg and Vladimir M. Khrustalev, *The Fall of the Romanovs: Political Dreams and Personal Struggles in a Time of Revolution* (New Haven and London, 1995), p. 282

15 McMeekin, *Heist*, pp. 21 and 91

16 For a brisk account, see *Izvestiia Tsentral'nogo Komiteta KPSS*, 1989, No. 10, pp. 60–63

17 Raskolnikov, *Kronstadt*, p. 345

18 [B. Nicolaevsky], *The Letter of an Old Bolshevik: A Key to the Moscow Trials* (Woking, 1938), p. 70

19 Victor Serge, *Memoirs of a Revolutionary* (Oxford, 1980), p. 228

20 Robert H. McNeal, *Bride of the Revolution: Krupskaya and Lenin* (London, 1973), p. 259

21 *Izvestiia Tsentral'nogo Komiteta KPSS*, 1989, No. 10, pp. 71–5

22 Cited in Roy Medvedev, *Let History Judge* (New York, 1989), p. 631

23 Ante Ciliga, *The Russian Enigma* (London, 1979), p. 227

24 Lerner, *Radek*, p. 154

25 Fayet, *Radek*, p. 719

26 Volkogonov, *Lenin*, p. 127

27 Lyandres, 'Inquiry', p. 22

28 Platten, *Lenin iz emigratsii*, note, p. 157

29 Kerensky, *The Catastrophe*, p. 322

30 Browder and Kerensky's three-volume classic, *Documents*. For a review, see Boris Elkin, 'The Kerensky Government and its Fate', *Slavic Review*, 23:4 (December 1964), pp. 717–36

31 http://alumni.stanford.edu/get/page/magazine/article/?article _id=38883 (accessed 23 July 2015)

32 [Nicolaevsky], *Letter of an Old Bolshevik*, p. 13

33 Trotsky, *My Life*, p. 427

34 *Pravda*, No. 15, 18 April 1997

35 For one such event (and a gallery of photographs of its big stars) I visited the site of Moscow's Museum of the Revolution at http://www.sovrhistory.ru/events/action/5562e87845bc1do f74adceb4

36 For cartoons, see http://vm.sovrhistory.ru/sovremennoy-istorii -rossii/specproekt-semnadcatiy-god/#/; for a short lecture on the events of 1917, visit http://vm.sovrhistory.ru/en/sovremennoy -istorii-rossii/interaktivniy-urok/1917/ and enjoy the pictures and clips. An interview of 2016 with Aleksei Levykin, the director of the State Historical Museum in Moscow, is a model of evasiveness regarding the hard questions about Lenin. See http://www.kommersant.ru/doc/2922745 (accessed March 2016)

37 *Novaia gazeta*, 25 March 2015, 'Biudzhet na revoliutsionnoe primirenie'

38 Cited in ibid.

39 http://www.scientificamerican.com/article/lenin-s-body-imp roves-with-age1/

40 http://grani.ru/Politics/Russia/President/m.247897.html (acc essed January 2016)

41 See remarks by Igor Chubais in the debate posted at http:// www.svoboda.org/content/transcript/27504159.html (accessed January 2016)

Suggestions for Further Reading

When it comes to the British, Sir Samuel Hoare is a good place to start, especially when thinking about the intelligence background and the gathering revolutionary situation in Petrograd. His book *The Fourth Seal* (London, 1930) remains a classic, to be supplemented by J. A. Cross, *Sir Samuel Hoare: A Political Biography* (London, 1977). On British intelligence, the best work is Keith Jeffery's official history, *MI6: The History of the Secret Intelligence Service, 1909–1949* (London, 2010), which is particularly strong on these earliest years. Other useful books include Michael Smith, *Six: The Real James Bonds, 1909–1939* (London, 2011) and Keith Nielson, *Strategy and Supply: The Anglo-Russian Alliance, 1914–17* (London, 1984).

Sir George Buchanan's memoirs (*My Mission to Russia and Other Diplomatic Memories*, 2 vols, London, 1923) are exactly like the man: sober, crisp and impeccable. The second volume covers the events of 1917. Maurice Paléologue's equivalent, *An Ambassador's Memoirs* (3 vols, London, 1923–5), gives an insight into French policy while leaving the reader in no doubt about the ambassador's own view of anyone to the left of the gentlest of conservatives. Still more entertaining are Robert Bruce Lockhart's *Memoirs of a British Agent* (London, 1974) and Arthur Ransome's *Autobiography of Arthur Ransome* (London, 1976), which can be supplemented by Hugh Brogan's *Signalling from Mars: The Letters of Arthur Ransome* (London, 1998). Sir Alfred Knox also wrote a memoir of his Russian adventures, *With the Russian Army, 1914–1917* (2 vols, London, 1921), which traces the decay that he deplored. On Scandinavia, see the second volume of Lord Esmé Howard's *Theatre of Life* (2 vols, London, 1935–6). For the British diplomatic effort in Russia generally, a good introduction is Michael Hughes, *Inside the Enigma: British Diplomats in Russia, 1900–1939* (London, 1997).

For Russian reform politics, a reader might begin with William J. Rosenberg, *Liberals in the Russian Revolution: The Constitutional Democratic Party, 1917–1921* (Princeton, 1974). Paul Miliukov wrote his own *Political Memoirs* (edited by Arthur P. Mendel, Ann Arbor, 1967). The literature on Russian politics in this period, even in English, is voluminous, and readers wishing to pursue it might like to consult J. D. Smele, *The Russian Revolution and Civil War: An Annotated Bibliography* (London, 2003), an excellent guide to English-language works on this and many other matters covered in my story.

When it comes to the Russian underground before and during the war, the choice is similarly vast. Parvus gets royal treatment in Z. A. B. Zeman and W. B. Scharlau, *The Merchant of Revolution: The Life of Alexander Israel Helphand (Parvus), 1867–1924* (London, 1965). For Fürstenberg, there are few English-language sources other than the final chapters of Michael Futrell's *Northern Underground: Episodes of Russian Revolutionary Transport and Communication through Scandinavia and Finland, 1863–1917* (London, 1963). Alfred Erich Senn examined the Russian exile community in *The Russian Revolution in Switzerland, 1914–1917* (Madison, 1971), while Israel Getzler's biography of Yuly Martov (Cambridge, 1967) sees their Menshevik section with a particularly sympathetic eye.

Germany's policies are charted through documents in Z. A. B. Zeman (ed.), *Germany and the Revolution in Russia,*

1915–1918: Documents from the Archives of the German Foreign Ministry (London, 1958). A flurry of publications at the same time made use of what was left of the relevant German archives (there was a fire at the Foreign Ministry before the Second World War, and then, in 1945, Berlin was all but razed). The most readable narrative is Alan Moorehead, *The Russian Revolution* (London, 1958), which was commissioned by *Life* magazine in an effort to prove Lenin's association with German finance. For a more recent account of Germany's Russian policy, see Wayne C. Thompson, *In the Eye of the Storm: Kurt Riezler and the Crises of Modern Germany* (Iowa City, 1980).

There are innumerable biographies of Lenin. A short introduction is provided by Robert Service's *Lenin: A Biography* (London, 2000), which condenses (and sometimes develops) themes in his earlier three-volume work. Dmitry Volkogonov's biography, which drew on secret archives but remained strangely flawed, was translated by Harold Shukman as *Lenin: Life and Legacy* (London, 1994). All Lenin fans should make a point of reading the great leader's entire forty-seven-volume *Collected Works*, of course (tantalized though some may be by the idea that there are fifty-five volumes in Russian), but those who can content themselves with less may enjoy Marcel Liebman's brilliant *Leninism under Lenin* (London, 1975) or Neil Harding's two-volume *Lenin's Political Thought: Theory and Practice in the Democratic and Socialist Revolutions* (Basingstoke, 1977 and 1981). A more recent selection of relevant writings, with commentary, is provided in Slavoj Žižek, *Revolution at the Gates: A Selection of Writings from February to October 1917* (London, 2002). For Lenin's life as an activist in Europe, a readable account is Helen Rappaport, *Conspirator: Lenin in Exile* (London, 2009).

Nadezhda Krupskaya's *Memories of Lenin* (London, 1970) provides a rather sentimental view of the Bolshevik leader, but is still vital for details only she could know. Krupskaya herself is the subject of a sympathetic biography by Robert H. McNeal, *Bride of the Revolution* (London, 1973). R. C. Elwood's biography of *Inessa Armand: Revolutionary and Feminist* (Cambridge, 1992) is excellent despite the unfortunate timing (after its completion) of the release of relevant Soviet archives. To make up for that, Elwood published a number of further essays, collected in one volume with the title *The Non-Geometric Lenin: Essays on the Development of the Bolshevik Party, 1910–1914* (London and New York, 2011), which are models of stylish research. Radek, meanwhile, has star billing in *Karl Radek: The Last Internationalist* by Warren Lerner (Stanford, Calif., 1970). Other passengers and fixers await their biographers in the English-speaking world, but Alexander Shlyapnikov's two-volume autobiographical history (in Russian) was abridged in an English edition (sadly missing many of the most interesting sections) as *On the Eve of 1917: Reminiscences from the Revolutionary Underground* (London and New York, 1982).

There is plenty of choice among the many excellent histories of Russia's February Revolution. The first and most detailed of archive-based studies is still Tsuyoshi Hasegawa, *The February Revolution: Petrograd, 1917* (Seattle and London, 1981), which is due to be reissued in 2017. In addition, comprehensive works by Richard Pipes (*The Russian Revolution, 1899–1919*, New York and London, 1990) and Orlando Figes (*A People's Tragedy: The Russian Revolution, 1891–1924*, London, 1996) cover the whole period from a number of perspectives. The most involving eye-witness account is Nikolai Sukhanov's *The Russian*

Revolution, 1917: A Personal Record (edited, abridged and translated by Joel Carmichael, London, 1955).

Lenin's journey was the subject of Michael Pearson's *The Sealed Train* (Newton Abbot, 1975), while Edmund Wilson used it as the pretext for an extended essay on revolutionary thinking: *To the Finland Station: A Study in the Writing and Acting of History* (New York, 1941). Apart from Shlyapnikov's memoirs, the other eye-witness accounts remain untranslated, but the story of the Bolsheviks in Russia is covered in Alexander Rabinowitch, *Prelude to Revolution: The Petrograd Bolsheviks and the July 1917 Uprising* (Bloomington, Ind., 1968).

For Russia's war, a classic work is Norman Stone, *The Eastern Front, 1914–1917* (London, 1975). The politics of the army are examined in Allan K. Wildman, *The End of the Russian Imperial Army* (Princeton, 1980) and (from a very different perspective) Joshua A. Sanborn, *Imperial Apocalypse: The Great War and the Destruction of the Russian Empire* (Oxford, 2014). On the German situation throughout the war, see Alexander Watson, *Ring of Steel: Germany and Austria-Hungary at War, 1914–1918* (London, 2014); on France, Elizabeth Greenhalgh, *The French Army and the First World War* (Cambridge, 2014). The agonies of peace-seeking politics are examined in Rex A. Wade, *The Russian Search for Peace, February–October 1917* (Stanford, Calif., 1968). More colourful accounts, however, come from the pen of 'Speedy' himself, in the form of A. Kerensky, *The Catastrophe: Kerensky's Own Story of the Russian Revolution* (New York, 1927) and *The Kerensky Memoirs: Russia and History's Turning-Point* (London, 1966).

There are innumerable accounts of the Bolsheviks' fortunes after July 1917, but they belong to other tales and different sorts of bibliography. For the atmosphere of this tense spring, a time when Britain still thought it held all the best trump cards, I can recommend few books more entertaining that John Buchan's *Greenmantle* (London, 1916), the work of Britain's wartime propaganda chief, and W. Somerset Maugham's semi-autobiographical *Ashenden, or, The British Agent* (London, 1928).

Acknowledgements

Like Lenin's, my journey was the work of many friends. I might still be on the quay at Trelleborg if Christina Haugen had not turned up on a wet Sunday night to drive me to Malmö, while Lena Amuren, her colleague at Historiska Media, helped with the introductions in Tornio. Yulia Matskevich was the best possible host in Petrograd, and John Nicolson provided magnificent accommodation at the Academy Garden on Vasilievsky Island.

My guide to Stockholm was Lars Ericson Wolke, who also helped with some of the important Swedish archives. I am also grateful to Christina Engström, of the Swedish Railway Museum in Gävle, for unearthing more archival treasures, including the timetables for the week of Lenin's Swedish odyssey. During my visit to Tornio, the staff of the Torne Valley Museum, especially Riikka Pyykkö, were very generous with their time and helped to produce several of the archive photographs that I have used. I also thank the curators of the many Lenin museums in and near St Petersburg who shared their expertise, showing me around with good-humoured thoroughness and helping me to get a sense of Lenin's life during the war. I learned a huge amount from each of them, and I was also able to form some idea of Lenin's reputation in Russia today. For the initial introductions, more thanks are due to Yulia Matskevich and also to Natalia Sidlina and Aleksandra Smirnova.

At home, I have had warm support and sage advice from

Gill Bennett, Victoria Bull, Valerie Holman, Sue Levene, Anne McIntyre, Nicola Miller, Anna Pilkington, Donald Rayfield, Ian Thomson, Alexandra Wachter and Mark White. The participants at the first ever Arvon history-writing course at The Hurst in November 2015 taught me at least as much as I was capable of teaching them; an added bonus was that I was able to spend time with Miranda France and Giles Milton. For academic hospitality, I thank the University of London's Institute for Historical Research, and especially David Cannadine and Lawrence Goldman, and I am also grateful to the Centre for History and Economics at Magdalene College, Cambridge. My particular thanks, as always, to Emma Rothschild and Inga Huld Markan.

The entire manuscript was read by Jon Smele, a man who has given half a lifetime to the study of Russia's revolution. His prompt and always tactful comments were especially impressive in the middle of a busy academic year. For more tact and an impeccable command of the historical context I am indebted to my editor, Simon Winder, who has encouraged this book from the start. It was a joy, as ever, to be working with the team at Penguin, and I particularly thank Maria Bedford, Richard Duguid and Peter James for their work on the final text and Penelope Vogler for her deft touch with publicity. I was also fortunate to have the assistance of Cecilia Mackay, who tracked down many of the photographs with a delightful sense for what might work. We had barely started to arrange the pictures, meanwhile, before the translators who had undertaken to turn my English into readable German, Swedish and Dutch had set to work under the pressure of a tight deadline. I thank them all, especially Bernd Rullkotter, and also Special Agent Melissa Chinchillo in New York. As ever, I am grateful to Peter Robinson, that most resourceful of literary agents, for his unfailing and good-humoured support.

The maps in this book are the work of the marvellous Frank Payne, as are many of the photographs. I thank him for his awesome skills with lens and screen, I thank him for his patience and his enterprise. But more than that, and always, I thank him for the shared adventure: haystack, *grechka*, reindeer gloves and all. Next time we really will spend longer in the Hermitage.

Index